GLENCOE

Native American Literature

 **Glencoe McGraw-Hill**

New York, New York   Columbus, Ohio   Woodland Hills, California   Peoria, Illinois

Program Advisors

Janice Brown
Houston ISD
Houston, Texas

Kay Licona
University of Phoenix
El Paso, Texas

Beverly Ann Chin
University of Montana
Missoula, Montana

William Ray
Lincoln-Sudbury Regional High School
Sudbury, Massachusetts

Rosa Fonseca
Franklin High School
El Paso, Texas

Jacqueline Jones Royster
Ohio State University
Columbus, Ohio

Acknowledgments

Interview with N. Scott Momaday, reprinted by permission of www.achievement.org. All rights reserved.

"The Journey" by Duane Big Eagle. Copyright © 1983 by Duane Big Eagle. Reprinted by permission of the author.

"Two Traditional Stories: Gluscabi and the Wind Eagle, and Old Man Coyote and the Rock" from *Keepers of the Earth*, copyright © 1991 by Joseph Bruchac. Reprinted by permission of Fulcrum Publishing.

Untitled poem from *My Horse and a Juke Box*, by Barney Bush. Reprinted by permission of the author.

❖ *cont. on page 290*

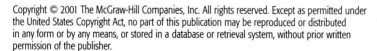

Glencoe/McGraw-Hill

A Division of The **McGraw·Hill** *Companies*

Send all inquiries to:
Glencoe/McGraw-Hill
8787 Orion Place
Columbus, Ohio 43240-4027

ISBN 0-07-822923-5

Printed in the United States of America

3 4 5 6 7 8 9 10   071   05 04 03 02 01

Contents

❖

Contents

❖

Contents

❖

Theme Four: Other Worlds

Theme Five: Change and Continuity

Alaskan Native Inupiat Dancer. Artist unknown. Bronze. Private collection.

Theme One

The Traditional World

I am saying, I will not let go . . .

— Diane Glancy

Before You Read

Four Songs

Traditional (Tohono O'odham)

"It has been a long time since the light began to show, my brother."

About the Tohono O'odham

The Tohono O'odham have long lived in what is now southern Arizona and northern Mexico. Formerly referred to as the Papago, from the name the Spanish explorers gave them, they officially adopted their traditional name, meaning "desert people," in 1986. At the time that Europeans first came to the Southwest, the Tohono O'odham lived by gathering desert plants, hunting desert animals, and growing maize, squash, and beans on irrigated farmland. They constructed dome-shaped houses, using a framework of saplings thatched with grass or shrubs.

Today, some 20,000 Tohono O'odham live in Arizona. Some reside on the three Tohono O'odham reservations, where cattle ranching provides the main source of income. Most, however, live and work off the reservations in Arizona's towns and cities.

Songs of Work and Dreams

The four songs you are about to read were collected and recorded in the 1920s by the musicologist Frances Densmore. In traditional Tohono O'odham culture, songs and music played an important part in the people's everyday lives. They sang while they worked, when they told stories, and as they played games. They had songs that were part of legends and songs that were part of ceremonies. They sang to bring rainfall and to make crops grow. They had healing songs, war songs, hunting songs, game songs, and songs for entertainment. Many of these songs were passed on from generation to generation, and individuals shared new songs believed to have been received in dreams. The Tohono O'odham accompanied their songs with one or two of their four main musical instruments: the gourd rattle, scraping sticks, basket drum, and flute.

Four Tohono O'odham Songs

— Traditional (Tohono O'odham)
Translated by Frances Densmore

The Sunset

LITERAL TRANSLATION

Tharai pi yoëwa himúna waha pi
Sun   is   slowly going   and   is

yoïvi ki hononye cucukûr nakamûrli
slower in setting   black   bats

nuïnakûr maïno   kuma   kokopa yaäli
will be swooping that is all spirit children

inowayiv̂urcov yahaiwara X   iyaälhimûr
beneath   moving around rolling

inowani wûrwûrmikûr viviki
around   among   tufts of eagle down

cucuökima
stuck up at intervals

FREE TRANSLATION

The sun is slowly departing,
It is slower in its setting,
Black bats will be swooping when the sun is gone,
   That is all.

The spirit children are beneath,
They are moving back and forth,
They roll in play among tufts of white eagle down,
   That is all.

Evergreen Trees Mountain

A cloud on top of Evergreen Trees Mountain is singing,
A cloud on top of Evergreen Trees Mountain is standing still,
It is raining and thundering up there,
It is raining here,
Under the mountain the corn tassels are shaking,
Under the mountain the horns of the child corn are glistening.

We Are Singing in the Night

Now as the night is over us we are singing the songs that were given
    to us.
You see the clouds beginning to form on top of the mountains.
They look like little white feathers.
You will see them shake like feathers in a wind.
Soon the raindrops will fall and make our country beautiful.

I Am Running Toward the Edge of the World

I am on my way running,
I am on my way running,
Looking toward me is the edge of the world,
I am trying to reach it,
The edge of the world does not look far away,
To that I am on my way running.

Responding to the Selection

Questions for Discussion

1. The words of songs reflect what is important to a particular group of people at a particular time. Why do you think the Tohono O'odham had songs for bringing rain?

2. On a literal level, what does "I Am Running Toward the Edge of the World" describe? What might the song mean figuratively? How are the words appropriate for a girl's coming-of-age ceremony?

3. In "The Sunset," what impression do you get of the "spirit children"? Do they seem like beings that would cause an illness? Why or why not?

4. What kind of imagery is predominant in these songs? What adjectives would you use to characterize these songs?

5. What are your favorite lines from the songs? Why do these lines appeal to you?

Activities

Creating a Song

1. Using these songs as models, make up a brief song that might be used to open a graduation ceremony, to request something vital in your life, or to bring relief from something that causes stress or illness in your life.

Discussing Traditional Music

2. Find and listen to a recording of Native American flute music or song from the Southwest. Select a short segment to share with the class and discuss its characteristics.

MEDIA connection

Television Transcript

This television documentary focuses on recent research into the architectural achievements of the ancient Hopewell Culture in the Midwest.

Searching for the Great Hopewell Road

Narrator: Today, on a clear Spring morning, archaeologist Dr. Bradley Lepper is conducting an aerial survey over central Ohio. He's searching the freshly-plowed fields and woodlands for remnants of the Ohio Hopewell, ancient Native Americans who once flourished in these fertile lands. Dr. Lepper is searching for traces of a road, a road connected to one of the Hopewells' most magnificent legacies—Octagon State Memorial in Newark, Ohio . . . a geometric enclosure of astonishing size and precision. Dr. Lepper is searching for traces of what he calls "the Great Hopewell Road," an ancient passageway that if found may shed light on a mystery that has puzzled archaeologists for centuries: the purpose of the Hopewells' massive geometric architecture.

. . .

Narrator: To prove his hypothesis, Dr. Lepper needed direct evidence from field excavations—evidence archaeologists call "ground truth." Yet after centuries of plowing, lines visible in infrared images are hard to spot in the soil.

Dr. Lepper: Well, we've identified the locations on the ground where we've seen some of the lines in the aerial photographs . . . And what we've done is measure out to the point where the lines should be. There are no traces visible on the surface, and what we're doing now is putting soil cores down at intervals to see if we can identify a soil change below the area of the plow zone. Hopefully we'll find some remnant of the foundation of the walls that framed the Hopewell Road.

Narrator: Excavations may confirm the evidence discovered in aerial photographs and written documents. However, archaeologists sometimes use other forms of evidence to investigate the past. Evidence that raises even more complex questions . . .

. . .

Narrator: Woodland tribes are revitalizing their culture at tribal centers throughout the Midwest . . . building language programs and libraries, preserving the past with a blend of modern technologies and traditional ways. Back in the Ohio

valley, tribal representatives are also attending cultural festivals and academic programs . . . providing different perspectives about the region's rich cultural heritage . . .

forts to sacred enclosures. Dr. N'omi Greber prefers a broader interpretation. She calls them "markers of knowledge."

Dr. Greber: We can never know the purpose of the . . . enclosures from their point of view . . . we can only estimate based on what we see some people do today still, or what we know about people in general, that we do still make great monuments.

. . .

Narrator: Most Woodland leaders believe all Woodland peoples share a common bond with the ancient peoples of the Ohio valley. Dr. Lepper has searched historical archives for Woodland traditions that may relate to the Great Hopewell Road. He . . . has uncovered several stories that express the importance of pathways and journeys.

. . .

Narrator: The complexity of Hopewell earthworks is only now coming to light . . . The exact purpose of these monumental geometric earthworks remains unknown. Over the centuries they've been called everything from

Dr. Ray Hively: The combination of scale, of precision, of intelligence and beauty that is embodied in these works makes them unique in all the world. This is more than just intellectual curiosity, there's some real feeling and passion involved here—because that is what inspires people to do great things, as the Hopewell did here at this site.
Chief Charles Dawes (Ottawa): We should preserve them if for no other reason than we don't know about them, we don't know enough about them. The quest for some knowledge in and of itself is enough. Certainly, historians and archaeologists and anthropologists have a need for this knowledge. And, indirectly, so do we.

Questions for Discussion

1. What kinds of evidence do archaeologists use in trying to reconstruct the past?

2. Is it important to try to learn what life was like long ago? Why or why not?

Before You Read

It Is Well

Rain-in-the-Face
c. *1835–1905*

> *"The man who preserves his selfhood ever calm and unshaken by the storms of existence . . . his is the ideal attitude and conduct."*
> — Dr. Charles A. Eastman (Ohiyesa)

About Rain-in-the-Face and Ohiyesa

Rain-in-the-Face, known in his own language as Itonagaju, was a member of the Hunkpapa tribe of the Sioux people, who lived in the Dakotas, Wyoming, and Montana. Many historians and contemporaries of Rain-in-the-Face, including General Custer's widow, believe that he killed Custer at the famous Battle of the Little Big Horn in 1876. In his own story, however, Rain-in-the-Face casts doubt on this. He suggests that in the melee of battle any of the warriors could have killed Custer.

Rain-in-the-Face's interviewer, Charles Alexander Eastman (Ohiyesa; 1858–1939), was a Woodland Sioux, born on the Santee Reservation in Minnesota. Eastman spent his first fifteen years following the traditional ways. His father then sent him for a "white man's" education, which led to his training as a medical doctor.

The Sioux Wars

Sioux, derived from a Chippewa word, is often used as the general name for a large group of loosely related tribes who call themselves the Dakota, Lakota, or Nakota—depending on their dialect—all meaning "Alliance of Friends."

The battles Rain-in-the-Face describes—the Fetterman Fight and the battle at the Little Big Horn—were two of many battles the Sioux fought with the U.S. government in the second half of the nineteenth century. The Sioux fiercely resented encroachment on their land. Their victory, in alliance with the Cheyenne, at Little Big Horn shocked the U.S. government. But the battle also stimulated the government to greatly increase its efforts to overcome their resistance.

It Is Well

— *Rain-in-the-Face*

As told to Charles Eastman (Ohiyesa)

"I was born near the forks of the Cheyenne River, about seventy years ago. My father was not a chief; my grandfather was not a chief, but a good hunter and a feast-maker. On my mother's side I had some noted ancestors, but they left me no chieftainship. I had to work for my reputation.

"When I was a boy, I loved to fight," he continued. "In all our boyish games I had the name of being hard to handle, and I took much pride in the fact.

"I was about ten years old when we encountered a band of Cheyennes. They were on friendly terms with us, but we boys always indulged in sham fights on such occasions, and this time I got in an honest fight with a Cheyenne boy older than I. I got the best of the boy, but he hit me hard in the face several times, and my face was all spattered with blood and streaked where the paint had been washed away. The Sioux boys whooped and yelled:

"'His enemy is down, and his face is spattered as if with rain! Rain-in-the-Face! His name shall be Rain-in-the-Face!'

"Afterwards, when I was a young man, we went on a warpath against the Gros Ventres. We stole some of their horses, but were overtaken and had to abandon the horses and fight for our lives. I had wished my face to represent the sun when partly covered with darkness, so I painted it half black, half red. We fought all day in the rain, and my face was partly washed and streaked with red and black: so again I was christened Rain-in-the-Face. We considered it an honorable name.

"I had been on many warpaths, but was not especially successful until about the time the Sioux began to fight with the white man. One of the most daring attacks that we ever made was at Fort Totten, North Dakota, in the summer of 1866.

"Hohay, the Assiniboine captive of Sitting Bull, was the leader in this raid. Wapaypay, the Fearless Bear, who was afterward hanged at Yankton, was the bravest man among us. He dared Hohay to make the charge.

It Is Well 9

It Is Well

Hohay accepted the challenge, and in turn dared the other to ride with him through the agency and right under the walls of the fort, which was well garrisoned and strong.

"Wapaypay and I in those days called each other 'brother-friend.' It was a life-and-death vow. What one does the other must do; and that meant that I must be in the forefront of the charge, and if he is killed, I must fight until I die also!

"I prepared for death. I painted as usual like an eclipse of the sun, half black and half red."

"Now the signal for the charge was given! I started even with Wapaypay, but his horse was faster than mine, so he left me a little behind as we neared the fort. This was bad for me, for by that time the soldiers had somewhat recovered from the surprise and were aiming better.

"Their big gun talked very loud, but my Wapaypay was leading on, leaning forward on his fleet pony like a flying squirrel on a smooth log! He held his rawhide shield on the right side, a little to the front, and so did I. Our warwhoop was like the coyotes singing in the evening, when they smell blood!

"The soldiers' guns talked fast, but few were hurt. Their big gun was like a toothless old dog, who only makes himself hotter the more noise he makes.

"How much harm we did I do not know, but we made things lively for a time; and the white men acted as people do when a swarm of angry bees get into camp. We made a successful retreat, but some of the reservation Indians followed us yelling, until Hohay told them that he did not wish to fight with the captives of the white man, for there would be no honor in that. There was blood running down my leg, and I found that both my horse and I were slightly wounded.

"Some two years later we attacked a fort west of the Black Hills [Fort Phil Kearny, Wyoming]. It was there we killed one hundred soldiers." [The military reports say eighty men, under the command of Captain Fetterman —not one left alive to tell the tale!] "Nearly every band of the Sioux nation was represented in that fight — Red Cloud, Spotted Tail, Crazy Horse, Sitting Bull, Big Foot, and all our great chiefs were there. Of course such men as I were then comparatively unknown. However, there were many noted young warriors, among them Sword, the younger Young-Man-Afraid, American Horse [afterward chief], Crow King, and others.

"This was the plan decided upon after many councils. The main war party lay in ambush, and a few of the bravest young men were appointed to attack the woodchoppers who were cutting logs to complete the building of the fort. We were told not to kill these men, but to chase them into the fort and retreat slowly, defying the white men; and if the soldiers should follow, we were to lead them into the ambush. They took our bait exactly as we had hoped! It was a matter of a very few minutes, for every soldier lay dead in a shorter time than it takes to annihilate a small herd of buffalo.

"This attack was hastened because most of the Sioux on the Missouri River and eastward had begun to talk of suing for peace. But even this did not stop the peace movement. The very next year a treaty was signed at Fort Rice, Dakota Territory, by nearly all the Sioux chiefs, in which it was agreed on the part of the Great Father in Washington that all the country north of the Republican River in Nebraska, including the Black Hills and the Big Horn Mountains, was to be always Sioux country, and no white man should intrude upon it without our permission. Even with this agreement Sitting Bull and Crazy Horse were not satisfied, and they would not sign.

"Up to this time I had fought in some important battles, but had achieved no great deed. I was ambitious to make a name for myself. I joined war parties against the Crows, Mandans, Gros Ventres, and Pawnees, and gained some little distinction.

"It was when the white men found the yellow metal in our country, and came in great numbers, driving away our game, that we took up arms against them for the last time. I must say here that the chiefs who were loudest for war were among the first to submit and accept reservation life. Spotted Tail was a great warrior, yet he was one of the first to yield, because he was promised by the Chief Soldiers that they would make him chief of all the Sioux. He would have stayed with Sitting Bull to the last had it not been for his ambition.

"About this time we young warriors began to watch the trails of the white men into the Black Hills, and when we saw a wagon coming we would hide at the crossing and kill them all without much trouble. We did this to discourage the whites from coming into our country without our permission. It was the duty of our Great Father at Washington, by the agreement of 1868, to keep his white children away.

"During the troublesome time after this treaty, which no one seemed to respect, either white or Indian [but the whites broke it first], I was like many other young men — much on the warpath, but with little honor. I had not yet become noted for any great deed. Finally, Wapaypay and I waylaid and killed a white soldier on his way from the fort to his home in the east.

"There were a few Indians who were liars, and never on the warpath, playing 'good Indian' with the Indian agents and the war chiefs at the forts. Some of this faithless set betrayed me, and told more than I ever did. I was seized and taken to the fort near Bismarck, North Dakota [Fort Abraham Lincoln], by a brother [Tom Custer] of the Long-Haired War Chief, and imprisoned there. These same lying Indians, who were selling their services as scouts to the white man, told me that I was to be shot to death, or else hanged upon a tree. I answered that I was not afraid to die.

"However, there was an old soldier who used to bring my food and stand guard over me—he was a white man, it is true, but he had an Indian heart! He came to me one day and unfastened the iron chain and ball with which they had locked my leg, saying by signs and what little Sioux he could muster:

"'Go, friend! take the chain and ball with you. I shall shoot, but the voice of the gun will lie.'

"When he had made me understand, you may guess that I ran my best! I was almost over the bank when he fired his piece at me several times, but I had already gained cover and was safe. I have never told this before, and would not, lest it should do him an injury, but he was an old man then, and I am sure he must be dead long since. That old soldier taught me that some of the white people have hearts.

"I went back to Standing Rock in the night, and I had to hide for several days in the woods, where food was brought to me by my relatives. The Indian police were ordered to retake me, and they pretended to hunt for me, but really they did not, for if they had found me I would have died with one or two of them, and they knew it! In a few days I departed with several others, and we rejoined the hostile camp on the Powder River and made some trouble for the men who were building the great iron track north of us [Northern Pacific].

"In the spring the hostile Sioux got together again upon the Tongue River. It was one of the greatest camps of the Sioux that I ever saw. There were some Northern Cheyennes with us, under Two Moon, and a few Santee Sioux, renegades from Canada, under Inkpaduta, who had killed white people in Iowa long before. We had decided to fight the white soldiers until no warrior should be left."

"Of course the younger warriors were delighted with the prospect of a great fight! Our scouts had discovered piles of oats for horses and other supplies near the Missouri River. They had been brought by the white man's fire-boats. Presently they reported a great army about a day's travel to the south, with Shoshone and Crow scouts.

"There was excitement among the people, and a great council was held. Many spoke. I was asked the condition of those Indians who had gone upon the reservation, and I told them truly that they were nothing more than prisoners. It was decided to go out and meet Three Stars [General Crook] at a safe distance from our camp.

"We met him on the Little Rosebud. I believe that if we had waited and allowed him to make the attack, he would have fared no better than Custer. He was too strongly fortified where he was, and I think, too, that he was saved partly by his Indian allies, for the scouts discovered us first and fought us first, thus giving him time to make his preparations. I think he was more wise than brave! After we had left that neighborhood he might have pushed on and connected with the Long-Haired Chief. That would have saved Custer and perhaps won the day.

"When we crossed from Tongue River to the Little Big Horn, on account of the scarcity of game, we did not anticipate any more trouble. Our runners had discovered that Crook had retraced his trail to Goose Creek, and we did not suppose that the white men would care to follow us farther into the rough country.

"Suddenly the Long-Haired Chief appeared with his men! It was a surprise."

"What part of the camp were you in when the soldiers attacked the lower end?" I [Charles Eastman] asked.

"I had been invited to a feast at one of the young men's lodges [a sort of club]. There was a certain warrior who was making preparations to go against the Crows, and I had decided to go also," he said.

"While I was eating my meat we heard the war cry! We all rushed out, and saw a warrior riding at top speed from the lower camp, giving the warning as he came. Then we heard the reports of the soldiers' guns, which sounded differently from the guns fired by our people in battle.

"I ran to my teepee and seized my gun, a bow, and a quiver full of arrows. I already had my stone war club, for you know we usually carry those by way of ornament. Just as I was about to set out to meet Reno, a body of soldiers appeared nearly opposite us, at the edge of a long line of cliffs across the river.

"All of us who were mounted and ready immediately started down the stream toward the ford. There were Ogallalas, Minneconjous, Cheyennes, and some Unkpapas, and those around me seemed to be nearly all very young men.

"'Behold, there is among us a young woman!' I shouted. 'Let no young man hide behind her garment!' I knew that would make those young men brave.

"The woman was Tashenamani, or Moving Robe, whose brother had just been killed in the fight with Three Stars. Holding her brother's war staff over her head, and leaning forward upon her charger, she looked as pretty as a bird. Always when there is a woman in the charge, it causes the warriors to vie with one another in displaying their valor.

"The foremost warriors had almost surrounded the white men, and more were continually crossing the stream. The soldiers had dismounted, and were firing into the camp from the top of the cliff."

"My friend, was Sitting Bull in this fight?" I inquired.

"I did not see him there, but I learned afterward that he was among those who met Reno, and that was three or four of the white man's miles from Custer's position. Later he joined the attack upon Custer, but was not among the foremost.

"When the troops were surrounded on two sides, with the river on the third, the order came to charge! There were many very young men, some of whom had only a war staff or a stone war club in hand, who plunged into the column, knocking the men over and stampeding their horses.

"The soldiers had mounted and started back, but when the onset came they dismounted again and separated into several divisions, facing different ways. They fired as fast as they could load their guns, while we used chiefly arrows and war clubs. There seemed to be two distinct movements among the Indians. One body moved continually in a circle, while the other rode directly into and through the troops.

"Presently some of the soldiers remounted and fled along the ridge toward Reno's position; but they were followed by our warriors, like hundreds of blackbirds after a hawk. A larger body remained together at the upper end of a little ravine, and fought bravely until they were cut to pieces. I had always thought that white men were cowards, but I had a great respect for them after this day.

"It is generally said that a young man with nothing but a war staff in his hand broke through the column and knocked down the leader very early in the fight. We supposed him to be the leader, because he stood up in full view, swinging his big knife [sword] over his head, and talking loud. Some one unknown afterwards shot the chief, and he was probably killed also; for if not, he would have told of the deed, and called others to witness it. So it is that no one knows who killed the Long-Haired Chief [General Custer].

"After the first rush was over, coups were counted as usual on the bodies of the slain. You know four coups [or blows] can be counted on the body of an enemy, and whoever counts the first one [touches it for the first time] is entitled to the 'first feather.'

"There was an Indian here called Appearing Elk, who died a short time ago. He was slightly wounded in the charge. He had some of the weapons of the Long-Haired Chief, and the Indians used to say jokingly after we came upon the reservation that Appearing Elk must have killed the Chief, because he had his sword! However, the scramble for plunder did not begin until all were dead. I do not think he killed Custer, and if he had, the time to claim the honor was immediately after the fight.

"Many lies have been told of me. Some say that I killed the Chief, and others that I cut out the heart of his brother [Tom Custer], because he had caused me to be imprisoned. Why, in that fight the excitement was so

great that we scarcely recognized our nearest friends! Everything was done like lightning. After the battle we young men were chasing horses all over the prairie, while the old men and women plundered the bodies; and if any mutilating was done, it was by the old men.

"I have lived peaceably ever since we came upon the reservation. No one can say that Rain-in-the-Face has broken the rules of the Great Father. I fought for my people and my country. When we were conquered I remained silent, as a warrior should. Rain-in-the-Face was killed when he put down his weapons before the Great Father. His spirit was gone then; only his poor body lived on, but now it is almost ready to lie down for the last time. *Ho, hechetu!* [It is well.]"

Responding to the Selection

Questions for Discussion

1. What is the relationship between Ohiyesa and Rain-in-the-Face?

2. What story does Rain-in-the-Face tell? What are some events of that story?

3. How does Rain-in-the-Face speak of the U.S. soldiers and officials in his story? What does this tell you about Rain-in-the-Face's character?

4. Based on his story, what quality do you think Rain-in-the-Face counted as most important in his life? Explain. Do you share his feelings about what is important in life?

Activities

Creating a Map

1. Read Rain-in-the-Face's battle accounts carefully. Then create a map of one battle, showing both U.S. and Sioux troop movements. Develop a color-coded key to indicate each army's positions and movements.

Writing a Memorial

2. Rain-in-the-Face is remembered as a great warrior, but there is more to a man's life than his bravery in battle. Think about the man revealed in the selection. Then write a brief memorial statement that captures both the warrior and the man.

Researching the Background

3. The autobiographical form of this selection necessarily limits the point of view through which readers learn of events. Briefly research either the Fetterman Fight or the Battle of the Little Big Horn. Then analyze Rain-in-the-Face's account for its objectivity and accuracy. (Remember that other accounts you read may also intend to convey a point of view.)

Before You Read

S'Klallam Spirit Canoe and Mine

Duane Niatum *(Born 1938)*
Diane Glancy *(Born 1941)*

"What is most difficult to face is not ourselves, but the pain of the ancestors in our dreams."

— Duane Niatum

About Niatum

Niatum was born in Seattle, Washington, where he has lived most of his life. After a sometimes difficult youth, during which he spent time in reform schools, he joined the navy at the age of seventeen. Having spent two years in Japan, he returned to the United States and earned a bachelor's degree in English from the University of Washington in 1970. He published his first collection of poetry the same year. Niatum served as the general editor of Harper and Row's Native American Authors Program, a publishing venture that stimulated what became known as the Native American Literary Renaissance of the 1970s and 1980s. Niatum continues to write and publish poetry and short stories.

About Glancy

A biography of Diane Glancy appears with her play *The Truth Teller* on page 211.

Heritages and Traditions

The two poems you are about to read reflect the different heritages of the two authors. Duane Niatum is a member of the people known in English as the Klallam, from *S'Klallam,* meaning "strong people." The Klallam originally lived in small villages along the shores of Washington state. From large dugout canoes, they hunted whales and fished for salmon, herring, cod, and other saltwater fish. Many Klallam still make their living from fishing today.

Diane Glancy is part Cherokee. The Cherokee originally lived in the Southeast, but most were forced to migrate to what is now Oklahoma in the 1830s: about one-fourth died on the way, along the infamous Trail of Tears.

S'Klallam
SPIRIT CANOE

— Duane Niatum

My paddle keeps to the sun's path,
pulls back home to sea,
my blood on its travels to the whirling depths.
From bow to stern our canoe drops and rises,
5   embraces each trough cleansed
by family singing from coastal cliffs.
We join our brothers and sisters
in canoes from other villages
in the circle of kelp and spray,
10   seal and whale; ride the moving hills,
slide sideways and down, then straight up,
each paddle touching sky.

The drumbeat slips beneath the current,
rattling from genes to prow,
15   returns to ancestral fire and form
emerging from the trail of cutwater.
From dawn to night we are the ribs
of great grandparents, soar like cormorants
on the green crest; offer our children
20   a dream stronger and bolder than rage or war.
Salt drying on our face and hands braids
our bodies into spirals of dusk,
evening star and Milky Way, hones
us for the split hurdle as we speak
25   with night weavers like the old growth
voice of red cedar dipping into light
who mirrors our coming-home story.

— Diane Glancy

I am saying, I will not let go.
This half-starved land,
A hole blown in its brown roof,
Trees clawing for a place.
5   Weeds quiver at the road.
A jig to some jive tune?
Ah, this West Pole.
Years of wind & desolation.
Sheets of dust
10 Blow from dirt roads
Across the highway.
Pink lightning like a roller rink
In a skating hall.
The part that sticks up,
15 An attic room
On the old house I didn't like.
The heavy cloud bank
Sweeps rain for miles over the land
Like curtains at the window.
20 Now the highway heads
For the mouth of the cave.
Ducking, my hands grip the wheel.
The pink lightbulb flashes overhead,
On & off,
25 The memory of my Mother
Trying to wake me for school,
Her pearly light all lizard-eyed.
The storm moves
With the whiz of roller-skates.
30 Onward, always onward.
A tumbleweed rushes across the road.
Skeletons of bushes hop jauntily.
I'm saying its mine.

Mine

All the dark caverns
35   This place offers.
An explorer who stabs the earth
With a flag pole.
Mine, the warped soil,
The leaning hills.
40   The rocks, mine.
Grasses, mine.
These winding roads over flat land.
Hairpin curves turning back
Into myself.
45   Mine, the arms,
The rope which pulls me through.
All of it, mine.

Responding to the Selection

Questions for Discussion

1. What is the speaker describing in the poem "S'Klallam Spirit Canoe"? What is the significance of the title of the poem?

2. In "S'Klallam Spirit Canoe," how is the action of the canoeists a "coming-home story"? What is the "dream stronger and bolder than rage or war"?

3. What is the speaker doing in "Mine"? What image of the land or environment do you get from "Mine"? What words or phrases help create that image?

4. How does the speaker in "Mine" feel about the land? Why might the speaker feel this way? Have you ever experienced such feelings about the area where you live or were born? Why or why not?

5. What message about traditions and homeland do these poems convey?

Activities

Writing a Report

1. Research the traditional way of life of the Klallam or the Cherokee and how these tribes are keeping their traditions alive. Present your findings in a report.

Creating a Diorama

2. Create a diorama depicting the action and setting of one of these poems.

Before You Read

In the Old Days

Anna Price
1837–1937

"When I was young I walked all over this country, east and west, and saw no people other than the Apache."
— Cochise, Chiricahua Apache leader

About Price

When Anna Price shared her memories with Grenville Goodwin, a student of Apache traditions, she was nearly one hundred years old. One way that Goodwin learned about Western Apache lifeways and history was to talk with older inhabitants. They shared with him their personal experience and their ancestral stories. Price became one of his most valuable sources. In Apache, her real name meant "Her Eyes Gray." She was the eldest daughter of a chief known by the Mexican name "Diablo," who was the most influential chief of the White Mountain Apache. Price's memories focus mostly on her father's deeds. They provide a window into life in the Southwest in the 1850s.

Western Apache Life

The Western Apache lived in present-day Arizona, with the White Mountain Apache living at the easternmost edge of the region. A nomadic people, the White Mountain Apache moved throughout the year, following animal food sources. They hunted, gathered wild plants, and grew some farm crops. At the time Price's story takes place, probably between 1855 and 1865, raiding also played a key role as a Western Apache food source. Usually, the Apache distinguished between raiding and warfare, with the former inspired by need and the latter inspired mostly by revenge. In this account, these two goals merge somewhat as Diablo leads the men on what begins as a purely military mission, but ends with the seizing of the enemy's cattle too.

In the Old Days

— *Anna Price*
As told to Grenville Goodwin

In the old days when a person got ready to be told a story, from the time the storyteller started no one there ever stopped to eat or sleep. They kept telling the story straight through till it was finished. Then when the story was through, the medicine man would tell all about the different medicines. There would be a basket of corn seeds there, and for each line that was spoken, that person who was listening would count out one corn seed. This way there would be sometimes two hundred corn seeds. Then that person would have to eat them all. If he could eat them, then he would remember all the words he had been told. If you fell asleep during this time, then the story was broken and was no good. That's the way we used to do.

This happened when my father was living on the East Fork. Some Navajo came to us to get mescal. They brought sheep hides and blankets to trade. My father and some of his men had gone hunting. These Navajo surrounded them at nighttime and started to fight just as our men were eating their supper of deer meat. Two of our men were killed. Another man shot at the Navajo, even though they could not be seen, and managed to kill one. Two days after the hunters returned home they sent word among all the people to assemble. They made a dance there, a war dance. They used shields to dance with, made of hide.

My father talked to the men before they left, "We are going after the Navajo. I don't know why they attacked us. We always treated them right before, but now we might just as well go and see them—fight them all."

They started and in two days arrived in the Navajo country. The Navajos had not gone far from where they killed our men on the other side of the White Mountains. Our people surrounded the camp and started the attack before dawn, while the Navajo were still asleep. All of them were killed. They tried to run off, leaving their guns and bows and quivers behind them. Our people set fire to their houses and burnt them up. They also set fire to the sheep corral.

During the battle my father talked to the Navajo, "This is what you want. You have asked me to come over to fight you. That's just the way it is. It used to be as if we ate together, but now I have come to fight you."

They captured one Navajo boy. He knew of another Navajo camp above this one, so they took him to guide them to it. The same day they arrived there at noon and started to fight immediately. The Navajo in the camp were all killed. A few who were herding sheep in the mountains not far off saved themselves. Thus they had fought in two places the same day, one in the morning and one at noon. We were lucky and not one of our people was killed. Whenever my father went to war a lot of men always accompanied him, lots of them, just like ants.

They had captured a second man at this Navajo camp who told them, "Some Navajo have been gone on the warpath for a long time. They went against the White people. One man has just returned ahead of the rest and has said the others will be in tomorrow and that they are bringing lots of cattle in two great herds, one in front of the other."

Two of our men were sent in search of them. The returning Navajo had sent two of their boys ahead to stop at a spring and prepare some meat for those who were coming behind. Our two men saw these boys, who went ahead and built the fire to prepare the meat. Our men knew that all the Navajo would be eating at that place. They set an ambush for them. It was almost sundown and they placed themselves about the spot where the cooking was going on.

Just about an hour later the cattle came up over the hill. One Navajo was riding in the lead, the chief of the party, I guess. They arrived and our men could see many Navajo gathered together by the fire. They started to eat all in a bunch and our men began to shoot. The Navajo got scared and not one fired a shot. A few of them who were herding the cattle saved themselves, but those who had been eating were slain. One Navajo spoke, " . . . you have killed us all."

My father spoke to his men, "Fifteen of you take those cattle home. We want to fight more. There is another herd of cattle coming. The rest of us will go and fight them again." A Navajo had told them these springs were the only ones in the region and that the second herd would certainly stop there in two days. They stayed only one night at the springs.

The next morning fifteen men took the cattle toward White River. The remainder went on ahead to intercept the Navajo. They kept the boy they had first captured. He wanted to show our men where a spring came out between two adjoining hills. At the foot of the one to the west was a little spring. When our men arrived there, the Navajo were bringing in their cattle at the same time and the two parties ran into each other. They saw the cattle coming and so formed a semicircle about the spring so that the Navajo might drive the cattle right into them. There was a bluff on one side and at its foot the spring. It was just like a corral and they had only to arrange themselves on one side because nothing could escape on the side of the bluff. A few were on top of the bluff.

The Navajo arrived and started to water. There were a lot of them. Just then, one of our men started to shoot. They were cut off on one side by the bluff and not one of them escaped—all were killed. At the end of the fight, two Navajo were still alive, one of them having had his side shot away, and the other shot through the leg. They both were sitting there and talked even though shot down. The one wounded in the leg said, "I have killed your men many times and left their bodies for the coyotes. But now you have done the same to me."

All our men gathered about them and my father, being chief, talked to the Navajo. "You have asked for me and for this fight. We used to be friends just as if we lived in the same camp. I don't know why you want to fight my people, so I fight you. The cattle herd ahead of you has been taken down to White River for me; the herd you were bringing home I'm going to take to my home also. You have done well for me and brought lots of cattle from the warpath. You can just sit there and tell your people. I want you to tell them about me. But you who are shot in the leg, side, arm, I am going to kill you." So he killed one, and the one who was left, the one who still sat there, said, "If any of you have some mescal, I wish you would give it to me. I want it. Then I will eat it up. Maybe that will bring me home to tell my people about you. I have had a hard time from your people. Give me some water." My father gave the Navajo some water. "Here," he said, "this will take you home to tell your people about us." Then the Navajo said, "All right, take your cattle home and I will talk to my people about you and also you tell your people about me. Put me in the shade. You have killed me. Put me in the shade of that pine." So they did. My father told him, "When you get home, tell your people about me and call my name. Tell them I am the one who got your cattle."

The fifteen men who took the first herd home got there first. The second bunch had been gone seven days when they got home with the cattle. They killed the Navajo boy when they left the spring.

My father had said when he started to war, "My heart is moving within me just as the sun moves overhead. That is the way the killing of my relatives makes me feel." When a man gets mad his heart beats fast and hard. This is what he meant.

Responding to the Selection

Questions for Discussion

1. Why do the Apache make war on the Navajo?

2. How does the battle progress? Describe each phase.

3. What emotions drive Diablo to battle with the Navajo? How, if at all, do his feelings affect his actions?

4. In her opening words, Anna Price says that stories lost their power—were "no good"—if listeners became distracted. What purpose do you think this story served for the Western Apache? Why was it told?

5. In the story's closing lines, Price says, "When a man gets mad his heart beats fast and hard." How is this statement demonstrated by the story? How, if at all, is such an emotional reaction specific to the Native American experience of the 1800s? Do you react this way when you get angry?

Activities

Writing a Review

1. Many critics consider Grenville Goodwin's collection of Western Apache memories an invaluable resource. Write your own review of Anna Price's account. What does it tell us about Western Apache life? What questions, if any, does it leave unanswered? Be sure to include a recommendation about reading the story.

Researching the Background

2. Using online or print reference sources, learn more about the history and lifeways of the White Mountain Apache or another Apache group. Present your findings in a 3–5 minute oral report, accompanied by visual materials such as maps or photos.

Creating a Song

3. Songs are often based on traditional stories. Create a song that conveys the story of Diablo's war raid. Use both words and music to capture the events and emotions of the story. If possible, share your song with classmates through a performance or recording.

Before You Read

The Warrior Maiden

Traditional (Oneida)

"The old ones speak
in thunder,
in the roots of the Great Wood
swelling beneath tar and steel."
— Roberta Hill Whiteman (born 1947),
Oneida poet

About the Oneida

The word *Oneida* comes from *Onayotekaono,* meaning "the People of the Standing Stone," referring to a huge boulder in their central New York territory. A founding member of the Iroquois League centuries ago, the Oneida lived in traditional Iroquois ways. Clustered along streams or rivers near Lake Oneida, they built elm-bark longhouses that housed several families. These families in turn belonged to clans linked by a common ancestor and symbolized by an animal. The Oneida were hunters—trapping forest animals both for food and for clothing—and also farmers.

During the Revolutionary War, the Oneida broke with the other Iroquois peoples, who favored the British, and provided military help and supplies to the colonists. However, in the 1820s and 1830s, under pressure from New York state authorities, the Oneida began to look for land west of their traditional territories. Today most Oneida live in Wisconsin.

Women of the Oneida

Women held much power among the Oneida. Like other Iroquois tribes, the Oneida were a matrilineal people. This means that a person's ancestry, and any privilege or status attached to it, followed the mother's descendents. Family names were passed along this way, for example. Women also played key roles in the political process. They selected sachems, or leaders, from among their clan. These sachems, in turn, made the important decisions for the tribe. Acknowledging the importance of the women's role, the Oneida referred to their most important crops—beans, corn, and squash—as the Three Sisters and gave crop ownership to the tribe's women.

The **Warrior** Maiden

— *Traditional (Oneida)*
Based on the version told by W. W. Canfield in 1902

Long ago, in the days before the white man came to this continent, the Oneida people were beset by their old enemies, the Mingoes. The invaders attacked the Oneida villages, stormed their palisades, set fire to their long-houses, laid waste to the land, destroyed the cornfields, killed men and boys, and abducted the women and girls. There was no resisting the Mingoes, because their numbers were like grains of sand, like pebbles on a lake shore.

The villages of the Oneida lay deserted, their fields untended, the ruins of their homes blackened. The men had taken the women, the old people, the young boys and girls into the deep forests, hiding them in secret places among rocks, in caves, and on desolate mountains. The Mingoes searched for victims, but could not find them. The Great Spirit himself helped the people to hide and shielded their places of refuge from the eyes of their enemies.

Thus the Oneida people were safe in their inaccessible retreats, but they were also starving. Whatever food they had been able to save was soon eaten up. They could either stay in their hideouts and starve, or leave them in search of food and be discovered by their enemies. The warrior chiefs and sachems met in council but could find no other way out.

Then a young girl stepped forward in the council and said that the good spirits had sent her a dream showing her how to save the Oneida. Her name was Aliquipiso and she was not afraid to give her life for her people.

Aliquipiso told the council: "We are hiding on top of a high, sheer cliff. Above us the mountain is covered with boulders and heavy sharp rocks. You warriors wait and watch here. I will go to the Mingoes and lead them to the spot at the foot of the cliff where they all can be crushed and destroyed."

The chiefs, sachems, and warriors listened to the girl with wonder. The oldest of the sachems honored her, putting around her neck strands of white and purple wampum. "The Great Spirit has blessed you, Aliquipiso, with courage and wisdom," he said. "We, your people, will always remember you."

The **Warrior** Maiden

During the night the girl went down from the heights into the forest below by way of a secret path. In the morning, Mingoe scouts found her wandering through the woods as if lost. They took her to the burned and abandoned village where she had once lived, for this was now their camp. They brought her before their warrior chief. "Show us the way to the place where your people are hiding," he commanded. "If you do this, we shall adopt you into our tribe. Then you will belong to the victors. If you refuse, you will be tortured at the stake."

"I will not show you the way," answered Aliquipiso. The Mingoes tied her to a blackened tree stump and tortured her with fire, as was their custom. Even the wild Mingoes were astonished at the courage with which the girl endured it. At last Aliquipiso pretended to weaken under the pain. "Don't hurt me any more," she cried, "I'll show you the way!"

As night came again, the Mingoes bound Aliquipiso's hands behind her back and pushed her ahead of them. "Don't try to betray us," they warned. "At any sign of it, we'll kill you." Flanked by two warriors with weapons poised, Aliquipiso led the way. Soundlessly the mass of Mingoe warriors crept behind her through thickets and rough places, over winding paths and deer trails, until at last they arrived beneath the towering cliff of sheer granite. "Come closer, Mingoe warriors," she said in a low voice, "gather around me. The Oneidas above are sleeping, thinking themselves safe. I'll show you the secret passage that leads upwards." The Mingoes crowded together in a dense mass with the girl in the center. Then Aliquipiso uttered a piercing cry: "Oneidas! The enemies are here! Destroy them!"

The Mingoes scarcely had time to strike her down before huge boulders and rocks rained upon them. There was no escape; it seemed as if the angry mountain itself were falling on them, crushing them, burying them. So many Mingoe warriors died there that the other bands of Mingoe invaders stopped pillaging the Oneida country and retired to their own hunting grounds. They never again made war on Aliquipiso's people.

The story of the girl's courage and self-sacrifice was told and retold wherever Oneidas sat around their campfires, and will be handed down from grandparent to grandchild as long as there are Oneidas on this earth.

The Great Mystery changed Aliquipiso's hair into woodbine, which the Oneidas call "running hairs" and which is a good medicine. From her body sprang honeysuckle, which to this day is known among her people as the "blood of brave women."

Responding to the Selection

Questions for Discussion

1. What problem faces the Oneida?
2. What decision do the sachems consider? Are there any other choices? What would you advise the sachems to do?
3. How does Aliquipiso propose solving her people's problem? Why do you think she chooses this path?
4. How does the story characterize Aliquipiso? How do her people regard her actions? Do you agree with their reactions?
5. How does the story present conflict between peoples? Do you agree with their view?

Activities

Writing a Dialogue

1. Aliquipiso faced a difficult personal decision. How do you suppose she explained that decision to her loved ones? Write a dialogue between Aliquipiso and a close relative or friend. Make sure that she explains her choice and the reasons behind it, while also responding to the other person's emotions.

Picturing the Story

2. When the Oneida retold the story of Aliquipiso's courageous actions, they may have used dance, costume, or other visual methods to help listeners picture the story. Create such a dance, costume, picture, or visual of your choice. Then present it with your own retelling of the story.

Writing an Essay

3. Aliquipiso became a heroic legend to her people. Look back at the story and identify her heroic qualities. What qualities made her seem larger than life, as heroes often are? Answer this question in a brief essay.

Before You Read

Soul Catcher

Louis Owens
Born 1948

> *"I know that we invent what we need to be true, imagining and rewriting until there is some kind of text that gives us back a self."*

About Owens

Louis Owens was born in 1948, inheriting Choctaw heritage from his father and Cherokee/Irish heritage from his mother. Owens spent his early years in California and in Mississippi. Third in a family of nine children, Owens was closest to his older brother Gene; the two were the first and only members of the family to graduate from high school. After working as a forest ranger and firefighter, Owens went on to receive a doctorate from the University of California. In addition to teaching at colleges and universities, Owens has written five novels, including *Nightland*, which received an American Book Award. His second novel, *The Sharpest Sight*, grew out of Gene's unexplained disappearance after surviving three tours of duty in Vietnam.

Soul Catchers

This story is based on a real event in Louis Owens's childhood. The event so struck Louis that it became "an image and theme that haunted my writing." It took place while the writer and his family were staying in an isolated cabin on the Mississippi swamps. As Owens recalls it, a black panther, or "painter," followed his father home from a hunting trip. His father managed to evade the animal and get into the cabin, whereupon the panther jumped onto the cabin roof, where it paced and howled at its loss all night long.

In the fictional story Owens crafted from this event, the hunter is a full-blooded Choctaw great-uncle who lives the traditional Native American life his nephew only knows from books. The uncle believes in the old stories and myths, like the *nalusachito*, or soul catcher, who feeds on the human spirit.

Soul Catcher

— *Louis Owens*

The old man held the rifle in one hand and walked bent over under the weight of the gunnysack on his back, as if studying the tangle of roots that was the trail. Behind him three lanky brown-and-black-and-white hounds crowded close to his thin legs and threw nervous glances at the wet forest all around. The only sound was that of the old man's boots and the occasional whine of one of the dogs. The sliver of moon had set, and the trail was very dark. The light from the carbide lamp on his hat cast a phosphorescent glow around the group, so that the old man, with his long silver hair, might have been one of the Choctaw shadows on the bright path home.

Out of the dark to the old man's right came a scream that cut through the swamp like jagged tin and sent the hounds trembling against his legs.

"Hah! Get back you!" he scolded, turning to shake his head at the cringing dogs. "That cat ain't going to eat you, not yet."

The dogs whined and pushed closer so that the old man stumbled and caught himself and the light from the headlamp splashed upon the trail. He shook his head again and chuckled, making shadows dance around them. He knew what it was that stalked him. The black *koi* hadn't been seen in the swamps during the old man's lifetime, but as a child he'd heard the stories so often that he knew at once what the *koi* meant. It was an old and familiar story. He'd felt the black one out there in the swamps for a long time. The bird, *falachito*, had called from the trees to warn him, and he had listened and gone on because what else was there to do? All of his life he had been prepared to recognize the soul catcher when it should come.

The old man also knew that the screamer was probably the panther that the fool white man, Reeves, had wounded near Satartia a couple of weeks before. He could feel the animal's anger there in the darkness, feel the hatred like grit between his teeth. And he felt great pity for the injured cat.

The boar coon in the sack was heavy, and the old man thought that he should have brought the boy along to help, but then the forest opened and he was at the edge of his cabin clearing, seeing the thread of his garden trail between the stubble of the past year's corn and the dried husks of melon and squash vines. Behind him, this time to his left, the panther screamed again. The cat had been circling like that for the past hour, never getting any closer or any farther away.

He paused at the edge of the clearing and spoke a few words in a low voice, trying to communicate his understanding and sympathy to the wounded animal and his knowledge of what was there to the soul catcher. For a moment he leaned the rifle against his leg and reached up to touch a small pouch that hung inside his shirt. All of his life the old man had balanced two realities, two worlds, a feat that had never struck him as particularly noteworthy or difficult. But as the cat called out once more, he felt a shadow fall over him. The animal's cry rose from the dark waters of the swamp to the stars and then fell away like one of the deep, bottomless places in the river.

When the old man pulled the leather thong to open the door, the hounds shot past and went to cower beneath the plank beds. He lowered the bag to the puncheon floor and pushed the door closed. After a moment's thought he dropped the bolt into place before reaching with one hand to hang the twenty-two on nails beneath a much larger rifle. Finally, he looked at the teenage boy sitting on the edge of one of the beds with a book in his lap. The lantern beside the boy left half of his upturned face in shadow, as if two faces met in one, but the old man could see one green eye and the fair skin, and he wondered once more how much Choctaw there was in the boy.

The boy looked up fully and stared at the old uncle. The distinct epicanthic fold of each eye giving the boy's face an oddly Oriental quality.

"Koi," the old man said. "A painter. He followed me home."

After a moment's silence, the boy said, "You going to keep him?"

The old man grinned. The boy was getting better.

"Not this one," he replied. "He's no good. A fool shot him, and now he's mad." He studied the air to one side of the boy and seemed to make a decision. "Besides, this black one may be *nalusachito*, the soul catcher. He's best left alone, I think."

The boy's grin died quickly, and the old man saw fear and curiosity mingle in the pale eyes.

"Why do you think it's *nalusachito*?" The word was awkward on the boy's tongue.

Soul Catcher

"Sometimes you just know these things. He's been out there a while. The bird warned me, and now that fool white man has hurt him."

"*Nalusachito* is just a myth," the boy said.

The old man looked at the book in the boy's lap. "You reading that book again?"

The boy nodded.

"A teacher give that book to your dad one time, so's he could learn all about his people, the teacher said. He used to read that book, too, and tell me about us Choctaws." The old man grinned once more. "After he left, I read some of that book."

The old man reached a hand toward the boy. "Here, let me read you the part I like best about us people." He lifted a pair of wire-rimmed glasses from a shelf above the rifles and slipped them on.

The boy held the book out and the old man took it. Bending so that the lantern-light fell across the pages, he thumbed expertly through the volume.

"This is a good book, all right. Tells us all about ourselves. This writer was a smart man. Listen to this." He began to read, pronouncing each word with care, as though it were a foreign language.

The Choctaw warrior, as I knew him in his native Mississippi forest, was as fine a specimen of manly perfection as I have ever beheld.

He looked up with a wink.

He seemed to be as perfect as the human form could be. Tall, beautiful in symmetry of form and face, graceful, active, straight, fleet, with lofty and independent bearing, he seemed worthy in saying, as he of Juan Fernández fame: "I am monarch of all I survey." His black piercing eye seemed to penetrate and read the very thoughts of the heart, while his firm step proclaimed a feeling sense of manly independence. Nor did their women fall behind in all that pertains to female beauty.

The old man looked at the boy. "Now there's a man that hit the nail on the head." He paused for a moment. "You ever heard of this Juan Fernández? Us Choctaws didn't get along too good with Spanish people in the old days. Remind me to tell you about Tuscaloosa sometime."

The boy shook his head. "Alabama?"

The old man nodded. "I read this next part to Old Lady Blue Wood that lives 'crost the river. She says this is the smartest white man she ever heard of." He adjusted the glasses and read again.

They were of such unnatural beauty that they literally appeared to light up everything around them. Their shoulders were broad and their carriage true to Nature, which has never been excelled by the hand of art, their long, black tresses hung in flowing waves, extending nearly to the ground; but the beauty of the countenances of many of those Choctaw and Chickasaw girls was so extraordinary that if such faces were seen today in one of the parlors of the fashionable world, they would be considered as a type of beauty hitherto unknown.

He handed the book back to the boy and removed the glasses, grinning all the while. "Now parts of that do sound like Old Lady Blue Wood. That unnatural part, and that part about broad shoulders. But she ain't never had a carriage that I know of, and she's more likely to light into anybody that's close than to light 'em up."

The boy looked down at the moldy book and then grinned weakly back at the old uncle. Beneath the floppy hat, surrounded by the acrid smell of the carbide headlamp, the old man seemed like one of the swamp shadows come into the cabin. The boy thought about his father, the old man's nephew, who had been only half Choctaw but looked nearly as dark and indestructible as the uncle. Then he looked down at his own hand in the light from the kerosene lantern. The pale skin embarrassed him, gave him away. The old man, his great-uncle, was Indian, and his father had been Indian, but he wasn't.

There was a thud on the wood shingles of the cabin's roof. Dust fell from each of the four corners of the cabin and onto the pages of the damp book.

"*Nalusachito* done climbed up on the roof," the old man said, gazing at the ceiling with amusement. "He moves pretty good for a cat that's hurt, don't he?"

The boy knew the uncle was watching for his reaction. He steeled himself, and then the panther screamed and he flinched.

The old man nodded. "Only a fool or a crazy man ain't scared when soul catcher's walking around on his house," he said.

"You're not afraid," the boy replied, watching as the old man set the headlamp on a shelf and hung the wide hat on a nail beside the rifles.

The old man pulled a piece of canvas from beneath the table and spread it on the floor. As he dumped the coon out onto the canvas, he looked up with a chuckle. "That book says Choctaw boys always respected their elders. I'm scared alright, but I know about that cat, you see, and that's the difference. That cat ain't got no surprises for me because I'm old, and I done heard all the stories."

The boy glanced at the book.

"It don't work that way," the old man said. "You can't read them. A white man comes and he pokes around and pays somebody, or maybe somebody feels sorry for him and tells him stuff and he writes it down. But he don't understand, so he can't put it down right, you see."

Soul Catcher

How do you understand? the boy wanted to ask as he watched the uncle pull a knife from its sheath on his hip and begin to skin the coon, making cuts down each leg and up the belly so delicately that the boy could see no blood at all. The panther shrieked overhead, and the old man seemed not to notice.

"Why don't you shoot it?" the boy asked, looking at the big deer rifle on the wall, the thirty-forty Krag from the Spanish-American War.

The old man looked up in surprise.

"You could sell the skin to Mr. Wheeler for a lot of money, couldn't you?" Mr. Wheeler was the black man who came from across the river to buy the coonskins.

The old man squinted and studied the boy's face. "You can't hunt that cat," he said patiently. "*Nalusachito's* something you got to accept, something that's just there."

"You see," he continued, "what folks like that fool Reeves don't understand is that this painter has always been out there. We just ain't noticed him for a long time. He's always there, and that's what people forget. You can't kill him." He tapped his chest with the handle of the knife. "*Nalusachito* comes from in here."

The boy watched the old man in silence. He knew about the soul catcher from the book in his lap. It was an old superstition, and the book didn't say anything about *nalusachito* being a panther. That was something the old man invented. This panther was very real and dangerous. He looked skeptically at the old man and then up at the rifle.

"No," the old man said. "We'll just let this painter be."

He pulled the skin off over the head of the raccoon like a sweater, leaving the naked body shining like a baby in the yellow light. Under the beds the dogs sniffed and whined, and overhead the whispers moved across the roof.

The old man held the skin up and admired it, then laid it fur-side down on the bench beside him. "I sure ain't going outside to nail this up right now," he said, the corners of his mouth suggesting a grin. He lifted the bolt and pushed the door open and swung the body of the coon out into the dark. When he closed the door there was a snarl and an impact on the ground. The dogs began to growl and whimper, and the old man said, "You, Yvonne! Hoyo!" and the dogs shivered in silence.

The boy watched the old man wash his hands in the bucket and sit on the edge of the other bed to pull off his boots. Each night and morning since he'd come it had been the same. The old uncle would go out at night and come back before daylight with something in the bag. Usually the boy would waken to find the old man in the other plank bed, sleeping like a small child, so lightly that the boy could not see or hear him breathe. But

Soul Catcher

this night the boy had awakened in the very early morning, torn from sleep by a sound he wasn't conscious of hearing, and he had sat up with the lantern and book to await the old man's return. He read the book because there was nothing else to read. The myths reminded him of fairy tales he'd read as a child, and he tried to imagine his father reading them.

The old man was a real Choctaw—*Chahta okla*—a full-blood. Was the ability to believe the myths diluted with the blood, the boy wondered, so that his father could, when he had been alive, believe only half as strongly as the old man and he, his father's son, half as much yet? He thought of the soul catcher, and he shivered, but he knew that he was just scaring himself the way kids always did. His mother had told him how they said that when his father was born the uncle had shown up at the sharecropper's cabin and announced that the boy would be his responsibility. That was the Choctaw way, he said, the right way. A man must accept responsibility for and teach his sister's children. Nobody had thought of that custom for a long time, and nobody had seen the uncle for years, and nobody knew how he'd even learned of the boy's birth, but there he was come out of the swamps across the river with his straight black hair hanging to his shoulders under the floppy hat and his face dark as night so that the mother, his sister, screamed when she saw him. And from that day onward the uncle had come often from the swamps to take the boy's father with him, to teach him.

The old man rolled into the bed, pulled the wool blanket to his chin, turned to the wall, and was asleep. The boy watched him and then turned down the lamp until only a dim glow outlined the objects in the room. He thought of Los Angeles, the bone-dry hills and yellow air, the home where he'd lived with his parents before the accident that killed both. It was difficult to be Choctaw, to be Indian there, and he'd seen his father working hard at it, growing his black hair long, going to urban powwows where the fancy dancers spun like beautiful birds. His father had taught him to hunt in the desert hills and to say a few phrases, like *Chahta isht ia* and *Chahta yakni,* in the old language. The words had remained only sounds, the powwow dancers only another Southern California spectacle for a green-eyed, fair-skinned boy. But the hunting had been real, a testing of desire and reflex he had felt all the way through.

Indians were hunters. Indians lived close to the land. His father had said those things often. He thought about the panther. The old man would not hunt the black cat, and had probably made up the story about *nalusa-chito* as an excuse. The panther was dangerous. For a month the boy had been at the cabin and had not ventured beyond the edges of the garden except to go out in the small rowboat onto the muddy Yazoo River that flanked one side of the clearing. The swampy forest around the cabin was

Soul Catcher

like the river, a place in which nothing was ever clear: shadows, swirls, dark forms rising and disappearing again, nothing ever clearly seen. And each night he'd lain in the bed and listened to the booming and cracking of the swamp like something monstrously evil and thought of the old man killing things in the dark, picturing the old man as a solitary light cutting the darkness.

The panther might remain, its soft feet whispering maddeningly on the cabin roof each night while the old man hunted in the swamp. Or it might attack the old man who would not shoot it. For the first time the boy realized the advantage in not being really Choctaw. The old uncle could not hunt the panther, but he could, because he knew the cat for what it really was. It would not be any more difficult to kill than the wild pigs he'd hunted with his father in the coastal range of California, and it was no different than the cougars that haunted those same mountains. The black one was only a freak of nature.

Moving softly, he lifted the heavy rifle from its nails. In a crate on the floor he found the cartridges and, slipping on his red-plaid mackinaw, he dropped the bullets into his pocket. Then he walked carefully to the door, lifted the bolt, stepped through, and silently pulled the door closed. Outside, it was getting close to dawn and the air had the clean, raw smell of that hour, tainted by the sharp odor of the river and swamp. The trees were unsure outlines protruding from the wall of black that surrounded the cabin on three sides. Over the river the fog hovered in a gray somewhat lighter than the air, and a kingfisher called in a shrill *kree* out across the water.

He pushed shells into the rifle's magazine and then stepped along the garden trail toward the trees, listening carefully for the sounds of the woods. Where even he knew there should have been the shouting of crickets, frogs, and a hundred other night creatures, there was only silence beating like the heartbeat drum at one of the powwows. At the edge of the clearing he paused.

In the cabin the old man sat up and looked toward the door. The boy had an hour before full daylight, and he would meet *nalusachito* in that transitional time. The old man fingered the medicine pouch on the cord around his neck and wondered about such a convergence. There was a meaning beyond his understanding, something that could not be avoided.

The boy brushed aside a muskedine vine and stepped into the woods, feeling his boots sink into the wet floor. It had all been a singular journey toward this, out of the light of California, across the burning earth of the Southwest, and into the darkness of this place. Beyond the garden, in the uncertain light, the trunks of trees, the brush and vines were like a curtain closing behind him. Then the panther cried in the damp woods somewhere in front of him, the sound insinuating itself into the night like one of the tendrils of fog that clung to the ground. The boy began to walk on the faint trail toward the sound, the air so thick he felt as though he were suspended in fluid, his movements like those of a man walking on the floor of the sea. His breathing became torturous and liquid, and his eyes adjusted to the darkness and strained to isolate the watery forms surrounding him.

When he had gone a hundred yards the panther called again, a strange, dreamlike, muted cry different from the earlier screams, and he hesitated a moment and then left the trail to follow the cry. A form slid from the trail beside his boot, and he moved carefully away, deeper into the woods beyond the trail. Now the light was graying, and the leaves and bark of the trees became delicately etched as the day broke.

The close scream of the panther jerked him into full consciousness, and he saw the cat. Twenty feet away, it crouched in a clutter of vines and brush, its yellow eyes burning at him. In front of the panther was the half-eaten carcass of the coon.

He raised the rifle slowly, bringing it to his shoulder and slipping the safety off in the same movement. With his action, the panther pushed itself upright until it sat on its haunches, facing him. It was then the boy saw that one of the front feet hung limp, a festering wound in the shoulder on that side. He lined the notched sight of the rifle against the cat's head, and he saw the burning go out of the eyes. The panther watched him calmly, waiting as he pulled the trigger. The animal toppled backward, kicked for an instant and was still.

He walked to the cat and nudged it with a boot. *Nalusachito* was dead. He leaned the rifle against a tree and lifted the cat by its four feet and swung it onto his back, surprised at how light it was and feeling the sharp edges of the ribs through the fur. He felt sorrow and pity for the hurt animal he could imagine hunting awkwardly in the swamps, and he knew that what he had done was right. He picked up the rifle and turned back toward the cabin.

When he opened the cabin door, with the cat on his shoulder, the old man was sitting in the chair facing him. The boy leaned the rifle against the bench and swung the panther carefully to the floor and looked up at the old man, but the old man's eyes were fixed on the open doorway. Beyond the doorway *nalusachito* crouched, ready to spring.

Responding to the Selection ───────

Questions for Discussion

1. What follows the old man to his cabin? In what ways does the old man explain its presence?

2. How does the boy respond to his great-uncle's explanations? Explain how the boy's life experiences contribute to his views and actions.

3. Why does the old man scoff at the boy's ideas?

4. How does the boy regard his heritage as the story progresses?

5. Have you ever been in a situation when you had to reconcile the real world with the world of traditional beliefs?

Activities

Imagining the Next Scene

1. Louis Owens's story has a cliff-hanger ending. What do you think happens next? What is crouching in the doorway? Is it really there, or is it only a vision? Write a scene that could come next in the story. Use information from the story to keep the characters believable.

Writing an Essay

2. Compare and contrast the two world views presented in the story. Begin by defining each view and then discuss the advantages and disadvantages you feel each view reflects. Conclude your essay by indicating which view most closely matches your own and explaining why.

Creating an Advertisement

3. Imagine that the story has been made into a film or a play. Create a visual advertisement for the show that captures its narrative tension and also suggests the larger philosophical questions it raises.

Focus on . . .
Coyote and Other Tricksters

Traditional Native American literature is filled with stories of the trickster. Among tribes from California, the Southwest, and the Central Plains, this character takes animal form as Coyote (sometimes "Old Man Coyote"). The trickster in the tales of Southeastern tribes is Rabbit, while Raven, Mink, or Blue Jay are the tricksters in stories of tribes from the Pacific Northwest. Sometimes, as with Gluscabi of the Northeast Woodlands, the trickster appears in human form.

Whatever the name, the trickster is a bundle of contradictory traits. He's neither good nor evil because he has no values or morals. He tricks other characters, but often falls for their schemes and gets tricked himself. He's a comic figure who teaches serious lessons. He's crafty but lacks wisdom. He's a hero and a fool. He's responsible for giving humans some basic things they need, such as fire and water, but he makes a mockery of social conventions. He has supernatural abilities, and yet he is always hungry and always on the prowl to satisfy his enormous appetite.

What purpose do the stories about such a wild character serve? The trickster is a comic character, and trickster stories are meant to be funny and entertaining. Most Native American trickster myths form a series, telling about the

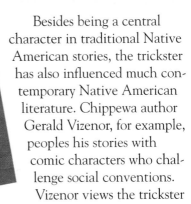

creation of the earth, how the earth was transformed, and how people's customs originated. The trickster is frequently the opposite of a role model. But even then, the character's actions focus attention on important beliefs and rules of behavior, and so the stories are passed on to instruct each new generation.

Literary critics have varying views on the role of the trickster. Some critics believe the trickster represents the dark side of people or of a culture. Others view trickster stories as a way for people to vent pent-up frustrations with social rules and obligations.

Besides being a central character in traditional Native American stories, the trickster has also influenced much contemporary Native American literature. Chippewa author Gerald Vizenor, for example, peoples his stories with comic characters who challenge social conventions. Vizenor views the trickster as playing a positive role—that of a liberator. In modern tales as well as traditional ones, the trickster makes people laugh as he teaches them.

Linking to . . .

- Think about what you've learned about the coyote and the trickster as you read the following selections.

Before You Read

Two Traditional Stories (Pawnee and Abenaki)

Joseph Bruchac
Born 1942

> " . . . *remember to listen.*
> *There are stories all*
> *around you.*"

About Bruchac

Joseph Bruchac is a storyteller, writer, publisher, and musician of Abenaki ancestry. Born in Saratoga Springs, New York, Bruchac was raised by his grandparents. He has lived most of his life in a house his grandfather built in Greenfield Center, a small town in the foothills of the Adirondack Mountains. Before he became a writer, Bruchac taught English in West Africa for three years. "I went to Africa to teach—but more than that, to be taught. It showed me many things. How much we have as Americans and take for granted. How much our eyes refuse to see because they are blinded to everything in a man's face except his color," he says. After returning from Africa, Bruchac and his wife started the Greenfield Review Press, which is dedicated to publishing multicultural literature.

Stories and Lessons

The two tales you are about to read come from *Native American Stories,* a collection of traditional stories retold by Bruchac. The first story, "Old Man Coyote and the Rock," comes from the Pawnee people of the Great Plains. Coyote, the main character in the story, is a trickster who appears in the oral literature of many Plains tribes. Coyote relies on his cleverness to try to fool others in order to get what he wants.

The second story, "Gluscabi and the Wind Eagle," comes from the traditions of the Abenaki people of New England. The character Gluscabi, whose name means "Teller of Stories," appears in many Abenaki stories. He is presented as a powerful but often misguided trickster who lived in a time before human beings existed. The stories are meant both to entertain and to help young people learn how to behave properly.

Two Traditional Stories

Old Man Coyote and the Rock

— Traditional (Pawnee)
Retold by Joseph Bruchac

Old Man Coyote was going along.

It was quite a while since he had eaten and he was feeling cut in half by hunger. He came to the top of a hill and there he saw a big rock. Old Man Coyote took out his flint knife.

"Grandfather," Old Man Coyote said to the rock, "I give you this fine knife. Now help me in some way, because I am hungry."

Then Old Man Coyote went along further. He went over the top of the hill and there at the bottom was a buffalo that had just been killed.

"How lucky I am," Old Man Coyote said. "But how can I butcher this buffalo without a knife? Now where did I leave my knife?"

Then Old Man Coyote walked back up the hill until he came to the big rock where his knife still lay on the ground.

"You don't need this knife," he said to the big rock.

Then he picked his flint knife up and ran back to where he had left the buffalo. Now, though, where there had been a freshly killed buffalo, there were only buffalo bones and the bones were very old and gray. Then, from behind him, Old Man Coyote heard a rumbling noise. He turned around and looked up. The big rock was rolling down the hill after him. GA-DA-RUM, GA-DA-RUM.

Old Man Coyote began to run. He ran and ran, but the stone still rumbled after him. GA-DA-RUM, GA-DA-RUM. Old Man Coyote ran until he came to a bear den.

"Help me," he called in to the bears.

The bears looked out and saw what was chasing Old Man Coyote. "We can't help you against Grandfather Rock," they said.

Two **Traditional** Stories

GA-DA-RUM, GA-DA-RUM. The big rock kept coming and Old Man Coyote kept running. Now he came to a cave where the mountain lions lived and he called out again.

"Help me," Old Man Coyote said. "I am about to be killed!" The mountain lions looked out and saw what was after Old Man Coyote. "No," they said, "we can't help you if you have angered Grandfather Rock."

GA-DA-RUM, GA-DA-RUM. The big rock kept rumbling after Old Man Coyote and he kept running. Now he came to the place where a bull buffalo was grazing.

"Help me," Old Man Coyote yelled. "That big rock said it was going to kill all the buffalo. When I tried to stop it, it began to chase me."

The bull buffalo braced his legs and thrust his head out to stop the big rock. But the rock just brushed the bull buffalo aside and left him standing there dazed, with his horns bent and his head pushed back into his shoulders. To this day all buffalo are still like that.

GA-DA-RUM, GA-DA-RUM. The big rock kept rolling and Old Man Coyote kept running. But Old Man Coyote was getting tired now and the rock was getting closer. Then Old Man Coyote looked up and saw a nighthawk flying overhead.

"My friend," Old Man Coyote yelled up to the nighthawk, "this big rock that is chasing me said you are ugly. It said you have a wide mouth and your eyes are too big and your beak is all pinched up. I told it not to say that and it began to chase me."

The nighthawk heard what Old Man Coyote said and grew very angry. He called the other nighthawks. They began to swoop down and strike at the big rock with their beaks. Each time they struck the big rock a piece broke off and stopped rolling. GA-DA-RUM, GA-DA-RUM. The rock kept rolling and Old Man Coyote kept running, but now the rock was much smaller. The nighthawks continued to swoop down and break off pieces. Finally the big rock was nothing but small pebbles.

Old Man Coyote came up and looked at the little stones. "My, my," he said to the nighthawks, "Why did you wide-mouthed, big-eyed, pinch-beaked birds do that to my old friend?" Then Old Man Coyote laughed and started on his way again.

Now the nighthawks were very angry at Old Man Coyote. They gathered all of the pieces of the big rock and fanned them together with their wings. The next thing Old Man Coyote knew, he heard a familiar sound behind him again. GA-DA-RUM, GA-DA-RUM. He tried to run, but he was so tired now he could not get away. The big rock rolled right over him and flattened him out.

❖

Gluscabi and the Wind Eagle

— Traditional (Abenaki)
Retold by Joseph Bruchac

Long ago, Gluscabi lived with his grandmother, Woodchuck, in a small lodge beside the big water.

One day Gluscabi was walking around when he looked out and saw some ducks in the bay.

"I think it is time to go hunt some ducks," he said. So he took his bow and arrows and got into his canoe. He began to paddle out into the bay and as he paddled he sang:

> Ki yo wah ji neh
> yo ho hey ho
> Ki yo wah ji neh
> Ki yo wah ji neh.

But a wind came up and it turned his canoe and blew him back to shore. Once again Gluscabi began to paddle out and this time he sang his song a little harder:

> KI YO WAH JI NEH
> YO HO HEY HO
> KI YO WAH JI NEH
> KI YO WAH JI NEH.

But again the wind came and blew him back to shore.

Four times he tried to paddle out into the bay and four times he failed. He was not happy. He went back to the lodge of his grandmother and walked right in, even though there was a stick leaning across the door, which meant that the person inside was doing some work and did not want to be disturbed.

"Grandmother," Gluscabi said, "What makes the wind blow?"

Grandmother Woodchuck looked up from her work. "Gluscabi," she said, "Why do you want to know?"

Then Gluscabi answered her just as every child in the world does when they are asked such a question.

"Because," he said.

Grandmother Woodchuck looked at him. "Ah, Gluscabi," she said. "Whenever you ask such questions I feel there is going to be trouble. And perhaps I should not tell you. But I know that you are so stubborn you will never stop asking until I answer you. So I shall tell you. Far from here, on top of the tallest mountain, a great bird stands. This bird is named Wuchowsen, and when he flaps his wings he makes the wind blow."

"Eh-hey, Grandmother," said Gluscabi, "I see. Now how would one find that place where the Wind Eagle stands?"

Again Grandmother Woodchuck looked at Gluscabi. "Ah, Gluscabi," she said, "Once again I feel that perhaps I should not tell you. But I know that you are very stubborn and would never stop asking. So, I shall tell you. If you walk always facing the wind you will come to the place where Wuchowsen stands."

"Thank you, Grandmother," said Gluscabi. He stepped out of the lodge and faced into the wind and began to walk.

He walked across the fields and through the woods and the wind blew hard. He walked through the valleys and into the hills and the wind blew harder still. He came to the foothills and began to climb and the wind still blew harder. Now the foothills were becoming mountains and the wind was very strong. Soon there were no longer any trees and the wind was very, very strong. The wind was so strong that it blew off Gluscabi's moccasins. But he was very stubborn and he kept on walking, leaning into the wind. Now the wind was so strong that it blew off his shirt, but he kept on walking. Now the wind was so strong that it blew off all his clothes and he was naked, but he still kept walking. Now the wind was so strong that it blew off his hair, but Gluscabi still kept walking, facing into the wind. The wind was so strong that it blew off his eyebrows, but still he continued to walk. Now the wind was so strong that he could hardly stand. He had to pull himself along by grabbing hold of the boulders. But there, on the peak ahead of him, he could see a great bird slowly flapping its wings. It was Wuchowsen, the Wind Eagle.

Gluscabi took a deep breath. "GRANDFATHER!" he shouted.

The Wind Eagle stopped flapping his wings and looked around. "Who calls me Grandfather?" he said.

Gluscabi stood up. "It's me, Grandfather. I just came up here to tell you that you do a very good job making the wind blow."

The Wind Eagle puffed out his chest with pride. "You mean like this?" he said and flapped his wings even harder. The wind which he made was so strong that it lifted Gluscabi right off his feet, and he would have been blown right off the mountain had he not reached out and grabbed a boulder again.

"GRANDFATHER!!!" Gluscabi shouted again.

The Wind Eagle stopped flapping his wings. "Yesss?" he said.

Gluscabi stood up and came closer to Wuchowsen. "You do a very good job of making the wind blow, Grandfather. This is so. But it seems to me that you could do an even better job if you were on that peak over there."

The Wind Eagle looked toward the other peak. "That may be so," he said, "but how would I get from here to there?"

Gluscabi smiled. "Grandfather," he said, "I will carry you. Wait here." Then Gluscabi ran back down the mountain until he came to a big basswood tree. He stripped off the outer bark and from the inner bark he braided a strong carrying strap which he took back up the mountain to the Wind Eagle. "Here, Grandfather," he said. "let me wrap this around you so I can lift you more easily." Then he wrapped the carrying strap so tightly around Wuchowsen that his wings were pulled in to his sides and he could hardly breathe. "Now, Grandfather," Gluscabi said, picking the Wind Eagle up, "I will take you to a better place." He began to walk toward the other peak, but as he walked he came to a place where there was a large crevice, and as he stepped over it he let go of the carrying strap and the Wind Eagle slid down into the crevice, upside down, and was stuck.

"Now," Gluscabi said, "It is time to hunt some ducks."

He walked back down the mountain and there was no wind at all. He walked till he came to the treeline and still no wind blew. He walked down to the foothills and down to the hills and the valleys and still there was no wind. He walked through the forests and through the fields, and the wind did not blow at all. He walked and walked until he came back to the lodge by the water, and by now all his hair had grown back. He put on some fine new clothing and a new pair of moccasins and took his bow and arrows and went down to the bay and climbed into his boat to hunt ducks. He paddled out into the water and sang his canoeing song:

> Ki yo wah ji neh
> yo ho hey ho
> Ki yo wah ji neh
> Ki yo wah ji neh.

But the air was very hot and still and he began to sweat. The air was so still and hot that it was hard to breathe. Soon the water began to grow dirty and smell bad and there was so much foam on the water he could hardly paddle. He was not pleased at all and he returned to the shore and went straight to his grandmother's lodge and walked in.

"Grandmother," he said, "What is wrong? The air is hot and still and it is making me sweat and it is hard to breathe. The water is dirty and covered with foam. I cannot hunt ducks at all like this."

Grandmother Woodchuck looked up at Gluscabi. "Gluscabi," she said, "what have you done now?"

And Gluscabi answered just as every child in the world answers when asked that question, "Oh, nothing," he said.

"Gluscabi," said Grandmother Woodchuck again, "Tell me what you have done."

Then Gluscabi told her about going to visit the Wind Eagle and what he had done to stop the wind.

"Oh, Gluscabi," said Grandmother Woodchuck, "will you never learn? Tabaldak, The Owner, set the Wind Eagle on that mountain to make the wind because we need the wind. The wind keeps the air cool and clean. The wind brings the clouds which gives us rain to wash the Earth. The wind moves the waters and keeps them fresh and sweet. Without the wind, life will not be good for us, for our children or our children's children."

Gluscabi nodded his head. "Kaamoji, Grandmother," he said. "I understand."

Then he went outside. He faced in the direction from which the wind had once come and began to walk. He walked through the fields and through the forests and the wind did not blow and he felt very hot. He walked through the valleys and up the hills and there was no wind and it was hard for him to breathe. He came to the foothills and began to climb and he was very hot and sweaty indeed. At last he came to the mountain where the Wind Eagle once stood and he went and looked down into the crevice. There was Wuchowsen, the Wind Eagle, wedged upside down.

"Uncle?" Gluscabi called.

The Wind Eagle looked up as best he could. "Who calls me Uncle?" he said.

"It is Gluscabi, Uncle. I'm up here. But what are you doing down there?"

"Oh, Gluscabi," said the Wind Eagle, "a very ugly naked man with no hair told me that he would take me to the other peak so that I could do a better job of making the wind blow. He tied my wings and picked me up, but as he stepped over this crevice he dropped me in and I am stuck. And I am not comfortable here at all."

"Ah, Grandfath . . . er, Uncle, I will get you out."

Then Gluscabi climbed down into the crevice. He pulled the Wind Eagle free and placed him back on his mountain and untied his wings.

"Uncle," Gluscabi said, "It is good that the wind should blow sometimes and other times it is good that it should be still."

The Wind Eagle looked at Gluscabi and then nodded his head. "Grandson," he said, "I hear what you say."

So it is that sometimes there is wind and sometimes it is still to this very day. And so the story goes.

Responding to the Selection

Questions for Discussion

1. Describe the traits of Old Man Coyote and the traits of Gluscabi. Think about how they act and what happens to them. What kind of people do you think these tricksters might represent?

2. What lessons might be learned from "Old Man Coyote and the Rock"? From "Gluscabi and the Wind Eagle"? Do you think these lessons are relevant today? Why or why not?

3. N. Scott Momaday, a well-known Native American writer and storyteller, says that these stories "center upon one of the most important of all considerations in human experience: the relationship between man and nature." What does each of these stories have to say about that relationship?

4. Discuss examples of other situations in which people have acted like Old Man Coyote and Gluscabi.

Activities

Telling a Story

1. Take on the role of a storyteller and practice and present one of these tales orally to your class. Joseph Bruchac offers this advice for telling a story: Read it several times so that you know it well. Speak slowly and clearly.

Creating a Comic Strip

2. Retell one of these stories in the form of a comic strip.

Rewriting a Traditional Story

3. Find a story that is part of your heritage and try rewriting it for a modern audience.

Before You Read

The Dog and the Wolf and The Oak and the Reed

Aesop
(c. 600–550 B.C.)

"Do not count your chickens before they are hatched."

— Aesop

About Aesop and la Fontaine

Aesop supposedly was a Greek slave famous for telling fables. If he did exist, he certainly was not an author in the usual sense, but a teller of stories from many sources. Aesop's fables express values that were held widely among ancient Greeks. Orators often quoted the fables in political speeches to make a point or support an argument. The fables were also appreciated simply for their entertainment value.

Many critics believe that Aesop's fables reached their highest form in the verse adaptations of Jean de la Fontaine.

Jean de la Fontaine
(1621–1695)

Although la Fontaine depended on earlier writers for material, his manner of telling fables was highly original. He enhanced the dramatic impact of these brief tales through subtle characterization and rich imagery.

In seventeenth-century France, fables were considered a minor literary form, not worth the attention of sophisticated readers. Jean de la Fontaine challenged this notion. His fables have become classics of French literature.

La Fontaine briefly studied theology and law, but found his true calling as a poet. He had difficulty supporting himself and relied mainly on the help of wealthy patrons in Paris. A charming and witty conversationalist, la Fontaine was popular in the literary salons of Paris.

The Dog and the Wolf

— *Aesop*
Retold by Joseph Jacobs

A gaunt Wolf was almost dead with hunger when he happened to meet a Housedog who was passing by. "Ah, Cousin," said the Dog, "I knew how it would be; your irregular life will soon be the ruin of you. Why do you not work steadily as I do, and get your food regularly given to you?"

"I would have no objection," said the Wolf, "if I could only get a place."

"I will easily arrange that for you," said the Dog; "come with me to my master and you shall share my work."

So the Wolf and the Dog went towards the town together. On the way there the Wolf noticed that the hair on a certain part of the Dog's neck was very much worn away, so he asked him how that had come about.

"Oh, it is nothing," said the Dog. "That is only the place where the collar is put on at night to keep me chained up; it chafes a bit, but one soon gets used to it."

"Is that all?" said the Wolf. "Then good-bye to you, Master Dog."

"Better starve free than be a fat slave."

❖

The Oak and the Reed

— *Jean de la Fontaine*
Translated by James Michie

One day the oak said to the reed:
"You have good cause indeed
To accuse Nature of being unkind.
To you a wren must seem
5   An intolerable burden, and the least puff of wind
That chances to wrinkle the face of the stream
Forces your head low; whereas I,
Huge as a Caucasian peak, defy
Not only the sun's glare, but the worst the weather can do.
10   What seems a breeze to me is a gale for you.
Had you been born in the lee of my leaf-sheltered ground,
You would have suffered less, I should have kept you warm;
But you reeds are usually found
On the moist borders of the kingdom of the storm.
15   It strikes me that to you Nature has been unfair."
"Your pity," the plant replied, "springs from a kind heart.
But please don't be anxious on my part.
Your fear of the winds ought to be greater than mine.
I bend, but I never break. You, till now, have been able to bear
20   Their fearful buffets without flexing your spine.
But let us wait and see." Even as he spoke,
From the horizon's nethermost gloom
The worst storm the north had ever bred in its womb
        Furiously awoke.

25   The tree stood firm, the reed began to bend.
       The wind redoubled its efforts to blow—
               So much so
               That in the end
       It uprooted the one that had touched the sky with its head,
30   But whose feet reached to the region of the dead.

Responding to the Selection ——————

Questions for Discussion

1. A fable is a brief story that teaches a moral, or lesson. The moral of "The Dog and the Wolf" is directly stated. What is a moral or lesson of "The Oak and the Reed"? How is the relationship between the two characters in each of these fables similar?
2. As a genre, how are the Native American trickster tales you have read similar to these European fables? Consider their purposes, titles, characters, and settings. How do they differ in style?
3. Think about the lessons that these four stories teach. What do the lessons have in common? Which story do you think most effectively demonstrates its lesson? Why?
4. Compare the main characters in these four tales. In which story or stories are the characters most fully developed? What human weakness do these main characters share?
5. Which of the four stories do you find the most entertaining and/or enlightening? Why?

Activities

Writing a Story

1. Think about a lesson you would like to teach new students coming to your school. Draw upon the common features of these Native American trickster tales and European fables to write a brief tale that teaches this lesson.

Creating an Illustration

2. For each of these stories, create an illustration portraying the main lesson, or moral.

Moonlight. Marvin Toddy (b. 1954). Oil on Canvas, 16 x 20 inches. La Fonda Indian Shop and Gallery, Santa Fe, NM.

Theme Two

The World of Home

*This house has survived,
with its many descendants . . .*

— Lucy Thompson

Before You Read

The Ancient Houses

Lucy Thompson
1853–1932

"Oh, how little we know of the depths of the ages gone; how wide, how profound and deep, is the knowledge we seek."

About Thompson

Lucy Thompson was a member of the Yurok, who have long lived along the Klamath River and the Pacific coast in northern California. Thompson was not a professional writer, but she published *To the American Indian* in 1916 because she believed the Yurok culture was on the verge of being wiped out by white American culture. She wrote the book to tell the "true facts" about her tribe's religion and culture before the knowledge was lost forever. As she wrote in the preface to her book, "My father . . . took me at a very early age and began training me in all of the mysteries and laws of my people. I can understand every word, every nod and gesture made in our language." Thompson was the first Native American woman in California to publish a book.

Thompson's Yurok name was Che-na-wah Weitch-ah-wah. At the age of 22, she married Milton James Thompson. The Thompsons had three children, but little else is known about their lives.

The Ancient White People

Like many other Native American tribes, the Yurok believed that a race of spirit beings lived on Earth at the beginning of time. Lucy Thompson calls these beings *Wa-gas* or "the Ancient White People." According to Yurok tradition, these first beings discovered the ideal way of life on Earth and passed on this knowledge to the Yurok. Then, for reasons unknown to the Yurok, the Wa-gas disappeared, promising to return some day. When they returned, it would signal the beginning of an age of peace and prosperity throughout the world.

The Ancient Houses

— *Lucy Thompson*

Many of the houses of the Klamath River Indians date back to the prehistoric centuries of the long, long ago, and have been repaired and rebuilt many generations. Some of them are hallowed with alluring traditions and inspiring history, when our people were powerful and ruled a mighty nation. The Indian name of these houses is Oc-lo-melth. One of these houses is situated at Wah-tec, less than two hundred yards from where the White Deerskin Dance is held, and is my mother's house, where she was born and where she first looked out upon the light of a strange world. The surroundings of this house are filled with the romance of centuries, together with the wonderful history of the passing ages, as it dates back before the Indians came to this land from Cheek-cheek-alth. They say the house first belonged to the Wa-gas, the white people that were here when they first arrived. The Wa-gas were very fond of pets, and while they lived in this house they kept a number of deer as pets.

When the Wa-gas left this land, they left behind at this place a young man that was half-Indian and half-white. He remained for some time and cared for the pets, as the Wa-gas cherished them. The young man became lonesome for his people, in spite of the fact that he was very devoted to the deer, and one day he answered the call of the Wa-gas and followed in their footsteps, to join them in the far north. As he was leaving, he asked the Indians of my ancient blood to care for his pets, as he would be absent and never return. This my people have done according to the request of the young man and out of their great friendship between the two races. This ancient house became a hallowed spot where sacred memories of a people that have passed away in silence long ago fill its every surroundings.

In one corner of this dwelling, within its walls, is a large stone trough which was made and placed there by the Wa-gas untold centuries ago, so they could feed their deer. The deer were fed upon the stalks of tobacco and the walth-pay, the stalks being pounded into fine meal, mixed together, and then placed in the stone trough for the deer to eat. It was said for ages, and up to the advent of the present white race, that the spirits of the departed Wa-gas would come earthward in the deep shadows of the evening-time and open a door, which was made in the corner of the house for that purpose, so the deer could come in at night and feed upon the meal. The deer would stealthily emerge from their forest homes at night and upon finding the door open would enter the house and eat the meal; then just before the break of day they would silently vanish into the forests, and the door would be closed when morning came. My mother has seen the deer coming toward the house in the dark shadows of evening, but she has not seen them for a good many years, as they have become hunted beasts of prey.

Through the memory of the passing ages the Wa-gas left this land before the world was covered with water, and according to these traditions this house goes back for hundreds of centuries. This house has survived, with its long line of descendents, but it is now fading in the storm of years that are passing, and the place of its ruins will soon be forgotten.

There are a number of these old houses in the different villages along the Klamath River, from its source to its mouth, and on the coast from Ah-man to Trinidad. At the present day most of them are deserted, and are left to sink into ruins and oblivion.

The rattlesnake is called May-yep-pere, and they make their dwelling places under the ground and in the dark recesses. The children born in this house are not afraid of these snakes, as they never harm them. The snakes crawl out and over the house without restraint. I had no thought of fear, as the blood of ages had made me a kin to these fierce reptiles, where my people had sheltered them and fed them for thousands of years. In olden times the whole family would go away and leave the house alone for several days, sometimes for two or three weeks, and during their absence the snakes would creep out over the house and lie about in numerous places. If a stranger tried to approach the house, they gave him warning, and if he attempted to enter, they would at once be aroused into a fury and would attack him. My mother says that strangers have attempted to enter the house while the family was away and have been severely bitten by the rattlers. Therefore, the door of this house was always left unlocked, as no one would ever attempt to enter it that knew its strange history. If the family was at home, strangers could come and go at their will, as it was never known that the snakes ever attempted to harm anyone while some member of the family was present.

The Ancient Houses

When the family would return from their sojourn, the head of the household, or someone who was born in this house, would precede the rest. I remember it was always my mother's duty upon reaching the door of the house, and she would begin talking in a low tone of voice, saying: "We are coming home; we are here now, and you must all go out of the way." Upon hearing her voice, the snakes would immediately begin to creep away to their hiding places. Upon entering, she would begin to tap lightly upon the floor with her cane and would keep talking until all the snakes would disappear, after which the rest of the family would enter the house, talking, laughing and playing without any thought of the snakes ever harming them.

This historical house is now owned by my mother, and in which she has not lived for fifteen years, but up until about five years ago she would go almost everyday and build a fire in it and sit around the house and weave baskets. In the past five years it has not been repaired and has racked into ruins, so bad that she does not care to enter it anymore, except on special occasions when she wants to break up something. For the past twenty years she has been breaking and pounding to pieces the stone bowls, trays and all the ancient implements that were left by the Wa-gas. She is endeavoring to destroy all these sacred reminiscences of the prehistoric days that they may never be ruthlessly handled and curiously gazed upon by the present white race. The stone trough that the deer fed out of is so large and heavy that she cannot break it to pieces, but is letting it sink into the ground; and it is being covered with rubbish, together with its strange charm and fascinating history, where my pen has failed to impress, this deep sentiment, therefore its wonderful tradition has faded with the closing of this chapter where a new era has dawned. My mother gave my husband two of the small stone bowls as relics of the days that are gone forever, and he keeps them as cherished memories.

Responding to the Selection

Questions for Discussion

1. What impressions of the Yuroks' home life and attachment to home do you get from reading "The Ancient Houses"?

2. Imagine walking into the old house of Lucy Thompson's mother. How would you feel? Why?

3. How would you describe the feeling toward home that an average American has today? How is it different from the feelings described by Lucy Thompson? What factors might account for the differences?

4. What do you think the story of the rattlesnakes means? Is it purely a legend or does it embody a message?

5. Discuss the reasons that Lucy Thompson's mother destroys old artifacts. Do you think it is better to let an ancient culture die out rather than preserve it as a museum exhibit? Why?

Activities

Writing a Script

1. Imagine that your home has been passed down through a long line of descendants. What features or items in your house would a future generation regard as significant or valuable? Why? Imagine that you are preparing the script for an archaeological documentary. Describe these features and items and their significance.

Writing Questions for an Interview

2. If you could interview Lucy Thompson, what questions would you ask her about her home, her culture, her life, or her beliefs? Write a list of interview questions.

Creating a Sign

3. Design a welcome and/or warning sign for the front door of the ancient house that Lucy Thompson describes. The Yurok did not have a written language, so use pictures and symbols rather than words in your sign.

Before You Read

Three Poems

Luci Tapahonso
Born 1953

> *"I write every day, and it's like eating and sleeping. I can't not do it."*

About Tapahonso

Luci Tapahonso grew up in a family of eleven children in Shiprock, New Mexico, on a Navajo reservation. Her love of language developed early, inspired by her family's storytelling and singing, and she began writing poetry when she was about eight years old. Tapahonso says, "The combination of song, prayer, and poetry is a natural form of expression for many Navajo people. A person who is able to 'talk beautifully' is well thought of and considered wealthy."

Tapahonso earned a master's degree in creative writing and English from the University of New Mexico and is an associate professor of English at the University of Kansas. The place of her birth and the traditions of her people continue to inspire her writing. Tapahonso says that her writing "becomes a prayer of sorts back to the land, the people, and the families from whence we came originally."

Navajo Lands and Traditions

The Navajo reservation covers sixteen million acres in New Mexico, Arizona, and Utah. Informally called the *rez,* it includes numerous sites with ruins that date back thousands of years. One of these sites is Canyon De Chelly, in northeastern Arizona. On ledges and at the base of the sheer red cliffs of Canyon De Chelly are village ruins of ancient people known as the Anasazi. Today, Canyon De Chelly is a national monument, but some Navajo still live and farm on the canyon floor.

Navajo traditions remain very much alive within the Navajo Nation today. The Navajo way of life centers on seeking harmony with all of nature and with other people. The most important ceremony or prayer of the Navajo is *hózhóójí,* or the blessing way. Its purpose is to achieve or restore *hózhó,* or a state of beauty, balance, or harmony.

Three Poems

— *Luci Tapahonso*

The Canyon Was Serene

Tonight as the bright moon fills the bed, I am certain I can't rise
and face the dawn. These dreams of Chinle and the mountains urge
    me to drive
back to the rez. My family knows why I left. But my husband's gentle
    horses
must wonder where he went. Since it happened, there has been no
    way to weave
5   this loneliness and the quiet nights into that calm state called
    beauty.
Hózhó. Maybe it doesn't exist. These days it makes me sad and
    jealous
that some Navajos really live by hózhóójí. Yes, I am jealous
of how the old ways actually work for them. They wake, rise,
and pray each morning knowing they are blessed. For me, the beauty
10   way is abstract most of the time. At dawn, I rush out and drive
to work, instead of saying a praying outside. They say we should
    weave
these ancient ways into our daily lives. Do you remember the horses
his mother gave at our wedding? They're traditional people, and
    brought horses
to my family. Such strong and exquisite animals. We heard people
    were jealous,
15   but we dismissed it. Back then, I rode horses for hours, and used to
    weave
until sunset each day. Once we went camping in Canyon De Chelly.
    The moonrise
was so bright, we could see tiny birds in the brush. The four-wheel
    drive
got stuck in the sand, and two guys helped push it out. That night
    the beauty

of the old canyon, the moon, and the surprise rescue proved that the beauty

20   the elders speak of, does exist. Late that night a small herd of wild horses
came to our camp. They circled and sniffed the worn-out four-wheel drive.
It smelled of gas and sweat. The canyon was serene. It's easy to be jealous
of the people who live there. How much more substantial the sunrise
blessings seem there. During those summers not long ago, it was easy to weave

25   that story and many others like it into my rugs. Back then I used to weave
and pray, weave and sing. The rhythm of the batten comb meant that beauty
was taking form. Nights like that and his low laughter made my rugs rise
evenly in warm delicate designs. Once I wove the colors of his horses
into a saddle blanket. He teased me and said my brother was jealous

30   because I had not made him one. Sometimes memories of his riding songs drive
me to tears. Whatever happened to that saddle blanket? Once on a drive
to Albuquerque, the long, red mesas and smooth cliffs showed me how to weave
them into a rug. I was so happy. Here I was sometimes frustrated and jealous
of older weavers who seem to live and breathe designs. I learned that beauty

35   can't be forced. It comes on its own. It's like the silky sheen of horses on cool summer mornings.
It's like the small breezes; the sway and rise of an appaloosa's back. Back then,
we drove the sheep home in the pure beauty of Chinle valley twilight.
Will I ever weave like that again? Our fine horses and tender love caused jealousy.
He's gone. From his grave, my tears rise.

All I Want

All I want is the bread to turn out like hers just once
            brown crust
            soft, airy insides
            rich and round
5   that is all.
    So I ask her: How many cups?
            Ah yaa ah, she says,
            tossing flour and salt into a large, silver bowl.
            I don't measure with cups,
10   I just know by my hands,
            just a little like this is right, see?
            You young people always ask
            those kinds of questions,
            she says,
15 thrusting her arms into the dough
    and turning it over and over again.
    The table trembles with her movements.
    I watch silently and this coffee is good,
                        strong and fresh.
            Outside, her son is chopping wood,
20   his body an intense arc.
            The dull rhythm of winter
            is the swinging of the axe
            and the noise of children squeezing in
            with the small sighs of wind
25   through the edges of the windows.

    She pats and tosses it furiously
    shaping balls of warm, soft dough.
            There, we'll let it rise,
            she says, sitting down now.
30   We drink coffee and there is nothing
            like the warm smell of bread rising
            on windy, woodchopping afternoons.

❖

I Am Singing Now

    the moon is a white sliver
    balancing the last of its contents
    in the final curve of the month
my daughters sleep
in the back of the pickup
breathing small clouds of white in the dark
they lie warm and soft
under layers of clothes and blankets
how they dream, precious ones, of grandma
    and the scent of fire
    the smell of mutton
    they are already home.

i watch the miles dissolve behind us
in the hazy glow of taillights and
the distinct shape of hills and mesas loom above
    then recede slowly in the clear winter night.

i sing to myself and
think of my father
    teaching me, leaning towards me
    listening as i learned.
    "just like this," he would say
    and he would sing those old songs

    into the fiber of my hair,
    into the pores of my skin,
    into the dreams of my children

and i am singing now
for the night
the almost empty moon
and the land swimming beneath cold bright stars.

❖

Responding to the Selection

Questions for Discussion

1. In the poem "The Canyon Was Serene," what is the difference between the speaker's present way of life and her former way of life? How would you characterize the speaker's state of mind in her former way of life? What caused the change?

2. The speaker in "The Canyon Was Serene" says "I learned that beauty can't be forced. It comes on its own." What does she mean? Do you agree?

3. What feelings about family and homeland does the speaker convey in the poem "I Am Singing Now"? How do the speaker's feelings compare with your own feelings for your family and homeland?

4. How would you describe the **mood** of "All I Want"? What kind of **attitude** toward life does the poem convey?

5. What similarities do you find in these three poems? Consider both the themes and the language.

6. How are these poems like "a prayer of sorts back to the land, the people, and the families"?

Activities

Creating a Poster

1. Research one of the Navajo traditions mentioned in these poems, such as religion, weaving, singing, or bread making and prepare an illustrated poster that describes the tradition.

Singing a Poem

2. Luci Tapahonso sometimes sings or chants her poems. Practice and present such an oral reading of one of these poems.

Before You Read

The Warriors

Anna Lee Walters
Born 1946

> *"Sometimes 'writing' seems to be an inappropriate word for living."*

About Walters

Anna Lee Walters was born in Pawnee, Oklahoma, of Pawnee and Otoe-Missouria heritage. She grew up hearing the traditional stories of these peoples. The influence of these stories persisted after she left Oklahoma, first to study creative writing in New England and then, after she married Harry Walters, a Navajo museum curator, to settle in Arizona. Over nearly thirty years, Walters has worked in the Native American arts and education communities. She has taught at Diné College, developed publications for Navajo Community College Press, and lectured on American Indian issues. At the same time, Walters pursued her own writing, shaping stories and crafting nonfiction that captured the unique voices of her heritage. *The Sun Is Not Merciful,* the short story collection from which "The Warriors" comes, received two literary prizes.

Traditional Storytelling

The Native American tradition, with its emphasis on oral storytelling, deeply affected Walters's approach to writing. For example, the narrator in "The Warriors" learns important lessons from an older relative who tells her stories. This oral tradition dates back to the earliest Native American literature, formulated as much as 28,000 years ago. These oral literatures expressed the themes a particular people held dear, themes such as how to live respectfully with nature and how to honor the rituals and traditions of the group. For the Pawnee, the people featured in this story, medicine men or priests traditionally performed ceremonies blending songs, poetry, and dance into stories explaining the Pawnee place in the universe.

The Warriors

— Anna Lee Walters

In our youth, we saw hobos come and go, sliding by our faded white house like wary cats who did not want us too close. Sister and I waved at the strange procession of passing men and women hobos. Just between ourselves, Sister and I talked of that hobo parade. We guessed at and imagined the places and towns we thought the hobos might have come from or had been. Mostly they were White or Black people. But there were Indian hobos, too. It never occurred to Sister and me that this would be Uncle Ralph's end.

Sister and I were little, and Uncle Ralph came to visit us. He lifted us over his head and shook us around him like gourd rattles. He was Momma's younger brother, and he could have disciplined us if he so desired. That was part of our custom. But he never did. Instead, he taught us Pawnee words. "*Pari* is Pawnee and *pita* is man," he said. Between the words, he tapped out drumbeats with his fingers on the table top, ghost dance and round dance songs that he suddenly remembered and sang. His melodic voice lilted over us and hung around the corners of the house for days. His stories of life and death were fierce and gentle. Warriors dangled in delicate balance.

He told us his version of the story of *Pahukatawa*, a Skidi Pawnee warrior. He was killed by the Sioux, but the animals, feeling compassion for him, brought *Pahukatawa* to life again. "The Evening Star and the Morning Star bore children and some people say that these offspring are who we are," he often said. At times he pointed to those stars and greeted them by their Pawnee names. He liked to pray for Sister and me, for everyone and every tiny thing in the world, but we never heard him ask for anything for himself from *Atius*, the Father.

"For beauty is why we live," Uncle Ralph said when he talked of precious things only the Pawnees know. "We die for it, too." He called himself an ancient Pawnee warrior when he was quite young. He told us that warriors must brave all storms and odds and stand their ground. He knew intimate details of every battle the Pawnees ever fought since Pawnee time began, and Sister and I knew even then that Uncle Ralph had a great battlefield of his own.

As a child I thought that Uncle Ralph had been born into the wrong time. The Pawnees had been ravaged so often by then. The tribe of several thousand when it was at its peak over a century before were then a few hundred people who had been closely confined for more than a hundred years. The warrior life was gone. Uncle Ralph was trapped in a transparent bubble of a new time. The bubble bound him tight as it blew around us.

Uncle Ralph talked obsessively of warriors, painted proud warriors who shrieked poignant battle cries at the top of their lungs and died with honor. Sister and I were little then, lost from him in the world of children who saw everything with children's eyes. And though we saw with wide eyes the painted warriors that he fantasized and heard their fierce and haunting battle cries, we did not hear his. Now that we are old and Uncle Ralph has been gone for a long time, Sister and I know that when he died, he was tired and alone. But he was a warrior.

The hobos were always around in our youth. Sister and I were curious about them, and this curiosity claimed much of our time. They crept by the house at all hours of the day and night, dressed in rags and odd clothing. They wandered to us from the railroad tracks where they had leaped from slow-moving boxcars onto the flatland. They hid in high clumps of weeds and brush that ran along the fence near the tracks. The hobos usually traveled alone, but Sister and I saw them come together, like poor families, to share a can of beans or a tin of sardines that they ate with sticks or twigs. Uncle Ralph also watched them from a distance.

One early morning, Sister and I crossed the tracks on our way to school and collided with a tall, haggard whiteman. He wore a very old-fashioned pin-striped black jacket covered with lint and soot. There was fright in his eyes when they met ours. He scurried around us, quickening his pace. The pole over his shoulder where his possessions hung in a bundle at the end bounced as he nearly ran from us.

"Looks just like a scared jackrabbit," Sister said, watching him dart away.

That evening we told Momma about the scared man. She warned us about the dangers of hobos as our father threw us a stern look. Uncle Ralph was visiting but he didn't say anything. He stayed the night and Sister asked him, "Hey, Uncle Ralph, why do you suppose they's hobos?"

Uncle Ralph was a large man. He took Sister and put her on one knee. "You see, Sister," he said, "hobos are a different kind. They see things in a different way. Them hobos are kind of like us. We're not like other people in some ways and yet we are. It has to do with what you see and feel when you look at this old world."

The Warriors

His answer satisfied Sister for a while. He taught us some more Pawnee words that night.

Not long after Uncle Ralph's explanation, Sister and I surprised a Black man with white whiskers and fuzzy hair. He was climbing through the barbed-wire fence that marked our property line. He wore faded blue overalls with pockets stuffed full of handkerchiefs. He wiped sweat from his face. When it dried, he looked up and saw us. I remembered what Uncle Ralph had said and wondered what the Black man saw when he looked at us standing there.

"We might scare him," Sister said softly to me, remembering the whiteman who had scampered away.

Sister whispered, "Hi," to the Black man. Her voice was barely audible.

"Boy, it's sure hot," he said. His voice was big and he smiled.

"Where are you going?" Sister asked.

"Me? Nowheres, I guess," he muttered.

"Then what you doing here?" Sister went on. She was bold for a seven-year-old kid. I was older but I was also quieter. "This here place is ours," she said.

He looked around and saw our house with its flowering mimosa trees and rich green mowed lawn stretching out before him. Other houses sat around ours.

"I reckon I'm lost," he said.

Sister pointed to the weeds and brush further up the road. "That's where you want to go. That's where they all go, the hobos."

I tried to quiet Sister but she didn't hush. "The hobos stay up there," she said. "You a hobo?"

He ignored her question and asked his own. "Say, what is you all? You not Black, you not White. What is you all?"

Sister looked at me. She put one hand on her chest and the other hand on me. "We Indians!" Sister said.

He stared at us and smiled again. "Is that a fact?" he said.

"Know what kind of Indians we are?" Sister asked him.

He shook his fuzzy head. "Indians is Indians, I guess," he said.

Sister wrinkled her forehead and retorted, "Not us! We not like others. We see things different. We're Pawnees. We're warriors!"

I pushed my elbow into Sister's side. She quieted.

The man was looking down the road and he shuffled his feet. "I'd best go," he said.

Sister pointed to the brush and weeds one more time. "That way," she said.

The Warriors

He climbed back through the fence and brush as Sister yelled, "Bye now!" He waved a damp handkerchief.

Sister and I didn't tell Momma and Dad about the Black man. But much later Sister told Uncle Ralph every word that had been exchanged with the Black man. Uncle Ralph listened and smiled.

Months later when the warm weather had cooled and Uncle Ralph came to stay with us for a couple of weeks, Sister and I went to the hobo place. We had planned it for a long time. That afternoon when we pushed away the weeds, not a hobo was in sight.

The ground was packed down tight in the clearing among the high weeds. We walked around the encircling brush and found folded cardboards stacked together. Burned cans in assorted sizes were stashed under the cardboards, and there were remains of old fires. Rags were tied to the brush, snapping in the hard wind.

Sister said, "Maybe they're all in the boxcars now. It's starting to get cold."

She was right. The November wind had a bite to it and the cold stung our hands and froze our breaths as we spoke.

"You want to go over to them boxcars?" she asked. We looked at the Railroad Crossing sign where the boxcars stood.

I was prepared to answer when a voice roared from somewhere behind us.

"Now, you young ones, you git on home! Go on! Git!"

A man crawled out of the weeds and looked angrily at us. His eyes were red and his face was unshaven. He wore a red plaid shirt with striped gray and black pants too large for him. His face was swollen and bruised. An old woolen pink scarf hid some of the bruise marks around his neck, and his topcoat was splattered with mud.

Sister looked at him. She stood close to me and told him defiantly, "You can't tell us what to do! You don't know us!"

He didn't answer Sister but tried to stand. He couldn't. Sister ran to him and took his arm and pulled on it. "You need help?" she questioned.

He frowned at her but let us help him. He was tall. He seemed to be embarrassed by our help.

"You Indian, ain't you?" I dared to ask him.

He didn't answer me but looked at his feet as if they could talk so he wouldn't have to. His feet were in big brown overshoes.

"Who's your people?" Sister asked. He looked to be about Uncle Ralph's age when he finally lifted his face and met mine. He didn't respond for a minute. Then he sighed. "I ain't got no people," he told us as he tenderly stroked his swollen jaw.

The Warriors

"Sure you got people. Our folks says a man's always got people," I said softly. The wind blew our clothes and covered the words.

But he heard. He exploded like a firecracker. "Well, I don't! I ain't got no people! I ain't got nobody!"

"What you doing out here anyway?" Sister asked. "You hurt? You want to come over to our house?"

"Naw," he said. "Now you little ones, go on home. Don't be walking round out here. Didn't nobody tell you little girls ain't supposed to be going round by themselves? You might git hurt."

"We just wanted to talk to hobos," Sister said.

"Naw, you don't. Just go on home. Your folks is probably looking for you and worrying 'bout you."

I took Sister's arm and told her we were going home. Then we said "Bye" to the man. But Sister couldn't resist a few last words, "You Indian, ain't you?"

He nodded his head like it was a painful thing to do. "Yeah, I'm Indian."

"You ought to go on home yourself," Sister said. "Your folks probably looking for you and worrying 'bout you."

His voice rose again as Sister and I walked away from him. "I told you kids, I don't have no people!" There was exasperation in his voice.

Sister would not be outdone. She turned and yelled, "Oh yeah? You Indian ain't you? Ain't you?" she screamed. "We your people!"

His topcoat and pink scarf flapped in the wind as we turned away from him.

We went home to Momma and Dad and Uncle Ralph then. Uncle Ralph met us at the front door. "Where you all been?" he asked looking toward the railroad tracks. Momma and Dad were talking in the kitchen.

"Just playing, Uncle," Sister and I said simultaneously.

Uncle Ralph grabbed both Sister and I by our hands and yanked us out the door. "*Awkuh!*" he said, using the Pawnee expression to show his dissatisfaction.

Outside, we sat on the cement porch. Uncle Ralph was quiet for a long time, and neither Sister nor I knew what to expect.

"I want to tell you all a story," he finally said. "Once, there were these two rats who ran around everywhere and got into everything all the time. Everything they were told not to do, well they went right out and did. They'd get into one mess and then another. It seems that they never could learn."

At that point Uncle Ralph cleared his throat. He looked at me and said, "Sister, do you understand this story? Is it too hard for you? You're older."

I nodded my head up and down and said, "I understand."

The Warriors

Then Uncle Ralph looked at Sister. He said to her, "Sister, do I need to go on with this story?"

Sister shook her head from side to side. "Naw, Uncle Ralph," she said.

"So you both know how this story ends?" he said gruffly. Sister and I bobbed our heads up and down again.

We followed at his heels the rest of the day. When he tightened the loose hide on top of his drum, we watched him and held it in place as he laced the wet hide down. He got his drumsticks down from the top shelf of the closet and began to pound the drum slowly.

"Where you going, Uncle Ralph?" I asked. Sister and I knew that when he took his drum out, he was always gone shortly after.

"I have to be a drummer at some doings tomorrow," he said.

"You a good singer, Uncle Ralph," Sister said. "You know all them old songs."

"The young people nowadays, it seems they don't care 'bout nothing that's old. They just want to go to the Moon." He was drumming low as he spoke.

"We care, Uncle Ralph," Sister said.

"Why?" Uncle Ralph asked in a hard, challenging tone that he seldom used on us.

Sister thought for a moment and then said, "I guess because you care so much, Uncle Ralph."

His eyes softened as he said, "I'll sing you an *Eruska* song, a song for the warriors."

The song he sang was a war dance song. At first Sister and I listened attentively, but then Sister began to dance the man's dance. She had never danced before and tried to imitate what she had seen. Her chubby body whirled and jumped the way she'd seen the men dance. Her head tilted from side to side the way the men moved theirs. I laughed aloud at her clumsy effort, and Uncle Ralph laughed heartily, too.

Uncle Ralph went in and out of our lives after that. We heard that he sang at one place and then another, and people came to Momma to find him. They said that he was only one of a few who knew the old ways and the songs.

When he came to visit us, he always brought something to eat. The Pawnee custom was that the man, the warrior, should bring food, preferably meat. Then, whatever food was brought to the host was prepared and served to the man, the warrior, along with the host's family. Many times Momma and I, or Sister and I, came home to an empty house to find a sack of food on the table. Momma or I cooked it for the next meal, and Uncle Ralph showed up to eat.

The Warriors

As Sister and I grew older, our fascination with the hobos decreased. Other things took our time, and Uncle Ralph did not appear as frequently as he did before.

Once while I was home alone, I picked up Momma's old photo album. Inside was a gray photo of Uncle Ralph in an army uniform. Behind him were tents on a flat terrain. Other photos showed other poses but only in one picture did he smile. All the photos were written over in black ink in Momma's handwriting. *Ralphie in Korea,* the writing said.

Other photos in the album showed our Pawnee relatives. Dad was from another tribe. Momma's momma was in the album, a tiny gray-haired woman who no longer lived. And Momma's momma's dad was in the album; he wore old Pawnee leggings and the long feathers of a dark bird sat upon his head. I closed the album when Momma, Dad, and Sister came home.

Momma went into the kitchen to cook. She called me and Sister to help. As she put on a bibbed apron, she said, "We just came from town, and we saw someone from home there." She meant someone from her tribal community.

"This man told me that Ralphie's been drinking hard," she said sadly. "He used to do that quite a bit a long time ago, but we thought it had stopped. He seemed to be all right for a few years." We cooked and then ate in silence.

Washing the dishes, I asked Momma, "How come Uncle Ralph never did marry?"

Momma looked up at me but was not surprised by my question. She answered, "I don't know, Sister. It would have been better if he had. There was one woman who I thought he really loved. I think he still does. I think it had something to do with Mom. She wanted him to wait."

"Wait for what?" I asked.

"I don't know," Momma said, and sank into a chair.

After that we heard unsettling rumors of Uncle Ralph drinking here and there.

He finally came to the house once when only I happened to be home. He was haggard and tired. His appearance was much like that of the whiteman that Sister and I met on the railroad tracks years before.

I opened the door when he tapped on it. Uncle Ralph looked years older than his age. He brought food in his arms. "*Nowa,* Sister," he said in greeting. "Where's the other one?" He meant my sister.

"She's gone now, Uncle Ralph. School in Kansas," I answered. "Where you been, Uncle Ralph? We been worrying about you."

The Warriors

He ignored my question and said, "I bring food. The warrior brings home food. To his family, to his people." His face was lined and had not been cleaned for days. He smelled of cheap wine.

I asked again, "Where you been, Uncle Ralph?"

He forced himself to smile. "Pumpkin Flower," he said, using the Pawnee name, "I've been out with my warriors all this time."

He put one arm around me as we went to the kitchen table with the food. "That's what your Pawnee name is. Now don't forget it."

"Did somebody bring you here, Uncle Ralph, or are you on foot?" I asked him.

"I'm on foot," he answered. "Where's your Momma?"

I told him that she and Dad would be back soon. I started to prepare the food he brought.

Then I heard Uncle Ralph say, "Life is sure hard sometimes. Sometimes it seems I just can't go on."

"What's wrong, Uncle Ralph?" I asked.

Uncle Ralph let out a bitter little laugh. "What's wrong?" he repeated. "What's wrong? All my life, I've tried to live what I've been taught, but Pumpkin Flower, some things are all wrong!"

He took a folded pack of Camel cigarettes from his coat pocket. His hand shook as he pulled one from the pack and lit the end. "Too much drink," he said sadly. "That stuff is bad for us."

"What are you trying to do, Uncle Ralph?" I asked him.

"Live," he said.

He puffed on the shaking cigarette a while and said, "The old people said to live beautifully with prayers and song. Some died for beauty, too."

"How do we do that, Uncle Ralph, live for beauty?" I asked.

"It's simple, Pumpkin Flower," he said. "Believe!"

"Believe what?" I asked.

He looked at me hard. "*Awkuh!*" he said. "That's one of the things that is wrong. Everyone questions. Everyone doubts. No one believes in the old ways anymore. They want to believe when it's convenient, when it doesn't cost them anything and they get something in return. There are no more believers. There are no more warriors. They are all gone. Those who are left only want to go to the Moon."

A car drove up outside. It was Momma and Dad. Uncle Ralph heard it too. He slumped in the chair, resigned to whatever Momma would say to him.

Momma came in first. Dad then greeted Uncle Ralph and disappeared into the back of the house. Custom and etiquette required that Dad, who was not a member of Momma's tribe, allow Momma to handle her brother's problems.

The Warriors

She hugged Uncle Ralph. Her eyes filled with tears when she saw how thin he was and how his hands shook.

"Ralphie," she said, "you look awful, but I am glad to see you."

She then spoke to him of everyday things, how the car failed to start and the latest gossip. He was silent, tolerant of the passing of time in this way. His eyes sent me a pleading look while his hands shook and he tried to hold them still.

When supper was ready, Uncle Ralph went to wash himself for the meal. When he returned to the table, he was calm. His hands didn't shake so much.

At first he ate without many words, but in the course of the meal he left the table twice. Each time he came back, he was more talkative than before, answering Momma's questions in Pawnee. He left the table a third time and Dad rose.

Dad said to Momma, "He's drinking again, Can't you tell?" Dad left the table and went outside.

Momma frowned. A determined look grew on her face.

When Uncle Ralph sat down to the table once more, Momma told him, "Ralphie, you're my brother but I want you to leave now. Come back when you're sober."

He held a tarnished spoon in mid-air and put it down slowly. He hadn't finished eating, but he didn't seem to mind leaving. He stood, looked at me with his red eyes, and went to the door. Momma followed him. In a low voice she said, "Ralphie, you've got to stop drinking and wandering— or don't come to see us again."

He pulled himself to his full height then. His frame filled the doorway. He leaned over Momma and yelled, "Who are you? Are you God that you will say what will be or will not be?"

Momma met his angry eyes. She stood firm and did not back down.

His eyes finally dropped from her face to the linoleum floor. A cough came from deep in his throat.

"I'll leave here," he said. "But I'll get all my warriors and come back! I have thousands of warriors and they'll ride with me. We'll get our bows and arrows. Then we'll come back!" He staggered out the door.

In the years that followed, Uncle Ralph saw us only when he was sober. He visited less and less. When he did show up, he did a tapping ritual on our front door. We welcomed the rare visits. Occasionally he stayed at our house for a few days at a time when he was not drinking. He slept on the floor.

He did odd jobs for minimum pay but never complained about the work or money. He'd acquired a vacant look in his eyes. It was the same look that

The Warriors

Sister and I had seen in the hobos when we were children. He wore a similar careless array of clothing and carried no property with him at all.

The last time he came to the house, he called me by my English name and asked if I remembered anything of all that he'd taught me. His hair had turned pure white. He looked older than anyone I knew. I marvelled at his appearance and said, "I remember everything." That night I pointed out his stars for him and told him how *Pahukatawa* lived and died and lived again through another's dreams. I'd grown, and Uncle Ralph could not hold me on his knee anymore. His arm circled my waist while we sat on the grass.

He was moved by my recitation and clutched my hand tightly. He said, "It's more than this. It's more than just repeating words. You know that, don't you?"

I nodded my head. "Yes, I know. The recitation is the easiest part but it's more than this, Uncle Ralph."

He was quiet, but after a few minutes his hand touched my shoulder. He said, "I couldn't make it work. I tried to fit the pieces."

"I know," I said.

"Now before I go," he said, "do you know who you are?"

The question took me by surprise. I thought very hard. I cleared my throat and told him, "I know that I am fourteen. I know that it's too young."

"Do you know that you are a Pawnee?" he asked in a choked whisper.

"Yes Uncle," I said.

"Good," he said with a long sigh that was swallowed by the night.

Then he stood and said, "Well, Sister, I have to go. Have to move on."

"Where are you going?" I asked. "Where all the warriors go?" I teased.

He managed a smile and a soft laugh. "Yeah, wherever the warriors are, I'll find them."

I said to him, "Before you go, I want to ask you . . . Uncle Ralph, can women be warriors too?"

He laughed again and hugged me merrily. "Don't tell me you want to be one of the warriors too?"

"No, Uncle," I said, "Just one of yours." I hated to let him go because I knew I would not see him again.

He pulled away. His last words were, "Don't forget what I've told you all these years. It's the only chance not to become what everyone else is. Do you understand?"

I nodded and he left.

I never saw him again.

The years passed quickly. I moved away from Momma and Dad and married. Sister left before I did.

The Warriors

Years later in another town, hundreds of miles away, I awoke in a terrible gloom, a sense that something was gone from the world the Pawnees knew. The despair filled days, though the reason for the sense of loss went unexplained. Finally, the telephone rang. Momma was on the line. She said, "Sister came home for a few days not too long ago. While she was here and alone, someone tapped on the door, like Ralphie always does. Sister yelled, 'Is that you, Uncle Ralphie? Come on in.' But no one entered."

Then I understood that Uncle Ralph was dead. Momma probably knew too. She wept softly into the phone.

Later Momma received an official call confirming Uncle Ralph's death. He had died from exposure in a hobo shanty, near the railroad tracks outside a tiny Oklahoma town. He'd been dead for several days and nobody knew but Momma, Sister, and me.

Momma reported to me that the funeral was well attended by the Pawnee people. Uncle Ralph and I had said our farewells years earlier. Momma told me that someone there had spoken well of Uncle Ralph before they put him in the ground. It was said that "Ralphie came from a fine family, an old line of warriors."

Ten years later, Sister and I visited briefly at Momma's and Dad's home. We had been separated by hundreds of miles for all that time. As we sat under Momma's flowering mimosa trees, I made a confession to Sister. I said, "Sometimes I wish that Uncle Ralph were here. I'm a grown woman but I still miss him after all these years."

Sister nodded her head in agreement. I continued. "He knew so many things. He knew why the sun pours its liquid all over us and why it must do just that. He knew why babes and insects crawl. He knew that we must live beautifully or not live at all."

Sister's eyes were thoughtful, but she waited to speak while I went on. "To live beautifully from day to day is a battle all the way. The things that he knew are so beautiful. And to feel and know that kind of beauty is the reason that we should live at all. Uncle Ralph said so. But now, there is no one who knows what that beauty is or any of the other things that he knew."

Sister pushed back smokey gray wisps of her dark hair. "You do," she pronounced. "And I do, too."

"Why do you suppose he left us like that?" I asked.

"It couldn't be helped," Sister said. "There was a battle on."

"I wanted to be one of his warriors," I said with an embarrassed half-smile.

She leaned over and patted my hand. "You are," she said. Then she stood and placed one hand on her bosom and one hand on my arm. "We'll carry on," she said.

The Warriors

I touched her hand resting on my arm, I said, "Sister, tell me again. What is the battle for?"

She looked down toward the fence where a hobo was coming through. We waved at him.

"Beauty," she said to me. "Our battle is for beauty. It's what Uncle Ralph fought for, too. He often said that everyone else just wanted to go to the Moon. But remember, Sister, you and I done been there. Don't forget, after all, we're children of the stars."

Responding to the Selection

Questions for Discussion

1. With whom are the narrator and her sister fascinated? Why?

2. What eventually links the girls closely to the hobos?

3. What lesson does Uncle Ralph try to teach the girls about life?

4. How does Uncle Ralph link the hobos to the place of Native Americans in larger society?

5. In what way are the narrator, Sister, and Uncle Ralph warriors? What do they fight for, and how?

Activities

Write a Character Sketch

1. In "The Warriors," Anna Lee Walters writes of one person's influence on her. Think about the people in your life and choose one that has strongly affected your thinking and life. Write a one-page **character description** of this person, including your thoughts on how he or she has influenced you.

Sharing a Culture

2. Uncle Ralph teaches the girls about their Pawnee heritage through music, dance, and story. Choose a culture you know well and share an aspect of its heritage through the medium of your choice—dance, music, visual arts, oral or written language.

Writing a Letter

3. Momma faces the difficult task of telling her brother that he isn't welcome unless he is sober. Write a **letter** in which she tells Uncle Ralph how she feels and why.

Before You Read

Love Orange

Olive Senior
Born 1943

> "*I want people to know that 'literature' can be created out of the fabric of our everyday lives, that our stories are as worth telling as those of Shakespeare.*"

About Senior

Olive Senior was born in a poor village in western Jamaica. One of ten children, she spent long periods living with her mother's relatives after she turned four. This arrangement allowed her to get a good education and escape poverty. However, she felt isolated among her urban, middle-class relatives. She took an interest in writing when she was in high school, and after graduating she was hired by a Jamaican newspaper. Later she studied journalism in Canada.

Senior is a highly regarded poet and short-story writer. She has also written studies of Jamaican culture and the role of women in the Caribbean. Her work is influenced by the oral culture of her parents' village, where people told stories in the African tradition. One critic has said that her stories "might serve as a kind of laboratory for examining Jamaican speech."

Jamaica

Jamaica, which is approximately the size of Connecticut, is the third largest island in the Caribbean. Its rugged, mountainous landscape is covered with green forests. When Columbus first saw it in 1494, he wrote that it was the most beautiful island in the world.

Jamaica's people are mostly of African heritage, with some Asian and European elements. The country has a strong sense of national unity, as expressed in its motto, "Out of Many, One People." Farming occupies the largest number of people, but mining and tourism are also important.

Christianity, in various denominations, is the religion of the vast majority of Jamaicans. There are also religions, such as Pocomania, based on a combination of Christian and traditional African beliefs.

Love Orange

— *Olive Senior*

> Work out your own salvation with fear and trembling.
> *Philippians*

Somewhere between the repetition of Sunday School lessons and the broken doll which the lady sent me one Christmas I lost what it was to be happy. But I didn't know it then even though in dreams I would lie with my face broken like the doll's in the pink tissue of a shoebox coffin. For I was at the age where no one asked me for commitment and I had a phrase which I used like a talisman. When strangers came or lightning flashed, I would lie in the dust under my grandfather's vast bed and hug the dog, whispering "our worlds wait outside" and be happy.

Once I set out to find the worlds outside, the horizon was wide and the rim of the far mountains beckoned. I was happy when they found me in time for bed and a warm supper, for the skies, I discovered, were the same shade of China blue as the one intact eye of the doll. "Experience can wait," I whispered to the dog, "death too."

I knew all about death then because in dreams I had been there. I also knew a great deal about love. Love, I thought, was like an orange, a fixed and sharply defined amount, limited, finite. Each person had this amount of love to distribute as he may. If one had many people to love then the segments for each person would be smaller and eventually love, like patience, would be exhausted. That is why I preferred to live with my grandparents then since they had fewer people to love than my parents and so my portion of their love-orange would be larger.

My own love-orange I jealously guarded. Whenever I thought of love I could feel it in my hand, large and round and brightly colored, intact and spotless. I had moments of indecision when I wanted to distribute the orange but each time I would grow afraid of the audacity of such commitment. Sometimes, in a moment of rare passion, I would extend the orange to the dog or my grandmother but would quickly withdraw my hand each time.

For without looking I would feel in its place the doll crawling into my hand and nestling there and I would run into the garden and be sick. I would see its face as it lay in the pink tissue of a shoebox tied with ribbons beside the stocking hanging on the bedpost and I would clutch my orange tighter, thinking that I had better save it for the day when occasions like this would arise again and I would need the entire orange to overcome the feelings which arose each time I thought of the doll.

I could not let my grandmother know about my being sick because she never understood about the doll. For years I had dreamed of exchanging homemade dolls with button eyes and ink faces for a plaster doll with blue eyes and limbs that moved. All that December I haunted my grandmother's clothes closet until beneath the dresses I discovered the box smelling faintly of camphor and without looking I knew that it came from Miss Evangeline's toy shop and that it would therefore be a marvel. But the doll beside the Christmas stocking, huge in a billowing dress and petticoats, had half a face and a finger missing. "It can be mended," my grandmother said, "I can make it as good as new. 'Why throw away a good thing?' Miss Evangeline said as she gave it to me."

But I could no longer hear I could no longer see for the one China blue eye and the missing finger that obscured my vision. And after that I never opened a box again and I never waited up for Christmas. And although I buried the box beneath the allamanda tree the doll rose up again and again, in my throat, like a sickness to be got rid of from the body, and I felt as if I too were half a person who could lay down in the shoebox and sleep forever. But on awakening from these moments, I could find safely clutched in my hands the orange, conjured up from some deep part of myself, and I would hug the dog saying "our worlds wait outside."

That summer I saw more clearly the worlds that awaited. It was filled with many deaths that seemed to tie all the strands of my life together and which bore some oblique relationship to both the orange and the doll.

The first to die was a friend of my grandparents who lived nearby. I sometimes played with her grandchildren at her house when I was allowed to, but each time she had appeared only as a phantom, come on the scene silently, her feet shod in cotton stockings rolled down to her ankles, thrust into a pair of her son's broken-down slippers. In all the years I had known her I had never heard her say anything but whisper softly; her whole presence was a whisper. She seemed to appear from the cracks of the house, the ceiling, anywhere, she made so little noise in her coming, this tiny, delicate, slightly absurd old woman who lived for us only in the secret and mysterious prison of the aged.

Love Orange

When she died it meant nothing to me, I could think then only of my death which I saw nightly in dreams but I could not conceive of her in the flesh, to miss her or to weep tears.

The funeral that afternoon was 5:00 P.M. on a hot summer's day. My grandmother dressed me all in white and I trailed down the road behind her, my corseted and whaleboned grandmother lumbering from side to side in a black romaine dress now shiny in the sunlight, bobbing over her head a huge black umbrella. My grandfather stepped high in shiny black shoes and a shiny black suit ahead of her. Bringing up the rear, I skipped lightly on the gravel, clutching in my hand a new, shiny, bright and bouncy red rubber ball. For me, the funeral, any occasion to get out of the house was a holiday, like breaking suddenly from a dark tunnel into the sunlight where gardens of butterflies waited.

They had dug a grave in the red clay by the side of the road. The house was filled with people. I followed my grandparents and the dead woman's children into the room where they had laid her out, unsmiling, her nostrils stuffed with cotton. I stood in the shadows where no one saw me, filled with the smell of something I had never felt before, like a smell rising from the earth itself which no sunlight, no butterflies, no sweetness could combat. "Miss Aggie, Miss Aggie," I said silently to the dead old woman and suddenly I knew that if I gave her my orange to take into the unknown with her it would be safe, a secret between me and one who could return no more. I gripped the red ball tightly in my hands and it became transformed into the rough texture of an orange; I tasted it on my tongue, smelled the fragrance. As my grandmother knelt to pray I crept forward and gently placed between Miss Aggie's closed hands the love-orange, smiled because we knew each other and nothing would be able to touch either of us. But as I crept away my grandmother lifted her head from her hands and gasped when she saw the ball. She swiftly retrieved it while the others still prayed and hid it in her voluminous skirt. But when she sent me home, in anger, on the way the love-orange appeared comforting in my hand, and I went into the empty house and crept under my grandfather's bed and dreamt of worlds outside.

The next time I saw with greater clarity the vastness of this world outside. I was asked to visit some new neighbors and read to their son. He was very old, I thought, and he sat in the sunshine all day, his head covered with a calico skull cap. He couldn't see very clearly and my grandmother said he had a brain tumor and would perhaps die. Nevertheless I read to him and worried about all the knowledge that would be lost if he did not live. For every morning he would take down from a shelf a huge Atlas and together we would travel the cities of the world to which he had been. I was very happy and the names of these cities secretly rolled off my tongue all day. I wanted very much to give him my orange but held back. I was not yet sure if he were a whole person, if he would not recover and need me less and so the whole orange would be wasted. So I did not tell him about it. And then he went off with his parents to England, for an operation, my grandmother said, and he came back only as ashes held on the plane by his mother. When I went to the church this time there was no coffin, only his mother holding this tiny box which was so like the shoe box of the doll that I was sure there was some connection which I could not grasp but I thought, if they bury this box then the broken doll cannot rise again.

But the doll rose up one more time because soon my grandmother lay dying. My mother had taken me away when she fell too ill and brought me back to my grandmother's house, even darker and more silent now, this one last time. I went into the room where she lay and she held out a weak hand to me, she couldn't speak so she followed me with her eyes and I couldn't bear it. "Grandma," I said quickly, searching for something to say, something that would save her, "Grandma, you can have my whole orange," and I placed it in the bed beside her hand. But she kept on dying and I knew then that the orange had no potency, that love could not create miracles. "Orange," my grandmother spoke for the last time trying to make connections that she did not see, "orange. . . . . . . ?" and my mother took me out of the room as my grandmother died. "At least," my mother said, "at least you could have told her that you loved her, she waited for it."

"But . . ." I started to say and bit my tongue, for nobody, not then or ever could understand about the orange. And in leaving my grandmother's house, the dark tunnel of my childhood, I slammed the car door hard on my fingers and as my hand closed over the breaking bones, felt nothing.

Responding to the Selection

Questions for Discussion

1. In "Love Orange" what impression do you gain of the narrator's life? Of her emotional state?

2. In "Love Orange" the narrator describes her grandmother's house as "the dark tunnel of my childhood." In "The Warriors" the narrator says that Uncle Ralph "was trapped in a transparent bubble of a new time" that "bound him tight." How is the young girl's "dark tunnel" like the "transparent bubble" that traps Uncle Ralph? How do they differ?

3. What similar problems do the narrator in "Love Orange" and Uncle Ralph in "The Warriors" face in their lives? How do their problems differ?

4. Contrast the family life of the young girl in "Love Orange" with the family life of the young girls in "The Warriors." In which family would you rather live? Why?

5. At the end of "Love Orange," the narrator breaks her fingers but feels nothing. Near the end of his life, Uncle Ralph acquires a vacant look in his eyes. How do you interpret their emotional states?

Activities

Writing a Letter

1. The narrator in "Love Orange" and Uncle Ralph in "The Warriors" both have difficulty fitting into the worlds in which they find themselves. Write a **letter** to one of these two characters describing a time when you felt as though you did not fit in.

Creating a Triptych

2. Select three important scenes from one of these stories and illustrate each one in a drawing. (Such a group of three related pictures is called a triptych.)

Newspaper Article

Language is an important part of a
culture's identity. This article profiles
a woman's efforts to help threatened
languages survive in the modern world.

O'odham poet strives to preserve languages

by Pila Martínez, The Arizona Daily Star

A Tohono O'odham linguist and poet
who has helped native communities
preserve their languages was named
today as one of the nation's new
MacArthur fellows.

Ofelia Zepeda, 45, joins a prestigious
group of scientists, scholars and artists
selected annually to receive the so-
called "genius grants"—five-year, no-
strings-attached awards worth hundreds
of thousands of dollars and given to
people judged to be among the most
creative in their fields.

In awarding Zepeda $320,000, the
John D. and Catherine T. MacArthur
Foundation stated that "her singular
work in advancing the field of native
language scholarship positions Zepeda

as a unique force on behalf of the continued life of endangered languages."

Zepeda, a linguistics professor at the
University of Arizona, spoke nothing
but O'odham until she entered grade
school in Stanfield, the town near Casa
Grande where she grew up. When she
enrolled at the UA as a young woman,
she declared sociology as her major but
continued studying her native language
on the side.

At the same time, the UA's bur-
geoning linguistics department was
recruiting students who were native
speakers, and one of the people Zepeda
had enlisted as a language tutor suggested she meet with one of the department's organizers.

Until then, she had never considered making a career out of her first language.

"I spoke the language and that was about it. I never thought about any of the possibilities . . . the fact that it could be studied," she said.

Many native languages are disappearing. Fewer than 1 percent of the Tohono O'odham people can read and write their language, according to Zepeda.

Zepeda has worked to reverse the trend from several angles. She helps put together an annual conference focused on preserving and teaching American Indian languages; conducts training seminars for American Indians interested in teaching; and has helped tribes develop native language programs for their schools.

Her own studies led her to American Indian writers, and the idea that providing native people with literature written in their own tongue could encourage them to learn to read it and write it.

She incorporated the concept into her O'odham language classes, which she began teaching as a graduate student.

Zepeda had her students write poetry and songs, and then she edited them, photocopied them, stapled them together and passed them out again. "And that was our reading material," she said.

Zepeda said she hopes her selection illuminates the need to preserve native languages.

"I certainly think that this award and the type of work that I've been involved with will bring . . . attention to our situation," she said.

Questions for Discussion

1. How do you feel about the language you grew up with at home? How important is it?

2. How important is a people's language to their identity as a group? Do you think languages that are in danger of dying out should be preserved?

Before You Read

Three Poems

Maurice Kenny
Born 1929

> *"I travel home . . . to the rebirth of chicory, burdock, tadpoles, otters, and the strawberry . . . 'Home' is with your people who stand on that earth and partake of its nourishment."*

About Kenny

Maurice Kenny, of Mohawk heritage, was born in 1929 in Watertown, New York. After studying poetry and literature at Butler University, Kenny left upstate New York. He lived in many places, including New York City, Mexico, and the Virgin Islands, becoming in his words a "Mohawk poet on the road." In the late 1990s, Kenny returned to his home region as poet-in-residence at North Country Community College. During his long career, he has written many poems, essays, and short stories. As a founder of the magazine *Contact II* and as editor for various literary journals, he has also guided other writers' works. Much of his work focuses on recognizing and appreciating Native American values and cultures. Nominated twice for the Pulitzer Prize, Kenny's work was recognized with an American Book Award in 1984.

Mohawk Heritage

The Akwesasne are a Mohawk group living along the St. Lawrence River; uniquely, their reservation covers land in both the United States and Canada. Members of the Iroqouis League, the Mohawks guarded the easternmost border of the League lands. In earlier times, the Mohawks followed traditional Iroquois lifestyles. They lived in longhouses clustered around the rivers of upstate New York, using elm-bark canoes to travel the waters. Though Kenny writes in his poems of not knowing the traditions of his people, in its own way his work helps keeps those traditions alive.

Three Poems

— *Maurice Kenny*

Black River—Summer 1981

For Patti-Lyn

       The evening river carries no sound . . .
       not the bark of this fox whose skull
       weights my hand,
       nor the wind of this hawk
5   feather tucked into the button hole of my shirt

       Rivers grumble and hiss and gurgle;
       they roar and sing lullabys;
       rivers rage and flow and dance
       like unseen wind;
10   in the dark they carry the eyes
       of stars and footprints of deer.

          I have slept on your arm,
          dawn sweetening my mouth,
          stiff in limb
15   and rose to your morning song.

Three Poems

I have watched geese fly over,
eels slither down stream,
bullheads defy rapids,
spiders ripple waves
20   in trapped inlets along the shore,
fireflies light paths
from murky banks
to mysterious islands
where witches live.

25   I have studied your waters.

Day-dreamed my watch to listen,
to feel your tremble,
to learn your summer,
touch your winter,
30   and be content.

Three Poems

Going Home

The book lay unread in my lap
snow gathered at the window
from Brooklyn it was a long ride
the Greyhound followed the plow
5   from Syracuse to Watertown
to country cheese and maples
tired rivers and closed paper mills
home to gossipy aunts . . .
their dandelions and pregnant cats . . .
10   home to cedars and fields of boulders
cold graves under willow and pine
home from Brooklyn to the reservation
that was not home
to songs I could not sing
15   to dances I could not dance
from Brooklyn bars and ghetto rats
to steaming horses stomping frozen
    earth
barns and privies lost in blizzards
home to a Nation, Mohawk
20   to faces I did not know
and hands which did not recognize me
to names and doors
my father shut

Three **Poems**

Friendship Days at Akwesasne

Summer of '84 . . . Annual Event
For Francis

    Humid afternoon by the St. Lawrence,
    women canoe-racers paddle the river;
    full of fry bread, soda and hot
    strawberry-rhubarb pie
5   I stumble under the cedar arbor
    to listen to the drum and singing.

    Outfitted Mohawks circle a "stomp dance."
    I take a place on a bench near
    an elder woman who asks in Mohawk,
10   what do I do? Tote bag slung over my
    left shoulder I figure I should own up.
    "I'm a writer." . . . in smiles.
    "What kind?" she asked, really curious.
    "A poet," I replied proudly . . .
15   to which she offered a grunt,
    got up from the bench and huffed off.

    Well, maybe she was right.

Responding to the Selection

Questions for Discussion

1. Describe the **setting** of each poem. How does the setting contribute to each poem's content?

2. How does the speaker view the river in "Black River–Summer 1981"? What **details** support your inference?

3. How do you think the speaker in "Going Home" feels about his heritage? What is your reaction to these feelings?

4. What is the **mood** of "Friendship Days at Akwesasne"? What do you think is the reason for the woman's reaction to Kenny's saying he is a poet? How does he react to her reaction?

5. Which is your favorite of these three poems? Why does this poem appeal to you most?

Activities

Creating a Poster

1. Using online or library sources, learn more about both historical and contemporary Mohawk lifestyles. Share your findings with the class in a visual format as a poster.

Writing an Essay

2. Examine Kenny's poems for sensory language. Then write a brief **essay** discussing that language. To which senses does Kenny appeal? Which images are most vivid?

Writing a Letter

3. In his poems, Kenny expresses some distance from his heritage. How do you respond to his feelings? Have you ever experienced similar feelings? Write a **letter** to Kenny in which you share your feelings.

Focus on . . .
The Land

Over the past few centuries millions of people have come to North America, fleeing repression, poverty, and lack of opportunity, in search of a new home. But the continent was already home to hundreds of different peoples, each one a nation with its own territory, history, and traditions: the Native Americans.

With the creation of the independent United States, many of the new-comers viewed the entire North American continent as theirs by right. The United States government gave Indian lands to veterans, encouraged settlers to push westward, and reserved only small tracts of land for Native Americans. But official policy was not entirely consistent. The Northwest Ordinance of 1787 declared that Native American "lands and property shall never be taken from them without their consent." In practice, however, this consent was obtained by any means necessary—by purchase or bribery, by promises or deceit, or simply by force. By setting aside land for reservations, the government hoped to eliminate conflicts between settlers and Native Americans. But as new settlements drew closer to Native American land, the reservations were reduced in size or the Native Americans were relocated entirely to less desirable areas.

As a result of the Indian Removal Act of 1830, most Native Americans in the East were forced to move to an area

of land west of the Mississippi called Indian Territory. Their arduous trip west became known as the Trail of Tears because so many died along the way. Indian Territory, which the government had pledged would belong to Native Americans forever, eventually filled with settlers too. It became part of the state of Oklahoma in 1907.

Questions of land ownership—and of control over natural resources—are still major issues for Native Americans today. Indian reservations are located in thirty-three states, and many Native

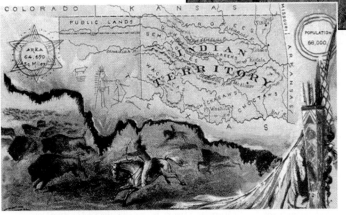

Americans regard these "islands" as crucial to maintaining their cultures. Some of the land on these reservations is held in trust by the U.S. government, some is owned either by the entire tribe or by individual tribal members, and some belongs to various government agencies. Throughout the country, Native Americans are working to gain more control over their own destinies. More emphasis is being placed on the concept of "tribal sovereignty" (Native American peoples usually entered into treaties with the United States as sovereign nations) and on the enforcement of treaty rights that have often been neglected or ignored for years.

Linking to . . .
• Think about this information as you read the selections in this theme.

Before You Read

At Last I Kill a Buffalo

Luther Standing Bear
1868–1939

"Earth was bountiful and we were surrounded with the blessings of the Great Mystery."

About Standing Bear

Luther Standing Bear's life straddled two centuries and two cultures. Born on the Pine Ridge Reservation in South Dakota, Standing Bear was first raised as a traditional Sioux. At the age of eleven, he was taken to the Carlisle Indian School in Pennsylvania, a government school whose purpose was to assimilate Indians into white society. After five years, he returned to the reservation. "While I had learned all that I could of the white man's culture, I never forgot that of my people," he wrote. Over the years Standing Bear worked as an assistant teacher, storekeeper, assistant minister, and rancher.

Later in life, Standing Bear became a Hollywood actor and worked actively to promote Native American rights. He published his first book about Sioux culture when he was nearly sixty years old and went on to publish three more.

Hunting the Buffalo

In the excerpt from "My Indian Boyhood" that you are about to read, Luther Standing Bear describes his first and only buffalo hunt. Such hunts were a vital part of a Sioux boy's passage into adulthood. A successful first hunt showed that a boy would be able to carry his weight in society. But even as Standing Bear's people were celebrating his success, the days of buffalo hunting were waning. Over-hunting by professional hunters from the East—sometimes encouraged by the government, in an effort to change the Plains tribes' lifestyle—was bringing the buffalo to the edge of extinction. Combined with the loss of much of their hunting territory, this brought drastic changes to the Sioux people. Standing Bear's generation was one of the last to experience the traditional life.

At Last I Kill a Buffalo

— Luther Standing Bear

At last the day came when my father allowed me to go on a buffalo hunt with him. And what a proud boy I was!

Ever since I could remember my father had been teaching me the things that I should know and preparing me to be a good hunter. I had learned to make bows and to string them; and to make arrows and tip them with feathers. I knew how to ride my pony no matter how fast he would go, and I felt that I was brave and did not fear danger. All these things I had learned for just this day when father would allow me to go with him on a buffalo hunt. It was the event for which every Sioux boy eagerly waited. To ride side by side with the best hunters of the tribe, to hear the terrible noise of the great herds as they ran, and then to help to bring home the kill was the most thrilling day of any Indian boy's life. The only other event which could equal it would be the day I went for the first time on the warpath to meet the enemy and protect my tribe.

On the following early morning we were to start, so the evening was spent in preparation. Although the tipis were full of activity, there was no noise nor confusion outside. Always the evening before a buffalo hunt and when every one was usually in his tipi, an old man went around the circle of tipis calling, 'I-ni-la,' 'I-ni-la,' not loudly, but so every one could hear. The old man was saying, 'Keep quiet,' 'Keep quiet.' We all knew that the scouts had come in and reported buffalo near and that we must all keep the camp in stillness. It was not necessary for the old man to go into each tipi and explain to the men that tomorrow there would be a big hunt, as the buffalo were coming. He did not order the men to prepare their weapons and neither did he order the mothers to keep children from crying. The one word, 'I-ni-la,' was sufficient to bring quiet to the whole camp. That night there would be no calling or shouting from tipi to tipi and no child would cry aloud. Even the horses and dogs obeyed the command for quiet, and all night not a horse neighed and not a dog barked. The very presence of quiet was everywhere. Such is the orderliness of a Sioux camp that men, women, children, and animals seem to have a common understanding and sympathy. It is no mystery but natural that the Indian and his animals understand each other very well both with words and without words. There are words, however, that the Indian uses that are understood by both his horses and dogs. When on a hunt, if one of the warriors speaks the word 'A-a-ah' rather quickly and sharply, every man, horse, and dog will stop instantly and listen. Not a move will be made by an animal until the men move or speak further. As long as the hunters listen, the animals will listen also.

The night preceding a buffalo hunt was always an exciting night, even though it was quiet in camp. There would be much talk in the tipis around the fires. There would be sharpening of arrows and of knives. New bowstrings would be made and quivers would be filled with arrows.

It was in the fall of the year and the evenings were cool as father and I sat by the fire and talked over the hunt. I was only eight years of age, and I know that father did not expect me to get a buffalo at all, but only to try perhaps for a small calf should I be able to get close enough to one. Nevertheless, I was greatly excited as I sat and watched father working in his easy, firm way.

Father sharpened my steel points for me and also sharpened my knife. The whetstone was a long stone which was kept in a buckskin bag, and sometimes this stone went all over the camp; every tipi did not have one, so we shared this commodity with one another. I had as I remember about ten arrows, so when father was through sharpening them I put them in my rawhide quiver. I had a rawhide quirt, too, which I would wear fastened to my waist. As father worked, he knew I was watching him closely and listening whenever he spoke. By the time all preparations had been made, he had told me just how I was to act when I started out in the morning with the hunters.

We went to bed, my father hoping that tomorrow would be successful for him so that he could bring home some nice meat for the family and a hide for my mother to tan. I went to bed, but could not go to sleep at once, so filled was I with the wonderment and excitement of it all. The next day was to be a test for me. I was to prove to my father whether he was or was not justified in his pride in me. What would be the result of my training? Would I be brave if I faced danger and would father be proud of me? Though I did not know it that night I was to be tried for the strength of my manhood and my honesty in this hunt. Something happened that

At Last I Kill a Buffalo

day which I remember above all things. It was a test of my real character and I am proud to say that I did not find myself weak, but made a decision that has been all these years a gratification to me.

The next morning the hunters were catching their horses about day-break. I arose with my father and went out and caught my pony. I wanted to do whatever he did and show him that he did not have to tell me what to do. We brought our animals to the tipi and got our bows and arrows and mounted. From over the village came the hunters. Most of them were leading their running horses. These running horses were anxious for the hunt and came prancing, their ears straight up and their tails waving in the air. We were joined with perhaps a hundred or more riders, some of whom carried bows and arrows and some armed with guns.

The buffalo were reported to be about five or six miles away as we should count distance now. At that time we did not measure distance in miles. One camping distance was about ten miles, and these buffalo were said to be about one half camping distance away.

Some of the horses were to be left at a stopping-place just before the herd was reached. These horses were pack-animals which were taken along to carry extra blankets or weapons. They were trained to remain there until the hunters came for them. Though they were neither hobbled nor tied, they stood still during the shooting and noise of the chase.

My pony was a black one and a good runner. I felt very important as I rode along with the hunters and my father, the chief. I kept as close to him as I could.

Two men had been chosen to scout or to lead the party. These two men were in a sense policemen whose work it was to keep order. They carried large sticks of ash wood, something like a policeman's billy, though longer. They rode ahead of the party while the rest of us kept in a group close together. The leaders went ahead until they sighted the herd of graz-ing buffalo. Then they stopped and waited for the rest of us to ride up. We all rode slowly toward the herd, which on sight of us had come together, although they had been scattered here and there over the plain. When they saw us, they all ran close together as if at the command of a leader. We continued riding slowly toward the herd until one of the leaders shouted, 'Ho-ka-he!' which means, 'Ready, Go!' At that command every man started for the herd. I had been listening, too, and the minute the hunters started, I started also.

Away I went, my little pony putting all he had into the race. It was not long before I lost sight of father, but I kept going just the same. I threw my blanket back and the chill of the autumn morning struck my body, but I did not mind. On I went. It was wonderful to race over the ground with all these horsemen about me. There was no shouting, no noise of any kind except the pounding of the horses' feet. The herd was now running and had raised a cloud of dust. I felt no fear until we had entered this cloud of dust and I could see nothing about me—only hear the sound of feet. Where was father? Where was I going? On I rode through the cloud, for I knew I must keep going.

Then all at once I realized that I was in the midst of the buffalo, their dark bodies rushing all about me and their great heads moving up and down to the sound of their hoofs beating upon the earth. Then it was that fear overcame me and I leaned close down upon my little pony's body and clutched him tightly. I can never tell you how I felt toward my pony at that moment. All thought of shooting had left my mind. I was seized by blank fear. In a moment or so, however, my senses became clearer, and I could distinguish other sounds beside the clatter of feet. I could hear a shot now and then and I could see the buffalo beginning to break up into small bunches. I could not see father nor any of my companions yet, but my fear was vanishing and I was safe. I let my pony run. The buffalo looked too large for me to tackle, anyway, so I just kept going. The buffalo became more and more scattered. Pretty soon I saw a young calf that looked about my size. I remembered now what father had told me the night before as we sat about the fire. Those instructions were important for me now to follow.

I was still back of the calf, being unable to get alongside of him. I was anxious to get a shot, yet afraid to try, as I was still very nervous. While my pony was making all speed to come alongside, I chanced a shot and to my surprise my arrow landed. My second arrow glanced along the back of the animal and sped on between the horns, making only a slight wound. My third arrow hit a spot that made the running beast slow up in his gait. I shot a fourth arrow, and though it, too, landed it was not a fatal wound. It seemed to me that it was taking a lot of shots, and I was not proud of my marksmanship. I was glad, however, to see the animal going slower and I knew that one more shot would make me a hunter. My horse seemed to know his own importance. His two ears stood straight forward and it was not necessary for me to urge him to get closer to the buffalo. I was soon by the side of the buffalo and one more shot brought the chase to a close. I jumped from my pony, and as I stood by my fallen game, I looked all around wishing that the world could see. But I was alone. In my determination to stay by until I had won my buffalo, I had not noticed that I was far from every one else. No admiring friends were about, and as far as I could see I was on the plain alone. The herd of buffalo had completely disappeared. And as for father, much as I wished for him, he was out of sight and I had no idea where he was.

I stood and looked at the animal on the ground. I was happy. Every one must know that I, Ota K'te, had killed a buffalo. But it looked as if no one knew where I was, so no one was coming my way. I must then take something from this animal to show that I had killed it. I took all the arrows one by one from the body. As I took them out, it occurred to me that I had used five arrows. If I had been a skillful hunter, one arrow would have been sufficient, but I had used five. Here it was that temptation came to me. Why could I not take out two of the arrows and throw them away? No one would know, and then I should be more greatly admired and praised as a hunter. As it was, I knew that I should be praised by father and mother, but I wanted more. And so I was tempted to lie.

I was planning this as I took out my skinning knife that father had sharpened for me the night before. I skinned one side of the animal, but when it came to turning it over, I was too small. I was wondering what to do when I heard my father's voice calling, 'To-ki-i-la-la-hu-wo,' 'Where are you?' I quickly jumped on my pony and rode to the top of a little hill nearby. Father saw me and came to me at once. He was so pleased to see me and glad to know that I was safe. I knew that I could never lie to my father. He was too fond of me and I too proud of him. He had always told me to tell the truth. He wanted me to be an honest man, so I resolved then to tell the truth even if it took from me a little glory. He rode up to me with a glad expression on his face, expecting me to go back with him to his kill. As he came up, I said as calmly as I could, 'Father, I have killed a buffalo.' His smile changed to surprise and he asked me where my buffalo was. I pointed to it and we rode over to where it lay, partly skinned.

Father set to work to skin it for me. I had watched him do this many times and knew perfectly well how to do it myself, but I could not turn the animal over. When the hide was off, father put it on the pony's back with the hair side next to the pony. On this he arranged the meat so it would balance. Then he covered the meat carefully with the rest of the hide, so no dust would reach it while we traveled home. I rode home on top of the load.

I showed my father the arrows that I had used and just where the animal had been hit. He was very pleased and praised me over and over again. I felt more glad than ever that I had told the truth and I have never regretted it. I am more proud now that I told the truth than I am of killing the buffalo.

It was late afternoon when we got back to camp. No king ever rode in state who was more proud than I that day as I came into the village sitting high up on my load of buffalo meat. It is not customary for Indian men to brag about their exploits and I had been taught that bragging was not nice. So I was very quiet, although I was bursting with pride. Always when arriving home I would run out to play, for I loved to be with the other boys, but this day I lingered about close to the tipi so I could hear the nice things that were said about me. It was soon all over camp that Ota K'te had killed a buffalo.

My father was so proud that he gave away a fine horse. He called an old man to our tipi to cry out the news to the rest of the people in camp. The old man stood at the door of our tipi and sang a song of praise to my father. The horse had been led up and I stood holding it by a rope. The old man who was doing the singing called the other old man who was to receive the horse as a present. He accepted the horse by coming up to me, holding out his hands to me, and saying, '*Ha-ye*,' which means 'Thank you.' The old man went away very grateful for the horse.

That ended my first and last buffalo hunt. It lives only in my memory, for the days of the buffalo are over.

Responding to the Selection

Questions for Discussion

1. What two tests does Luther Standing Bear face? How does he fare in each? Of which is he the proudest? Which would have been the harder test for you? Why?

2. Judging from this passage, how did Indian boys learn the skills they needed? What values and standards of behavior were they taught? Which of these skills, values, and standards are emphasized in American homes and schools today?

3. What impressions of everyday life in a Sioux camp did you gain from this passage? What aspects of that life, if any, appeal to you? Why?

4. Describe the relationship between Luther Standing Bear and his father. How would you characterize the way that the father relates to his son?

5. What do you think of the custom of a father giving away something valuable, like a horse, when his child achieves something?

Activities

Writing a Narrative

1. Write a personal **narrative** describing an incident that tested your character. For example, you may have resisted a temptation to cheat on a test, you may have defended a friend who was a victim of gossip, or you may have performed well under pressure to win a close game in a sport.

Designing a Shield

2. Design a buffalo hide shield for Luther Standing Bear that commemorates his first buffalo hunt.

Before You Read

I Remember Mama

Lynette Perry
Born 1914

"I believe the world I grew up in has something to say to the very different world I've aged into. You can decide whether I'm right . . . ."

About Perry

Lynette Perry was born in rural Oklahoma, with the Delaware name of Pima Pen Okwe. Her mother was a full-blooded Delaware, of the Turtle clan, her father a white man named Amos Reeve. The family lived near Dewey, Oklahoma, on the banks of Coon Creek, in an area mostly populated by Delaware and their Cherokee neighbors. "Delaware, Cherokee, white, Osage," she writes, "it didn't much matter to us. We pretty much accepted our neighbors as folks . . . "

Perry and her family lived simply off the land, with help from her father's pay as an oil pump tender. Delaware traditions such as Saturday night's stomp dance were a vital part of Perry's childhood.

The Delaware and Their Dolls

Perry's Unami, or Turtle, clan had a history similar to other Delaware. With continuing white settlement, the Delaware relocated inland and then westward to Ohio and Indiana. Perry's grandmother was born in Indiana and during her lifetime followed further migrations to Missouri, Kansas, and finally to the Indian Country (now Oklahoma). At that time— around 1868—the Delaware bought lands from the Cherokee Nation who then owned the Indian Territory. Though part of the Cherokee Nation's political structure, many Delaware still practiced their own traditional rituals. One such ritual was keeping the Ohtas, or Delaware dolls. Perry's grandmother kept these dolls, a man and a woman, during the tribe's most recent wanderings. Each spring, she hosted the Doll Dance, in which the dolls' healing and fertility powers were honored.

I Remember Mama

— *Lynette Perry*

She stands in my memory this way: framed in the doorway of Saint Paul's Episcopal Church in Dewey, wearing her Sunday best—a navy blue dress with white polka dots, white collar, and brooch. It was a dress she sewed herself, as she made all our clothes. Her long, coarse black hair glistens in the sun. A touch of rouge awakens the copper in her cheeks; charcoal from a burnt match darkens her eyebrows and shadows her lids. She has no vanity, but she has regard for beauty, even her own. Her face is broad; prominent cheekbones frame her dark, penetrating eyes; her skin is smooth as a peach. She's a woman of average height, my height, but there's something commanding about her presence. Her figure is full, not supple anymore, but graceful and strong. Mama is a fine-looking woman; in all that congregation no one holds a candle to her.

Most of the Episcopalians at Saint Paul's were white, fair-skinned women unsuited to the sun. Our Oklahoma summers sucked the juice out of them, fried them and dried them. Mama, who was as much an outlander as any of the European women, had skin as smooth as beaten copper. She was a full-blood Delaware, her beauty perfectly suited to the ferocity of our summer sun. When I was a girl this part of the country had its share of full-bloods—handsome, dignified men and women with wise, serious eyes. You'd be hard pressed now to fill even a little room with full-blood Delawares.

Our family, along with Aunt Shirley and Uncle Joe, made up the full complement of Indians in the congregation. I don't know that Mama felt she was in a spotlight. I do know that she was careful to dress her four daughters in the latest styles, perfectly copied from the Sears catalog— the arbiter of fashion in our world. Phoebe Whiteturkey Reeve was a good Christian woman, kind and loving in all her ways, and she was respected in the church for her character. Even so, it was important to her to make certain no family painted a prettier, more up-to-date picture than her girls.

Church has been important to me all my life. The first church, Saint Paul's Episcopal, offered comforts of its own. It was a big, high-ceiling room of polished wood; the altar and the benches and the door lintels and ceiling rafters gleamed from constant rubbing. Reflected in the high-backed benches we could see the darling little hats Mama made us. They were pink georgette built on a frame of wire, but of course no hint of the wire showed. She crocheted flowers and sewed ribbons onto our hats; I felt wonderful just sitting and looking at mine, perched on my head and mirrored in the bright mahogany.

Another thing I remember about church is seeing my mama's hands folded in prayer. They were strong hands, work-worn, but they could be so gentle and looked graceful when she prayed. I think I'm struck by that because it may be the only time I ever saw her hands at rest. When she wasn't at church or asleep, Mama was perpetually at work.

Phoebe Whiteturkey Reeve was an accomplished woman. There was nothing a rural wife was called on to do that she didn't do well. But let's stop calling her Phoebe. That's the name on her grave marker, but it's not the name anyone called her. Mama's Delaware name was Weetdolly, and family and friends called her Dolly. Aunt Dolly she was to all our little playmates. So, from here on it's Dolly Reeve who flashes us a smile as she hurries past, always busy with something.

They don't hand out gold medals for the things Dolly Reeve was good at. She didn't expect anything like that; I doubt she ever thought of herself that way. And yet I know it was important to her to do well the tasks of a woman as the white world reckoned them. I've told you already about our clothes. Mama made every stitch we wore, from rough-and-ready work clothes to dresses that were the pride of the countryside. She sewed our bonnets, our coats, our mittens, all.

Sewing was likely the first skill Dolly mastered; when she was fourteen, Grandpa Sam bought her a Singer sewing machine. The Singer was a proud thing—heavy steel, black with delicate little flowers painted on, that folded into a wooden case. Mama pumped the treadle as she nimbly pulled and turned the cloth. Singers were almost unbreakable; Mama used her machine to make . . . it must have been hundreds of things over the years. To own such a machine was an obligation. Tailors had them and almost no one else. Mama had to sew as well as a tailor, and she did. Without benefit of form or frame, she studied a picture, took her measurements, cut patterns out of newspaper, and worked her magic. I don't think there was anything she couldn't make.

Mama not only sewed our clothes, she washed them. Now, that was an entirely different proposition in those days than it is today. First she had to make the soap, a concoction of lye from wood ash mixed with rendered fat.

I Remember Mama

She boiled the white things in a big galvanized tub, stirred the soap in with a thick ladle, took them down to the well to rinse. In summer we hung them up on the line, in winter the wet clothes dried around our fire. The colored things we took down to a big old washer by the well. Mama, Indie, Ruth, and I would load up the tub, pour in soap and bluing. Henry would draw water from the well and heat it up with a torch. He'd sit atop the machine, working the agitator by hand. It took plenty of elbow grease to get those coloreds clean.

Most of what we ate we raised right on our place. Which is to say that Mama brought our food out of the ground. She planted two gardens, more than an acre in all of corn and potatoes, tomatoes, squash, beans, okra, beets, poke, onions. She put the seeds into the earth with a little prayer, a dusting of pollen, a dried fish in each pile of corn seeds. Then she pulled weeds, every day inspecting and digging out the unwanted greens and milkweed, thistles and wild flowers. We had an old scarecrow, very unconvincing I thought, and a dog on guard to run off the cotton-tails and other hungry critters. We didn't water the garden, couldn't, but relied on the rains—fierce and driving in the spring—and the rhythms of flood and drought. Coon Creek spilled over its banks during the spring rains to soak the soil that held the seed. It must not have happened often in late summer, though. I recall one time, when I was eight or so, when the flood began rising toward our ripening field. I guess I thought the water would rot our crop; I got all the baskets and buckets I could find and rushed out to pick beans. By the time the water reached my bare feet, I'd pretty well cleared the field of squash and tomatoes too. I felt enor-mously proud of having rescued the harvest, and Mama took me seriously enough to heap praise on my heroic efforts. Of course the flood would have done no harm, as I learned soon enough. I always thought of myself as being helpful, but I don't think I ever again worked quite so hard to bring in the crops for Mama.

Cooking, cleaning, washing, mending, sewing, planting, harvesting, can-ning, gathering eggs, and on and on . . . the woman's work that kept Dolly Reeve's hands so busy that I only remember seeing them still at church, in prayer. But I don't want to give you the idea that her life, her accomplish-ment, was confined to the domestic. Mama was the daughter of a time and place that held Annie Oakley to be a model woman, and she could shoot a gun and ride a horse with the best of them. She'd sit Old Brownie just as pretty as a picture and put that horse through his paces. And Mama could shoot, pistol or rifle, with dead-eye accuracy. Papa used to say that his Dolly could shoot a jackrabbit from a galloping horse with a .38. I don't know if he ever saw her make that shot, I never did, but it shows the regard he held her in. He couldn't have made such a shot himself, I'm sure of that.

I Remember Mama

If a woman were her work and nothing more, my portrait of Phoebe Reeve would be complete. But a woman is always more than her work, even in frontier Oklahoma. I think that a woman is always her love first and foremost, and then, often, her mystery.

Mama's work and Mama's love. I accepted them, never questioned them; they supported my world. But Mama's mystery . . . that's another matter. That I've just discovered, thinking about her now, so many years later, as I prepare to put my memories on paper.

I'm not talking about feminine wiles, though Dolly Reeve certainly possessed those. She did all she could to make herself up real pretty when she went to town, even if she had to use the charcoal from a burnt match to darken her brows. I don't think Papa was a sympathetic audience for what he liked to call "women's nonsense." In fact I remember once he found rouge in Mama's bag and threw it out in the field, making a great show of righteous indignation. They were strong, opinionated people, both of them—sometimes strong in their folly. Mama didn't snap back, even under such extreme provocation. What she did was to take her case before the Reeve women and, with the support of Papa's mother and sisters, force Amos into full-scale retreat. The women on the frontier did what they could to further the feminine mystique, as women have in all times and all places.

But Mama's mystery had to do with the makeup of her personality, not with powders and shadows and such frivolous things. Let me place before you two women—separated by just a few years—and you'll see what I mean. The first is the fourteen-year-old Phoebe Whiteturkey who flirted with Amos Reeve. Raised by Grandma Wahoney, she spoke Delaware fluently. Because Grandma relied on her, she didn't go off to Haskell like her sister Mamie. She had only our local one-room school, and her English was halting and unsure. She worshiped at the Delaware Big House. She wore traditional Delaware camp dresses, bright as flower gardens. She was skilled in basketmaking, weaving watertight baskets from the split bark of the hackberry bush.

The second is the Dolly Reeve I knew growing up. She spoke Delaware with the old people, or when she wanted to keep things from us kids. Her English was better than Papa's—a big vocabulary, very good usage and grammar. She was a loyal Episcopalian, a regular churchgoer, who never attended a Big House ceremony in my lifetime. She wore the latest fashions and favored tasteful black-and-white polka dot outfits. She wove no baskets but was skilled at many crafts, and her bonnets were as neatly made as any basket.

Ten years separate the two women. Ten years and a tremendous act of will. How did my Mama work such a change in herself? She was a highly capable woman, as I think I've made plain. And she must have been fiercely motivated. Therein lies her mystery. What was it that urged her to the transformation, especially when her striking Delaware full-blood looks proclaimed her Indian at the moment of first meeting? I'm not going to be able to answer the question; I don't know if Mama could. But I can make some suggestions.

Surely her marriage to Amos Reeve was one thing that urged her. Not that he would ask her to change or be put off by things Indian. He grew up in Indian country, after all. His brother Hank married Mama's cousin; his sister Shirley married a Cherokee man. And yet things most definitely were expected from the wife of Amos Reeve, from her church membership to her mastery of the domestic arts.

Part of the reason for Mama's change must lie in the burial of the Delaware dolls. The dolls were lost on Mama's watch, if I can put it that way. If Grandma Wahoney had banded her dolls on to Mama, it might have come out different. But she didn't do that; she took the dolls with her into the grave. She was telling Mama that the Delaware time was over, that Mama should live her life in the modern world. "The past is dead; the past is buried. The dolls, which are the health of the tribe, the future of the tribe, are in the ground with me." That was Grandma's last message. I don't know if she was right; as I look back over my life, our lives, I'm not sure she was. But it was a powerful message, and Mama took it to heart. That was another thing.

I probably come closest to understanding Mama's mystery when I remember a look in her eyes. I saw the look when Grandma Reeve brought home my big sister, Indie, and displayed her with a kind of hesitant pride, to show off surprising blond highlights in her hair. It turned out that Aunt Marianne and Grandma Reeve had tried to make Indie look a little more like the cute blond girls who were turning all the boys' heads. They washed her hair and rinsed it in lemon juice. And I guess it did put some touches of blond—more like auburn probably—into her long, dark hair.

I don't remember Mama saying much about it. I do remember her cupping Indie's head in her hands and looking long into my sister's dark eyes. The hurt that was in Mama's eyes, the way she shook her head so slow and resigned . . . it was as if in that moment she opened a window onto a sealed room in her soul. Her look seemed to say that even the best (I know she believed that Papa's people were the best) could be cruel without realizing. I never saw that look again. As far as I know, Mama was comfortable with her life, content with her lot. But sometimes I wonder if she was hiding a hurt and trying to protect us from being touched by the same prejudice.

I Remember Mama

For the reasons I've mentioned, and some I may never understand, Dolly Reeve backed away from her heritage and taught herself the ways of the white world. She was good at it. But of course you can never transform yourself altogether; it's impossible. Mama remained the girl Grandma Wahoney raised up, and our house was more Delaware than she would ever have admitted.

Responding to the Selection

Questions for Discussion

1. Who tells this story? Who is it mostly about?

2. How would you describe Dolly Reeve's character?

3. What was Dolly Reeve's life like before her marriage? How did it change afterward?

4. How would you describe Perry's attitude toward her mother? Do you agree with her estimation? Why or why not?

5. Toward the end of the selection, Perry says that her Grandma Wahoney took the Delaware Dolls into the grave with her. Grandma said, "The past is dead; the past is buried." What do you think Grandma meant by this? Do you think Grandma made the right choice about the dolls?

Activities

Researching History

1. Part of the Delaware heritage is a document that offers a look at their history. Originally engraved on wood, the *Walum Olum* or "Red Score" is a pictographic recording of the tribe's history. At the library or online, learn more about the Walum Olum. Choose a section to recount orally for classmates.

Composing an Epitaph

2. Use the information about Dolly Reeve in the selection to write an epigraph for her grave stone. Try to focus on the qualities that made her unique, but keep your epitaph under twenty-five words.

Writing an Essay

3. Lynette Perry paints a very vivid picture of her mother. Write a brief essay in which you analyze her language. What verbs and descriptive words does she use to bring her mother so entirely to life?

Before You Read

I See the Fusing

Barney Bush
Born 1946

> *"A native person is anyone who is from this earth and does not seek power over the lives of others."*

Born in Illinois, Barney Bush is of Shawnee and Cayuga ancestry. After graduating from high school, Bush spent several years hitchhiking across the United States. Since then, he has traveled the country on foot and by car, bus, train, airplane, raft, and canoe.

Bush started his writing career while studying art and history at Fort Lewis College in Durango, Colorado. After graduating from college, he became active in the American Indian Movement and taught Native American studies at several colleges. He earned a master's degree in English and fine arts from the University of Idaho in 1980.

Bush's poetry has appeared in many anthologies and magazines, and he has given readings and workshops throughout the country. Bush also composes, performs, and records his own music.

Background

In this untitled poem from his second book, *My Horse and a Jukebox,* Bush combines elements of traditional and contemporary Native American life, slowly building toward an understated but moving climax as a group waits for a family member to return from a war. Historically, Native Americans have provided the United States military with more personnel in relation to their total numbers than any other group. In the poem Bush makes references to burning cedar and to sweetgrass, an aromatic herb. According to Native American tradition, the scents of cedar smoke and sweetgrass please the Creator and so are used in prayers. Cedar smoke is a signal of friendship with the thunder spirits. Sweetgrass is meant to communicate a person's needs to the Creator.

I See the Fusing

— Barney Bush

I see the fusing
   of images
beyond the hills

Winter hides us in
5   the shelter of dreams

Smoke curling from among
   yellow aspens smells
   of the cedar I burn
   for you

10   It is getting so cold
   the horses are restless

We are all watching the
   valley for your
   headlights breaking through
15   the pines

We keep watching but
   all that approaches

is the grey blueness
   of the storm

20   The rain and sleet beat
   against the house

I built up the fire
and laid out the starblanket
Grandmother made for you

25   Our faces in the windowpane
       stare at the shining darkness
       broken by the beams
of father's truck

Your brothers, we stare at
30   each other

And help to carry your
    flag draped body
    into the house

Grandfather caressed the
35   box, gave sweetgrass to
    our mother

Your horses, silent now,
are standing in the rain.

Responding to the Selection ——————

Questions for Discussion

1. What happens in this poem? What facts are unspoken but implied?
2. How would you describe the **mood** of this poem? What words or images help create this mood?
3. How do the horses reflect the behavior or mood of the people?
4. How does the speaker express himself? How effective is this style of expression?
5. Where do you imagine the **setting** of this poem to be? What clues to the setting do you find in the poem?
6. How does this poem combine traditional and contemporary aspects of Native American life?

Activities

Writing a Journal Entry

1. Imagine that you are the speaker in this poem. Write a **journal entry** in which you describe how you felt as your brother's body was brought into the house.

Illustrating the Poem

2. Draw or paint a picture to illustrate this poem. Copy the poem in calligraphy next to your picture.

Spirits of the Last Light-Steamboat. Baje Whitehorne. Acrylic on canvas, 60 x 40 in.
Collection of the artist.

Theme Three

The Natural World

The sky's height stirs me . . .

— *Uvavnuk*

Before You Read

Traditional Inuit Songs

> *"All my being is song, and I
> sing as I draw breath."*
>
> — Orpingalik, Inuit shaman

The Importance of Songs

The Inuit, also called Eskimos, have lived in the Arctic regions of Alaska, Canada, and Greenland for at least four thousand years. Before the Inuit had extensive contact with Europeans, one of their chief forms of entertainment was singing. During the long, dark winters, they held lengthy song festivals. Members of a village would gather in a large snowhouse for hours to listen to one another perform.

The Inuit admired people who composed good songs, and the composition of a song was considered an important task. Typically, a composer would go off alone into the wilderness to work on the words to fit a tune he or she had earlier composed. The Inuit had great respect for the masterful use of language, and songs were put together with as much care as might be given to building a boat or a house. Each song belonged to its composer, and no one else could sing it during the composer's lifetime.

Since the Inuit had no system of writing, people would memorize their songs and practice them over and over. In the evenings, the individual snowhouses in a village would be filled with the singing of family members. Men and women also hummed songs as they went about their work. When performing a song before an audience, the composer would often play a drum and dance while singing.

The songs you are about to read were collected in the early 1900s by Knud Rasmussen, a Danish-Eskimo explorer and scientist who studied Inuit culture. Before the songs Orpingalik, one of the poets Rasmussen studied, tells how a song comes into being.

Traditional Inuit Songs

Eskimo Song

— *Orpingalik*
Translated by Tom Lowenstein

Songs are thoughts which are sung out with the breath when people let themselves be moved by a great force, and ordinary speech no longer suffices.

A person is moved like an ice-floe which drifts with the current. His thoughts are driven by a flowing force when he feels joy, when he feels fear, when he feels sorrow. Thoughts can surge in on him, causing him to gasp for breath, and making his heart beat faster. Something like a softening of the weather will keep him thawed. And then it will happen that we, who always think of ourselves as small, will feel even smaller. And we will hesitate before using words. But it will happen that the words that we need will come of themselves—

When the words that we need shoot up of themselves—we have a new song.

A Forgotten Man's Song About the Winds

— Translated by Tom Lowenstein

(Nobody knows who the composer of this song was,
but his words are remembered.)

      I wonder what the dear south wind
      has on its mind
      as it blows past?
      Does it think about the small people
5   who live north of us?
      Does it think of them,
      as it blows past?

      I wonder what the dear east wind
      has on its mind
10   as it blows past?
      Does it think of the small people
      who live west of us?
      Does it think of them,
      as it blows past?

15   I wonder what the dear north wind
      has on its mind
      as it blows past?
      Does it think of the small people
      who live south of us?
20   Does it think of them,
      as it blows past?

Traditional Inuit Songs

<pre>
        I wonder what the dear west wind
        has on its mind
        as it blows past?
25   Does it think of the small people
        who live east of us?
        Does it think of them,
        as it blows past?

        And what is on my mind
30   as I roam the land?
        I think of all the living things
        that can be seen:
        the musk oxen that crowd together
        in clusters on the tundra,
35   and the reindeer
        lifting their antlers
        above the mountain-tops!
        It's precious game
        I think of as I wander.
</pre>

Bird Song

— *Tatilgak*
Translated by Tom Lowenstein

The great gull hovers
on wings spread wide
above us, above us.
He stares, I shout!
5 His head is white,
his beak gapes,
his small round eyes
look far, look sharp!
Qutiuk! Qutiuk!

10 The great skua hovers
on wings spread wide
above us, above us.
He stares, I shout!
His head is black,
15 his beak gapes,
his small round eyes
look far, look sharp!
Ijoq! Ijoq!

The great raven hovers
20 on wings spread wide
above us, above us.
He stares, I shout!
His head is blue-black,
his beak is sharp
25 (does it have teeth?)
His eyes squint!
Qara! Qara!

And then there is the owl,
the great owl!
30   He hovers
on wings spread wide
above us, above us.
He stares, I shout!
His head is swollen,
35   his beak is hooked,
and his round eyes
have lids turned inside out,
red and heavy!
    Oroq! Oroq!

Delight in Nature

— *Tatilgak*
Translated by Tom Lowenstein

Isn't it delightful,
little river cutting through the gorge,
when you slowly approach it,
and trout hang behind stones
5   in the stream?
    Jajai-ija.

Isn't it delightful,
that grassy river bank?
Yet Willow Twig,
10   whom I so long to see again,
is lost to me.
So be it.
The winding of the river
through the gorge is lovely enough.
15   Jajai-ija.

Isn't it delightful,
that bluish island of rocks out there,
as you slowly approach it?
So what does it matter
20   that the blowing spirit of the air
wanders over the rocks:
the island is so beautiful,
when, driving steadily,
you gain on it.

Moved

— Uvavnuk
Translated by Tom Lowenstein

(A song that would always send the shaman
Uvavnuk into a trance.)

The great sea stirs me.
The great sea sets me adrift,
it sways me like the weed
on a river-stone.

The sky's height stirs me.
The strong wind blows through my mind.
It carries me with it,
so I shake with joy.

Delight in Singing

— *Piuvkaq*
Translated by Tom Lowenstein

It's wonderful
to make up songs:
but all too many of them fail.

It's wonderful
5   to have your wishes granted:
but all too often
they slip by.

It's wonderful
to hunt reindeer:
10   but all too seldom
you succeed,
standing like a bright fire
on the plain.

Responding to the Selection

Questions for Discussion

1. Orpingalik says that the Inuit "always think of ourselves as small." On the basis of what you know about their environment, why might they think that way?

2. What is the source of most of the images in the songs? Explain why Inuit songs might be full of such imagery.

3. What kinds of feelings about life, or attitudes toward life, do these songs convey?

4. The Inuit poet Kilime wrote: "let me cleave words, / sharp little words, / like the firewood / that I split with my axe." How does this attitude towards poetry compare to Orpingalik's? Which attitude about poetry is closer to your own?

5. Which of the songs do you like best? Why?

Activities

Writing a Poem

1. Compose a poem of your own, patterning it after one of these Inuit songs. You might use the form or the subject matter of one of the selections.

Arranging a Song

2. Set one of the songs to music and perform it for the class.

Writing an Essay

3. Reread Orpingalik's remarks. Then write one or two paragraphs giving your own thoughts as to what a song or poem should be.

Before You Read

Pied Beauty and My Heart Leaps Up

Gerard Manley Hopkins
1844–1889

"Come forth into the light of things, let Nature be your teacher."

— William Wordsworth

About Hopkins

Like many writers, British poet Gerard Manley Hopkins did not know fame during his lifetime. His poetry was not published until nearly thirty years after his death.

Hopkins was born into a middle-class Anglican family that shared a love of literature, art, and music. He began writing as a child and won a poetry prize when he was fifteen. He went on to study Latin and Greek at Oxford University.

Longing for a more spiritual life, at twenty-two Hopkins converted to Roman Catholicism against the wishes of his family. He died of typhoid at forty-four.

William Wordsworth
1770–1850

About Wordsworth

Early in life, William Wordsworth suffered two tragedies: the death of his mother when he was eight and the death of his father five years later. Though Wordsworth grieved over his loss, he came to love school and the people and the beauty of the Lake District where he lived. His passion for poetry, simple country living, and the natural world influenced him for the rest of his life.

Wordsworth believed that poetry springs from the "spontaneous overflow of powerful feelings" that the poet "recollect[s] in tranquility." He was one of the first poets to set down the principles of a new trend in poetry, called Romanticism.

Pied Beauty

— *Gerard Manley Hopkins*

Glory be to God for dappled things—
    For skies of couple-color as a brinded cow;
        For rose-moles all in stipple upon trout that swim;
Fresh-firecoal chestnut-falls; finches' wings;
5   Landscape plotted and pieced—fold, fallow, and plow;
    And all trades, their gear and tackle and trim.

All things counter, original, spare, strange;
    Whatever is fickle, freckled (who knows how?)
      With swift, slow; sweet, sour; adazzle, dim;
10   He fathers-forth whose beauty is past change:
             Praise him.

My Heart Leaps Up

— William Wordsworth

My heart leaps up when I behold
   A rainbow in the sky:
So was it when my life began;
So is it now I am a man;
So be it when I shall grow old,
   Or let me die!
The Child is father of the Man;
And I could wish my days to be
Bound each to each by natural piety.

Responding to the Selection

Questions for Discussion

1. What is the theme of "Pied Beauty"? Of "My Heart Leaps Up"? How are their themes similar? How are they different?

2. How do Wordsworth's ideas about the source of poetry compare with Orpingalik's ideas about the source of songs? How do you think Wordsworth would have reacted to "Eskimo Song"?

3. Compare and contrast the style of language of the Inuit songs with that of "Pied Beauty" and "My Heart Leaps Up." Which style of language do you prefer? Why?

4. Which of these songs and poems best expresses a feeling or belief you share? Give reasons for your answer.

Activities

Writing an Essay

1. Think about the process you go through in composing a poem or a song. Write a brief essay describing this process and telling where your ideas come from.

Creating a Travel Poster

2. Investigate the landscape of the Lake District in England and the Inuit lands in the Arctic region. Prepare a travel poster highlighting the natural beauty of one of these areas.

Before You Read ──────────

The Hunter

Larry Littlebird

About Littlebird

Larry Littlebird has developed his talents in many areas. He is a poet, storyteller, film and television writer, filmmaker, and actor. He starred in the movie version of the novel *House Made of Dawn* by Kiowa author N. Scott Momaday. Littlebird promotes the oral tradition of Native Americans through an educational organization he founded called Coyote Gathers His People. He grew up in the Pueblo communities of Laguna and Santo Domingo in New Mexico. He now lives in Santa Fe, New Mexico. His forthcoming book *Hunting Sacred—Everything Listen* will use words, music, and art to show how the Pueblo oral tradition can be a guide to living in harmony with nature.

The Pueblo Background

"The Hunter" is a short story set in New Mexico, where the varied landscape includes flat-topped hills called mesas and dry streambeds called arroyos. New Mexico has nineteen pueblos where people still maintain many of their old traditions. The "Pueblo" are not a tribe as such; they comprise several different language groups, for example. But they are linked by their lifestyle and by many of their beliefs. One basic tenet of the Pueblo way of life is that a person's spiritual life is not separate from his or her "everyday" life. The Pueblo believe that the Creator, or Great Spirit, is present everywhere throughout the natural world, and so Earth and all creatures and natural objects have a spirit, or divine essence. Thus, a person's spiritual life focuses on becoming fully aware of his or her relationship and responsibility to all life.

The Hunter

— *Larry Littlebird*

Maybe it was because I was a child and saw it that way, or maybe it really is the way I remember it, growing up in my mother's village.

It is fall. There is a special clarity in the way light appears at this time of year. And it gives my memory a sense of another time, a time when my young eyes can see beyond the haze and the world stands out, still, brilliant, and defined. In the fall, all talk and thoughts turn to hunting. As the stories of the deer and the hunter unfold detail by detail, in my child's mind, images of the deer appear and take shape.

They say the deer is a spirit. A creature of God's creation, it needs supplication, understanding, and reverence. It is a blessing, a gift bestowed upon humankind as a remembrance of our own life's interconnected course, an interwoven thread from the beginning of all living time. It is meat for the body and soul.

Endowed with a keen sense of sight, smell, and hearing plus additional uncanny abilities beyond human dimension, this creature cannot be simply slaughtered and used. The deer's realm is the pristine spaces of mountain and plain, its very domain is a sanctuary. Its essence is life; to kill it is to waste it.

This new and wondrous creature begins to occupy me, looming magnificently magnified and imagined in my thoughts as I roam mesas and arroyos playing, as I eat and sleep.

I want to be a hunter, one of the men afield in the fall, gun in hand, bandolier of shiny bullets around my waist, a bright red kerchief about my head. Can I be a man who will endure the rigors of the hunt? The all-night prayer and singing? A man who from daylight till sunset, without food, without drink, will evidence the stamina of a strong people? I wonder.

With a child's anticipation and delight, the fall evenings are spent around the little outdoor fires on the village edge waiting into the night for the signal that will tell everyone a hunter returns. For seeming nights on end, we wait until at last the bright orange spark that lights the shadow of the far southern hill sends me scurrying with the other boys and girls toward the only road by which the hunters will enter. Gathering excitedly at the road's edge, laughing and whispering, speculating about which party of men are returning, our noisy exuberance is suddenly cut silent. A low murmuring sounds from the far deep night. The joyous rise of men's voices singing their songs of the deer coming home to our village reaches us through the darkness.

Someday I will arrive home like these men, my face painted to signify my sacred purpose, greeted reverently by the people, blessed and made welcome. I dream of that day, but how?

One day my grandmother simply tells me, "Day by day, little by little, you will learn. Keep your eyes open, your mouth shut and become obedient to those in authority around you. Life is sacred to us, and you are sacred. You carry it in your heart the best you can. Treat all things as you want to be treated, then some day you will be ready." It is simple and I believe her. But I still want to kill a deer.

With a little boy's forgetfulness, these questions I ponder so seriously easily give way to other equally important concerns as the season passes. Will there be enough snow this year for my homemade sled I've worked so hard to find enough scrap boards to make? Will I ever learn to spin my brightly painted wooden top, whipping it off the tight string as accurately as my older cousin? Will my small frail hand ever grasp the correct grip on the beautiful glass marble that would allow me to win a few? The seasons come and go, invisibly blending one into another, and even though I still leave more marbles in the ring than fill my pockets, visions of the deer never quite leave me.

During this time I learn to use a homemade inner tube band slingshot until cans, bottles, even objects tossed into the air are accurately and consistently knocked down. After that, proficiency with a rifle comes easily. Even then, something tells me hunting is more than expertise with a weapon. Gradually, I am obsessed by one recurrent thought, "to kill a deer without wasting it."

The year of my first deer hunt, my uncles carefully instruct me on what a man does when he wants to hunt. I do as I am taught; I do it all correctly but I don't kill a deer.

"Killing a deer isn't everything to hunting," my uncles say. "Fasting and praying, a man works hard giving his self to the spirit the deer belongs to. We are only human, we cannot say what our giving should bring. Yes, we want badly to bring home that big buck; we can only work truthfully at doing that. The Creator will see our honesty; we must believe our reward will come about. There should be no disappointment."

The Hunter

Trying not to feel disappointed, I think all this over. I prepared so carefully—my rifle, my bullets, my actions, my thoughts, my prayers. Where am I at fault? Then I remember.

I remember that little boy sitting by the outdoor fires watching for the returning hunters. I remember what he felt in his heart when he saw the stripe-painted faces of the men arriving home from the deer's mountain sanctuary, their beings permeated with invisible blessings, strength, well-being.

I remember water that is made holy as the paint is washed from their faces by the women. I remember the little boy who is told to drink that sacred water. I remember eagerly drinking that murky brown liquid, the taste of sweet sediment in my mouth. The grown-ups laugh and make joking remarks but I drink it anyway because I believe them when they tell me it will make me a strong hunter. I feel my body shudder as the essence touches my young heart that wants only to be a hunter.

It is the desire to be a hunter who will not waste a deer's life that I remember. My feet have touched the mountains where deer live; I have breathed in the same air and drunk of their water. I've gotten close, yet no deer has come to my hungry gun. There is no fault. Had I killed a deer that first year, would I have recalled the little boy who wanted to be a hunter? Or remembered the child who believed the stories old men and old women tell in that other long ago time?

Surely, the deer is a spirit, and I must die if I am to be one. Day by day, little by little, as I embrace and struggle with this gift, my worldly desires must die, my physical needs must die. I must die to the selfish lusts that would entice my body and entrap my soul, until at last, unthinking and clear-eyed, innocent like a child, I am free to believe and know the secret pulsing in the hot flowing blood the hunter hunts. And, somewhere, the red living waters of the pure-eyed deer wait for me.

Responding to the Selection ───────

Questions for Discussion

1. In "The Hunter," how does a hunter prepare to hunt a deer? What is the purpose of these preparations?

2. How do the people view the deer they hunt? Why is it important to kill a deer without "wasting" it?

3. The pristine land of the deer is called a "sanctuary." What attitude toward nature is reflected in this choice of words?

4. This story portrays hunting as a sacred act. How or why might it be considered so? By hunting the deer, what does the hunter seek union with? What do such phrases as "the secret pulsing in the hot flowing blood" and the "red living waters of the pure-eyed deer" refer to?

Activities

Writing an Essay

1. Conduct further research on the religious philosophy of the Pueblo people and write an essay describing how "The Hunter" reflects this philosophy.

Creating an Illustration

2. Illustrate the story in a way that shows what you think of the story's environment and message.

Before You Read

Four Poems

Linda Hogan
Born 1947

> *"When I was a child,
> I knew that my journey
> through life was going to be
> a spiritual one."*

About Hogan

Linda Hogan is an active environmentalist who believes that people are meant to be appreciative caretakers of life on Earth. She says, "Many of us in this time have lost the inner substance of our lives and have forgotten to give praise and remember the sacredness of all life."

At the age of fifteen, Hogan quit school and worked as an aide in a nursing home. "I was engaged young and I wanted to get married. I didn't know anyone who went to college, or even what it was," she says. Hogan held a series of low-paying jobs before she went to college and obtained a master's degree in English and creative writing from the University of Colorado at Boulder.

The Chickasaw in Oklahoma

The poems you are about to read come from Linda Hogan's first collection of poetry, *Calling Myself Home*. At the time she wrote these poems, Hogan was working with handicapped children and wrote during her lunch hours. The poems were inspired by her remembrances of her grandparents' home on Chickasaw land in Oklahoma.

The Chickasaw have lived in Oklahoma since the late 1830s, but their original homeland was in Mississippi. After the United States gained its independence, settlers flocked to what was then the Southwest Territory. Conflicts with the Native American inhabitants arose, and the newly established state of Mississippi urged the federal government to expel the Native Americans. Eventually, in exchange for a payment of $3,000,000 and the promise of permanent land rights, the Chickasaw agreed to move to Oklahoma.

Four Poems

— Linda Hogan

Arrowhead

I hear the soft breath
of horses,
ghosts resting in heat,
the muffled hooves
5   turning from the sun.

Here
where the smell of pine is thick,
I rest beneath this tree
holding broken flint.

10   Eyes closed,
I see a woman grinding corn
in a round stone basin
and soft feet hit earth
dry as the air.

15   In the breeze
are the sounds of this man
chipping stone,
his old knees bent
and birds
20   falling
down his mind.

Thanksgiving

Turkey, blue head on the ground
body in a gleaming white tub
with lion claw feet.
Heat rises in the yard
5   melting crystals of ice
and there are feathers, bronze,
metallic blue and green
that were his strong wings
which never flew away.

10   And we give thanks for it
and for the old woman
shawl pulled tight around her
she sits
her teeth brown
15   her body dry
her spoons
don't match.

Some geese, last stragglers
trickling out of Canada
20   are flying over.
Noisy, breaking the glass sky
grey
they are grey
and their wings are weightless.

Man in the Moon

He's the man who climbs his barn
to look down on the fields,
the man leading his horse from the barn
that finally fell down.

5   When I'm quiet he speaks:
we're like the spider
we weave new beds around us
when old ones are swept away.

When I see too much
10   I follow his advice
and close my worn-out eye.

Yesterday he was poor
but tomorrow he says his house
will fill up with silver
15   the white flesh will fatten on his frame.

Old man, window in a sky
full of holes
I am like you
putting on a new white shirt
20   to drive away on the fine roads.

hackberry trees

We walk small
over the dry pond,
old bowl of earth.
We walk over the fine bones of fish
5   buried in powdered silt
beside hooks.

This summer the turtle is gone,
pupil in the eye we called water
that watched us grow dry.

10   The trees are all that's left of water.
Beneath them the crickets
are sawing their legs
dust for rosin.
Turn up a stone and they keep silent.

15   On the dark trunks of trees
shells of bronze insects
are open at the back.

We are like the trees,
they have been in this place so long
20   their yellow hearts could open.
The insects walk over our warm skin.
They think we are the earth.

Responding to the Selection ─────────────

Questions for Discussion

1. What kind of connection, and to whom, does the speaker in the poem "Arrowhead" experience? What sparks this connection? Have you ever had a similar experience? What sparked it, and what was the experience like?

2. How does the speaker in the poem "Man in the Moon" relate to the Moon? What attitude toward time and change does the poem convey?

3. In the poem "Thanksgiving," what impressions do you gain of the speaker's experience of a Thanksgiving? Why do you think Hogan describes the slaughtered turkey as well as the geese flying south?

4. What kind of relationship between people and the natural world does the poem "hackberry trees" portray? How would you describe your own sense of your relationship to nature?

5. What common qualities do you notice in these four poems? For example, how would you describe the mood, or the feeling the poet creates, in these poems? How are the subjects and the themes similar?

Activities

Writing a Poem

1. Write a free-verse poem that captures a childhood remembrance you have of a particular place or an experience of nature.

Creating a Book Jacket

2. On the basis of the feeling you get from these poems, design a book jacket for Hogan's collection *Calling Myself Home.*

Before You Read

A Song of the Gotal Ceremony

Traditional (Mescalero Apache)

> *"There is one God looking down on us all."*
>
> — Geronimo, Apache leader

About the Mescalero

The Mescalero Apache are one band of the Apache tribe. Before the Spanish came to the Southwest, the Mescalero roamed over a large area covering parts of present-day Colorado, New Mexico, Texas, and Mexico. As nomadic hunters, they followed the buffalo herds for nine months of the year, sometimes traveling over forty miles a day on foot. During the hunting season, they lived in tipis on the plains. In the winter, they built shelters in the mountains or deserts.

For many centuries, the Apache lived as nomadic hunters and gatherers. Organized in small bands, they had no central authority. This made it difficult for the Spanish, Mexican, and United States governments to reach a lasting agreement with them; one band might be considered "renegades" for not obeying a treaty that had been agreed to by an entirely different group. In 1873, after many conflicts, the Mescaleros as a whole agreed to accept the boundaries of their present reservation.

Religious Traditions

Traditionally, the Mescalero believe in a Great Spirit who created the world in four days, and the number four figures prominently in their religious rituals. They saw the Great Spirit as being manifest in the natural universe, and they paid homage to the movements of the Sun and Moon.

An important Mescalero religious ritual was a ceremony held for each girl when she came of age. The ceremony lasted four days and nights, reflecting the four days of creation. Within a sacred lodge especially built for the ceremony, a medicine man sang and prayed for the girl. The girl wore a yellow dress, the color of pollen, and danced throughout much of the ceremony. The song you are about to read was sung on the last morning of the ceremony just at sunrise.

A Song of the Gotal Ceremony

— *Traditional (Mescalero Apache)*
Translated by Pliny Earle Goddard

The black turkey-gobbler, under the East, the middle of his tail;
    toward us it is about to dawn.
The black turkey-gobbler, the tips of his beautiful tail; above us
    the dawn whitens.
The black turkey gobbler, the tips of his beautiful tail; above us
    the dawn becomes yellow.
The sunbeams stream forward, dawn boys, with shimmering shoes of
    yellow;
5 On top of the sunbeams that stream toward us they are dancing.
At the East the rainbow moves forward, dawn maidens, with
    shimmering shoes and shirts of yellow, dance over us.
Beautifully over us it is dawning.
Above us among the mountains the herbs are becoming green;
Above us on the tops of the mountains the herbs are becoming
    yellow.
10 Above us among the mountains, with shoes of yellow, I go around
    the fruits and herbs that shimmer.
Above us among the mountains, the shimmering fruits with shoes
    and shirts of yellow are bent toward him.
On the beautiful mountains above it is daylight.

Responding to the Selection

Questions for Discussion

1. What does the tail of the turkey represent in this song? How are sunbeams personified?

2. What is the dominant color mentioned in the song? What might that color have represented to the Mescalero?

3. What does this song celebrate? What attitude toward nature does the song express? How is the song appropriate for celebrating a girl's coming to maturity?

4. In line 11, who is the "him" toward which the fruits bend?

5. Which are your favorite lines in this song? Why?

Activities

Writing a Poem

1. Using this song as a model, write a poem that celebrates the sunset.

Creating an Illustration

2. Create a work of art that captures the spirit of the song. You may research traditional Apache art and use that style in your work, or you may interpret the song in a style of your own or in the style of another tradition.

Newspaper Article

Many Native American peoples think of natural features as sacred places. This article discusses conflicts that can arise because of this feeling.

Rock climbers, Washoe Indians clash over Cave Rock

Los Angeles Times

How would you react if teen-agers slung ropes over the Western Wall to practice rappelling? Or rock climbers took to scaling the steeple of the National Cathedral? What if dirt bike racers rumbled each weekend through the somber fields of Gettysburg?

How would you feel?

Indignant, maybe? Appalled?

Good. Then the Washoe Indians who posed those questions have made their point. They have forced you to consider how they feel watching rock climbers crawl over one of their most sacred sites—a towering plug known as Cave Rock that juts up from the eastern shore of Lake Tahoe.

But before signing on with the Washoe cause, consider the climbers.

They, too, revere the rock. From around the globe, they come to worship it in their own way, through sweat and strain, by hauling themselves up its steep forbidding crags. Cave Rock offers some of the most challenging climbs in the world, and the athletes have marked each one by drilling 300 bolts into the landmark's surface.

And so two cultures stake claims to this one rock.

The Washoe want the climbers out. The climbers refuse to abandon their routes. Both sides are angry. And it's up to the U.S. Forest Service, which manages the rock, to find a solution.

According to Washoe tradition, Cave Rock is so charged with spiritual energy that only certain elders dare approach it. Even they must tread with care. Darriel Bender, a Washoe elder, recalls that his uncle, a Washoe medicine man, would spend days working his way up to the top of the rock, pausing often for spiritual renewal.

But climbers contend the rock lost its spiritual and cultural significance decades ago, when the state punched two freeway tunnels through the lower cave. Traffic now rumbles through those tunnels at all hours; some motorists honk their horns to bounce an echo off the rock. A nearby boat launch adds to it.

The Washoes agree that the tunnels destroy Cave Rock's calm. But that desecration, they argue, only makes the rest of the rock all the more precious—and all the more deserving of protection.

"You can see what has been done to it and that speaks to us, telling us this shouldn't happen anywhere else," said A. Brian Wallace, the tribe's elected chairman.

Questions for Discussion

1. What arguments could you make for and against the Washoe position? For and against the rock climbers?

2. How would you solve the dispute?

Before You Read

Three Essays

Louise Erdrich
Born 1954

" . . . *if I started thinking about all the things that other people tell you to write about or do, I would've never written in the first place.*"

About Erdrich

A member of the Turtle Mountain Band of Chippewa, Louise Erdrich comes from a family of storytellers and writers. She has said that people in Native American families "make everything into a story." Born in Little Falls, Minnesota, Erdrich grew up in a family of seven children in Wahpeton, North Dakota, where her parents taught in a school operated by the Bureau of Indian Affairs. She began writing stories as a small child, earning a nickel a story from her father.

While attending Dartmouth College, Erdrich met Michael Dorris, who was then the founding director of the Native American Studies Program at Dartmouth. Erdrich and Dorris later married and developed a literary partnership in which they collaborated on most of their writing, publishing under the name of the one who wrote the first draft. Erdrich became a critically acclaimed, best-selling author with such novels as *Love Medicine, The Beet Queen,* and *Tracks.*

A Writer at Home

Although Louise Erdrich is best known as a novelist, she also writes nonfiction and poetry. The selections you are about to read come from her collection of essays *The Blue Jay's Dance,* written while she lived with her husband and six children in a farmhouse in New Hampshire. The essays deal with her life as a mother and writer in the 1980s and early 1990s. During this time, she did her writing in an office across the road from her home.

Besides relating the joys and frustrations of raising a family while maintaining a career as a writer, Erdrich also reflects on the natural world outside her country home.

Three Essays

— *Louise Erdrich*

Local Deer

The fat lady thins suddenly. A new company of woodchucks appears. There are five, and they tumble beneath my feet, knocking against the boards of the crawl space, chewing up the raisins and apples I leave by their hole. I begin to worry that the whole house may plunge into the earth. Week after week I watch the fat pups spill into the yard, tumbling onto one another, end over end, weaving themselves into a ball of woodchucks. They play under the house, sometimes right below my feet. No matter how hard I stomp they continue to loll and dig and play. They knock into the underground gas furnace, and love the big noise. I leave sliced apples outside the door. Cracked corn. Stale bread. I spread the contents of a box of half-petrified prunes on the old wooden step. All of this they gobble down, running from below the house before I've even gone inside again. After a while they become tame as children and will approach my foot to take a peanut from the toe of my boot.

So here I sit, with a peanut on my foot, as though I'm not a writer, as though I've got nothing to do but watch these careful nuisances steal toward me one muscle at a time. I should be working because our baby is asleep, but I am too busy training woodchucks. It is late summer now, the air filled with a round clarity. I'm thinking of a sentence, businesslike, a thing I can write down, when I look up from my woodchuck.

A young buck deer is watching me.

I've never seen one here before, although they leave their tracks, two split moon, at the edge of the field and far from the road. I've fixed No Hunting signs into the sides of the trees. I've watched. I've waited the way my father taught me to wait for deer. But New Hampshire's deer herd is about half the size of Vermont's and they are nowhere near the nuisance they are in the northeastern suburbs. Simple politics. I live in a section of the state where for the price of a license a hunter can shoot any deer, doe, or fawn. Vermont has more restrictive laws, it also has a bigger winter kill-off. Deer eat rare plants as well as boring shrubs, so I know they're a mixed blessing. It is our human fault that they're now pests in many areas. At any rate, the deer I see are an unusual presence in my hunted-down stretch of the Northeast.

The young buck stands fifteen feet away, under the old apple tree some-one planted here a hundred years ago. His antlers are small, still cased in velvet. He is the bronze of dead pine needles and his eyes are black rimmed in black, still and large. His neck is limber and strong. When a car passes, he freezes, but he does not move. I don't move either. He watches me care-fully and then with nervous care he reaches down and picks up a hard, green apple. His head jerks up and he looks straight at me, the apple round and whole in his teeth, like the apple in the mouth of a suckling pig.

The apple begins to vanish. His tongue extends and pushes the whole thing back into his throat. I am alarmed, suddenly, as when one of my children bites off a piece of something too large to swallow. I mentally review the Heimlich maneuver. But the apple vanishes. He reaches down for another. And then, through the wide screen door, he hears the baby shake her rattle. She has awakened and she brandishes her toy at the buck. He takes one step backward, and stands in an attitude of absolute alert-ness, testing the noise. The rattle spins again. He turns. He walks carefully into the trees.

Deer return until the apples are gone, a doe with the young buck. She is the same shade of russet, her wide-set ears flickering and nervous, all air and grace. I look up and she is watching me, her eyes deep-water mussels, endless and grave, purple-black. She moves from the brush. Her tail is long, a dog's tail, curved and sinuous, tipped with black. She sweeps it back and forth as she browses. I grow used to them and soon I find that the deer are there, always there, in the shadows and the shapes of other things. Invisible and obvious, gray as talc and calm as sand, the deer divide themselves from the spars and bones of trees. They make themselves whole suddenly. I am not looking, and then I am looking into their eyes.

Three Essays

The Chickadee's Tongue

We shall never know how often birds fly into things, whether, in the woods, they misjudge distances rarely or often and crash. My windows are a particular hazard before I paste the cutout shadow of a hawk into the corner of glass. Today a chickadee hits the window with a small, surprising thunk. I walk outside, pluck it off the warming earth. The bird is stunned, blinking, undamaged. I stand motionless with the bird in my hand, examining it carefully, but not a feather seems to have snapped or ruffled. I think of Pretty Shield, a Crow Indian woman interviewed by Frank Linderman before the turn of the century. Her people had great regard for the chickadee, and so do I, for it is a tough, cheerful, weightless survivor of the harshest winters, and its call seems always pleasantly friendly and encouraging. Linderman, professing to know much of chickadees, whistled the little bird's spring song to Pretty Shield. Her face became animated. Then she asked, to his intrigue, if he had seen the chickadee's tongue.

The bird was a calendar to the Crow people. If one forgot the month, one caught a chickadee and looked at its tongue. Through the winter, she said, it develops up to seven tiny bristles in its mouth.

I have always wanted to catch a chickadee and look at its tongue, but now that I've got one, my hands seem as big and clumsy as paws. I don't dare try to open its beak. Regaining its wits, the bird seems to trust me—it vibrates, its breath spins, its heart ticks too fast to apprehend, but it doesn't leave the palm of my hand. I wouldn't close my fingers on it for anything, and it knows. It looks up at me, alert and needle-sharp, but very calm, and I feel suddenly that I am an amazingly fortunate woman.

Three Essays

Morning Glories and Eastern Phoebes

Each spring for the past eight years, I've nicked the tough morning glory seeds with a knife and pushed them deep into the soil beside the doorway. Now I know exactly how it will happen, how they will grow. For two months, the shoots will twist and creep, flowing at last up the trellis in tiny bursts, then wild, incredible twisting ropes, until finally in the last weeks of summer they'll blare open. With the sun's passage, we will watch the blossoms rotate wide in the morning and shut at dusk like silken valves. Their color will be celestial, bluer than their namesake heaven.

Within and among the flowers, black and yellow Argiope spiders will set up their webs. They are swift, streamlined, handsome black and yellow with red-orange bands on their legs. Every year they loom four or five webs in the quiet sunstruck windows facing east, right in the middle of the morning glories. The eggs hatched last winter, the young over-wintered in their sacs and even now they are dispersing, already in them the knowledge of how male and female will fix and weave their webs together with an unusual seam—a zigzag up the middle, reinforced, as if stitched by a machine.

Walking over to my office, I play a cat and mouse game with a pair of eastern phoebes. The two birds nest every year on a crossbar on the small latticed lean-to outside the door. Each morning, I duck in quickly with baby in my arms, and then all day as I work, they work, building their nest with dabs of mud taken from a low, swampy part of the yard or the pond behind the house. As we all work, as the baby naps restlessly, pouring her cries out from time to time, I learn what they can see, what is in their line of vision. Each time I rise I make myself part of something else—the wall, the door brace—and move with slow care.

The nest sprouts moss immediately and becomes an emerald cup. The eggs are laid. I can tell because now the female sits as often as she can, her cool gray back smooth above the moss. When she leaves to hunt with the male they perch together on the electrical wire, a graceful duet. They hover and drop on invisible gnats, snatch food from the air, then exhibit the self-satisfied tail bobbing of their species. Discreet birds, I never know it when the eggs do hatch. I can detect no change in his or her behavior.

Two weeks pass and I despair. Though watching carefully, I can see no young. I think perhaps blue jays, the huge feral tomcat that haunts this place, or maybe my own disturbances have doomed the clutch of eggs.

And so my curiosity at last overcomes me. One afternoon, when she flies off, I step outside my door and tap my finger lightly on the crosspiece of wood below the nest. At once, four heads shoot out of the nest, beaks open, raving for food.

Responding to the Selection ———————

Questions for Discussion

1. In "Local Deer," how does Erdrich gain the trust of the woodchucks? Of the deer? What do you think Erdrich sees when she looks into the eyes of the deer?

2. In "The Chickadee's Tongue," why does Erdrich find the chickadee interesting and worthy of regard? As Erdrich holds the chickadee, why do you think she feels that she is "an amazingly fortunate woman"?

3. In "Morning Glories and Eastern Phoebes," what is the connection between the morning glories, the Argiope spiders, and the eastern phoebes? How is Erdrich's life like that of the eastern phoebes?

4. How would you characterize the way in which Erdrich relates to the woodchucks, the deer, the chickadees, and the eastern phoebes? What do you learn about Erdrich from the way in which she relates to the natural world around her?

5. Erdrich once wrote, "I am not a scientist, not a naturalist, not a chef, not an expert, not the best or worst mother, but a writer only, a woman constantly surprised." Based on what you have read, what qualities does she seem to have that would make her a person capable of being "constantly surprised"?

Activities

Keeping a Log

1. Take the time to observe an animal in a natural setting as Erdrich does—perhaps a bird or a squirrel in your backyard or in a park. Keep a log of your observations for a week.

Writing an Essay

2. Write a short essay describing and reflecting on your observations of an animal. Reread Erdrich's essays, paying attention to the kinds of details she includes. If you wish, try to model your writing after hers.

How the Horse Brought Changes

Consider the effect the automobile has had on everyday life. It has influenced where and how people live, work, shop, and travel—almost every aspect of people's social and recreational activities. The horse had this kind of far-reaching impact on the lives of Native Americans after the Spanish reintroduced the animal to the Western Hemisphere.

Although small horses, the ancestors of today's horses, roamed the West long ago, they became extinct about the same time as the mastodons and saber-toothed tigers. For centuries, the only beast of burden in North America was the dog. In the 1500s, Spanish explorers brought modern horses with them to Mexico. Over time many escaped, and by the mid-1700s herds of wild horses had spread all the way to Canada.

The coming of the horse helped create the golden age of Plains culture. Previously, the peoples there depended largely on farming for subsistence. They did hunt the great herds of buffalo that ranged over the plains, but hunting these massive animals on foot was not easy. A lone hunter might spend hours stalking one buffalo. Sometimes an entire village might be able to stampede a herd over a cliff or into a corral. But hunting on horseback proved much easier and more productive. A mounted hunter could overtake a running buffalo and get close enough to shoot it. Some tribes on the Plains, such as the Cheyenne, gave up farming after they learned to ride horses. A Cheyenne woman described some of the changes the horse brought:

My grandmother told me that when she was young . . . people themselves had to walk. In those times they did not travel far nor often. But when they got horses, they could move more easily from place to place. Then they could kill more of the buffalo and other animals, and so they got more meat for food and gathered more skins for lodges and clothing.

With this increased prosperity and with horses to carry bigger loads, tipis became larger and possessions more numerous. People also had more spare time; more art was created, and tribes gathered more frequently for sacred ceremonies.

Traveling on horseback, tribes could follow the buffalo herds as they migrated across the wide open plains. This mobility resulted in increased contact between tribes and more frequent disputes over territory. In addition, tribes raided one another for horses, which were prized possessions, and warfare among tribes intensified.

The Plains warrior gained a reputation for being an exceptionally skilled horseman, and a strong bond often developed between horse and rider. The Crow chief Plenty Coups, speaking of his horse as a brother, said: "I have been told that the white man . . . does not believe that the horse has a spirit. This cannot be true. I have many times seen my horse's soul in his eyes."

How the Horse Brought Changes 153

Before You Read

The Hawk Is Hungry

D'Arcy McNickle
1904–1977

> "I am writing of the West, not of the Indians primarily, and certainly not of the romantic West which the best-selling authors have exploited."

About McNickle

D'Arcy McNickle rose above a difficult childhood to become an influential writer, historian, anthropologist, and advocate of Native American self-determination. He grew up in the area of the Flathead Reservation in Montana until his parents divorced in 1914. After a bitter custody battle, the three McNickle children were taken from their mother and sent to an Indian boarding school.

McNickle went on to study English literature and creative writing at the University of Montana and at Oxford University in England. Later, he worked as an editor, writing in his spare time. In 1936 he published his first novel, *Surrounded,* which critics consider his masterpiece.

McNickle's Montana

The physical environment plays a major role in McNickle's short story "The Hawk Is Hungry," which is set in the 1930s in eastern Montana. This region consists of mostly dry, flat grassland with scattered hills. Precipitation averages only about thirteen inches a year. The winters are bitterly cold, while the summer temperatures can reach above 100 °F. Farmers and ranchers in Montana typically experience cycles of good and bad years for crops, depending on the rainfall.

For a brief period in the early 1900s, people flocked to the plains of Montana to start grain farms, taking advantage of the Homestead Act that allowed people to gain title to public land if they lived on it for five years and improved it. Many of the homesteaders' farms succeeded for a few years, but then a number of dry years caused crops to fail. Many people then abandoned their farms and left the state.

The Hawk Is Hungry

— *D'Arcy McNickle*

My sister had come to spend the summer at my Montana ranch. It was a long ten years since I had seen her, I was fond of her, and I was hoping to keep her in the West. I wasn't subtle about it. I was bragging shamelessly about our advantages, I was ready to lie if need be.

My sister is an attractive person. She is young, she will always be young, she is pleasing to look at, and she enjoys herself. Her name is Anne Elizabeth, after a great-grandmother, whom she resembles, if the painting which hung in the library of our Connecticut home is to be trusted.

As I say, I wasn't being subtle in my campaign of persuasion. Every day I thought up something for the purpose.

"You laugh when you hear mention of the 'great open spaces,' but the fact remains, this is the place to live." I would make such a remark during our morning's ride—she likes horses and I had done everything to cultivate this interest.

"I know—splendid air—open-hearted people."

My fondness for Anne runs to such foolish lengths that she may take any sort of liberty with me—she always ends by regretting it and treating me with tender regard.

"Nonsense!" After one of her digs I tried to be stern. "We are really a free people out here. The American spirit is making its last stand here. Every man is his master. He believes in himself. We don't know anything about tenement life, ward politics, the factory system—all that. . . ."

Then she would smile, and I would know that she was ready to squash me once more. "Yes, you know so little about these things that you've let the Easterners get control of your power sites, your mines, and your politics. As for tenement life, look at your farmers. . . ."

"Ranchers, Anne!"

She gave me her broadest smile, in which, I suspected, was hidden a good bit of amused tolerance. We had reached home after the ride and we were hungry. We smelled our breakfast coffee as we came near the ranch

The Hawk Is Hungry

house. If I have not already given myself away, I will make it clear that I am a bachelor, and that I keep a man and wife to cheer me up and to do the hard work. And after smelling the coffee, who could continue the argument? For once she did not wind up by calling me a romancer, a hopeless romancer, her pet term for me.

On that day I had promised to take Anne to visit the Brown sisters, Matilda and Beth. I had counted on the Browns to help me persuade Anne about the freedom of the West. They, like Anne, had been teaching school in one of those New York beehives; they had wearied of it, as her letters told me she had; and they had struck for freedom, coming here and taking up a homestead. They had talked to me about that. "We needed a change," they had said during one of our first conversations. "The city was stifling us and we needed a little free movement—needed to get our hands in the dirt." I had remembered their words. It wasn't any of my romancing. I had admired their courage. My coming to the West had been forced upon me by a physical and nervous system which had collapsed without much warning. The Browns had come by choice. That was what mattered.

Their homestead is high on a hillside. Some people have been unkind enough to speak of this as a piece of stupidity. "Who in hell would try to farm a hilltop, if he was in his right mind!" I've heard people say it. That wasn't fair. There wasn't much homestead land left when the girls came, and their choice was not the worst they might have made.

Their only water is a sluggish spring, and the soil up there is coarse and thirsty. In a dry summer—most of our summers are dry—they have the tedious task of carrying water to their garden. But what prejudiced people was the fact that the Browns had planted, and watered, a flower garden as well as the indispensable vegetable plot.

I told Anne about this and was surprised by my own vehemence in defending them against the harsh comments I had heard. These I put down to ignorance laughing at what it could not understand. High art in low company is nonsense. "You can see why they were misunderstood," I appealed to Anne.

I don't know what I had expected of her. A nod of the head, if it had been sympathetic, would have sufficed. All she said was, "You must take me to see them sometime."

That cooled me. I believe I changed the subject. At least I didn't tell her any more stories about the Browns, and there were more. There was one about the time Matilda washed the two pigs they had just bought, because "pigs are naturally clean" if given a chance, as their books on agricultural science informed them. And there was the time they were taken in by a rustic wag and on his advice had tried to buy "side-hill cattle," the kind with legs shorter on one side to make side-hill grazing more convenient. Without investigating these stories, I had dismissed them as fabrications; but the fact that I withheld them from Anne would indicate, I suppose, that I wasn't sure.

Still, I had introduced the subject of the visit and I wasn't permitted to let it drop. I suspect that Anne thought she might have some fun out of me. She had said, "I would like to see that flower garden built in defiance of the laws of nature, to say nothing of realistic neighbors."

Laughter and scepticism lay behind those words, and I shied. "All right, Anne. But I warn you, you may not enjoy them."

At that she did laugh. "I believe you're afraid to show them off!" I protested that I was nothing of the sort.

We drove the ten miles behind my fast bay team, setting out right after breakfast. On the way we talked about our childhood Connecticut, always a safe topic.

I am now coming to the part of this record which decidedly I do not like to recall. Our visit went so suddenly from a commonplace friendly call to—well, let's call it ridiculous and let it go at that.

The Brown place looked especially forlorn that morning. I had been there before, but I must admit that I had not noticed details. I suppose I was always full of thoughts about their independence of spirit and their making their own fate.

Their house was built of slab siding, refuse which most mills either burn or throw away, and the roof of a single slope was covered with tar-paper. Beside the house there was a shed for the chickens, which but for being smaller was equal to their own living quarters. The chicken house was shaded by a growth of wild elderberry bushes, around the roots of which the hens dusted themselves in holes worn by their bodies. There was a shed for the cow, a plain cow, no fantastic "side-hill" beast. Then there was a berry patch, with many dead bushes, the vegetable garden which gave them sustenance, and finally the flowers—against the walls of the house, in a round bed in the center of the yard, and a perfect nest of hollyhocks against the outhouse.

The eye took all this in in a single glance. I saw Anne look, and then look at me. I looked dead ahead. "This," she was saying silently (in my mind, of course), "you call superior to tenement conditions? It's true there is an abundance of fresh air! What a lot of fresh air!"

I had managed to get word to the sisters by calling their nearest neighbor on the telephone. So they were expecting us that Saturday morning. When they came out of the house a minute or two after we drew up, they had tidy aprons over their freshly ironed gingham dresses.

Anne slides very easily into any situation, and I should have known that there would be no difficulty in getting acquainted and settling ourselves. But I had become so apprehensive about Anne and the impression she would get of my prize exhibits that I did nothing but fidget.

"You've been here three years now, if I remember correctly," I observed at the first opportunity. I don't know what I expected them to say. I suppose Anne knew. I suppose it was written all over my face and in my manner, my eagerness to hear the Brown girls get rapturous over their manner of life. The words would not matter.

That was when things began to get ridiculous.

Matilda, the younger and the more quick-spoken, snapped me up. "Three of the dreariest years mortals ever endured. If you called it half a century it wouldn't seem wrong."

Her voice was absolutely flat. For a moment we all only stared at her, Anne and I—more especially I—trying to get at her meaning. How seriously did she intend her words?

"Really," I said, trying to ignore that flatness in her voice, "it hasn't been that bad! Whenever I've seen you, you've both looked cheery— I would say happy. Always some new thing happening. . . ."

"Mr. Buck, you've seen very little of us—and you've never seen us after a broiling day when we've come in broken-backed from carrying water to our garden—you've never seen me get raving mad when that murderous chicken hawk carries off one of our precious few hens. . . ."

I was ready to drop the subject. It was the elder sister, Beth, who made the shift and got us back on safe ground.

I had noticed before that if at any time Matilda failed to make herself understood, or if one questioned her reasoning in a discussion, Beth came to her aid, perhaps not consciously. Matilda of course resented intrusions of that sort, and I had seen her contradict herself, apparently simply to embarrass her sister. Beth was mild and warm and devoted; Matilda was lean-faced, impetuous, argumentative, caustic, demanding.

"Everybody tells us we arrived in the driest years this country has ever seen. This hill, they tell us, used to be green all summer through. Maybe they're right. We only know what we've seen." She let it go at that and got Anne to talking about Connecticut, which was their homeland as well as ours. They came from Meriden, we from Hartford. Since they had been teaching in New York City not so many years before, it soon turned out that Anne and they had common acquaintances. After that, things went along pleasantly, almost gaily, for a while.

Matilda shook off the gloom which had resulted from our first exchange and was most eager in her questioning about life "back there."

"You've no idea what a treat it is to hear you talk," she said suddenly, her eyes shining.

The Hawk Is Hungry

The simple luncheon they served was made an occasion for bringing out their linen (they had a few pieces buried in a trunk) and silver, nice old-fashioned flatware. While the sisters worked at setting things in place and getting the food served up, Anne and I tossed words at them, never looking at each other. I saw her examine the surroundings in quick, shielded glances. I looked about too and felt depressed. The house inside lacked the shabbiness of the yard and garden, and it was scrubbed clean, but it was depressing.

The room in which we sat was hardly more than ten feet square and it was full of evidence of that rejected world (I could see now, realistically, that what had been left behind was more real, better understood, and better loved, than what they had come to)—an album of photographs, framed etchings and prints, a plaster cast of the Apollo Belvedere, Breton earthenware on a plate rail, and of course books, shelved against every vacant wall. I also saw a bookcase in the small room adjoining, the bedroom, and no doubt there were books stored away in boxes.

We looked at these things, Anne and I, and tried to make conversation. She avoided my eyes. She smiled gently when she caught the glances of the sisters. She was moved to tenderness. In fact, her reactions were what mine should have been, since I am supposed to be the more feeling person and she the more rational. And there I was, glum and depressed.

The table was set in the doorway, but it might as well have been on top of the stove. There was no shade outside but there even the noon sun was sufferable. As for that cabin, with its thin walls, low roof and small square windows, it was a perfect heat trap. We sat about the table and perspired, eating making it worse, and only slavish obedience to social custom kept us fully clothed and amiable.

Matilda took command of the conversation at the table. It seemed that we had all been in Brittany, at different times, and the talk turned first to the Quimper plates on the rack.

"We did get about," Matilda was saying. "Our two salaries combined meant an occasional summer in Europe, Christmas with our Connecticut folks, Easter in Bermuda. It wasn't bad, teaching."

I squirmed, not looking at Anne.

"There was that time we made an excursion in the Hautes Alpes. Motorbus trip. Remember, Beth? Like today, there were heat waves, layer on layer, and the peasants were on the mountainside above us, scything hay. We were in the last seat of the autobus, watching them. It was intolerable when we stopped, heat and dust, and burnt petrol. We wondered if the peasants did not hate us for carrying that smell into their mountains. Remember? We watched them, like brown moles on the mountainside, swinging their scythes. We said something like 'How patient and enduring. . . .' I often think of that when we're blistering on our hillside. Not very enduring, I'd say."

We laughed a little, without gaiety.

As we sat there I noticed a hen, a grouchy-looking bird of a dirty brown color, walk or rather stroll across the yard, obviously intent on looking us over. Coming near, she cocked her head at us and stood with one foot raised.

Beth saw me look. "That's Molly, the boss of the hencoop. She heard strange voices and has come round to investigate. None of the others, not even Tom the rooster, would stir about in this heat."

When Beth tossed out a crumb, Molly the hen showed some of her quality. If she had run excitedly for the tidbit, she would have attracted attention in the hencoop. Instead, she walked quietly toward the crumb, looked back once to make sure she was unobserved, then deftly clipped it with her beak and turned once more toward the humankind.

We all commented.

"A creature of sense."

"You could call it insight."

"Oh, Molly," Beth exclaimed. "She never makes a false move!"

It was left for Matilda to make the wry comment. "You see what we have come to. The neighbors think us fantastic, so they avoid us. Result, we're reduced to making conversations with the barnyard folk. You should hear us carry on. Some days you'd think we were a family of ten, the way we call out names. 'Tom, get out of the garden this minute! Susiebell—that's the guinea-hen—stop that racket!'"

Beth looked a little stung. "But they are like people! We've known people just like Molly. Bossy, fussy, always wanting her way, and getting it. Even Tom the old rooster has a way of giving in. The young rooster positively avoids her. He has his younger set. But that Molly—she'll even fight off the chicken hawk! The others, with old Tom in the lead, the silly thing, run at the first sight of his shadow."

That left us wondering what to say next. A kind of embarrassment had come upon me and I supposed that Anne shared it. I felt that under the surface of this neighborly visit were many quirky currents of meaning, hidden eddies of the subject which somehow one must avoid, deep pools of resentment and frustration. I began to wish we could be on our way—and we hadn't yet reached the dessert course.

Now it was Touraine, the château at Loches, and the little blue room with fleur-de-lys on the walls where Anne of Brittany had sat looking out upon the Loire flowing toward the sea—as the guide told it.

"At Chenancoux we stood in the room of that Medici woman. It was so different from Anne's little blue room . . . ," Matilda chanted, remembering more of her guidebook. "When we got bored by French chatter, we had tea at Thomas Cook's, upstairs. The English make those snug upstairs tea shops all over France."

If we could have kept to France and Bermuda and teaching in New York, all would have been well, and at the proper moment Anne and I would have started for home. Instead, we were swept suddenly into the full current of their hidden, complex lives.

It began when a shadow drifted across the yard. But before that, the rooster, with some of his hens in tow, had wandered out to share whatever entertainment Molly had found. They were together in a group, midway across the parched yard. Their beaks hung open. It was wretchedly hot just then. The sun blast withered every living thing, blinding animal eyes and giving a droop to green leaves. The utter quiet of the willows at the spring showed how breathless was the air. The faint piping whistle of a threshing machine in the valley announced the end of the noon rest. There was work to do. We at the table were wilted.

Molly the hen suddenly jerked her head erect. She looked toward the cabin, then off to the spring. Then a quick step of alarm. A moment later all the chickens had caught her awareness. Heads poked high. The rooster gave a throaty warning.

From my position at the table I had the best view of the yard and had seen that first stir of alarm. Matilda must have seen it almost as soon as I, for she reacted before the others. Her breath caught on a half-uttered sound.

The shadow streaked across the yard, was lost, then drifted back again from a different angle. It came to a pause. The hawk was directly overhead, descending.

Matilda reared up, on the point of screaming, but no sound coming. Her face, when I glanced up, was intense with pain. It chilled me.

The outcry of the chickens was shrill and wild. Wings fluttered, feathered bodies hurtled through the air, stirring small whirls of dust. The noontime stillness was suddenly loud with terror.

Molly gave ground slowly, backing away, wings spread and head lowered, scolding loudly. And then the bolt of death struck her, sprawling in the dust. A shower of feathers and scattering pebbles marked her last fight. Great wings flapped again. The sky raider was struggling upward. The hapless Molly screeched despairingly, her scolding tone beaten out of her. She rasped weakly. The sound rose higher and higher, and before any of us moved, it had stopped altogether. A few feathers floated earthward.

Matilda in this moment of stress was incoherent. She was the first to reach the yard, where she grabbed up a few stray brown feathers. The hawk was already out of sight.

"The beast! The—the beast!" It was as much as she could pronounce.

Beth had reached her by then, stretched out a hand to her floundering sister, thought better of it. For a moment she stood there empty-handed. Then her trick of explaining her sister asserted itself. She turned to us.

"It is hard to make you understand, I suppose, how terrible this is. Molly was so much—almost a person. We've been so alone here. And so, this, well. . . ."

That effort of Beth's to explain the situation finally aroused Matilda. She came at us fiercely, fairly shouting. She was oblivious of us, of course. Her quarrel was with that miserable hillside shack, with the years of dreariness. But she explained it better.

"Damnation! It was more than that! You make us seem like two old maids talking to ourselves. I say *no* to that and damn the notion! That hen was an idea. The idea of personal integrity. Standing alone and damn the consequences. Men try to live like that. Few do. Very few. The hen did. Did you see her? And this hawk, he's the witless brute force that insults us all. The best of us! We put ourselves above the beast, but when the hawk is hungry he comes for us. And what are we then?

"We liked Molly because we fancied ourselves her kind of a person. That's the truth of the matter. Birds of her feather! How do you like that?"

With an expression of disgust, she stopped short and snapped her head earthward, letting fall the few feathers which old Molly had lost in her fatal encounter.

I heard Anne's soft voice and when I looked up from a study of the ground at my feet, I saw that she had approached Matilda, put her hand out to her.

"Why don't you come home, to Connecticut? That's what you want to do, isn't it? Come home with me."

The sisters seemed to fold up at that. Perhaps it had been in their minds for a long time and they had never spoken of it aloud. Perhaps. I don't know. They seemed to get limp, Matilda and Beth together, and they slumped into chairs at the table. Neither spoke until they had sat reflecting for moments. Brittany, peasants on the mountainside, the Bermuda sands, winter in the Connecticut hills—it must all have been in their minds. Perspiration poured down their faces without distracting their thought.

"But we couldn't," Matilda spoke her thought aloud. "We couldn't—any more than Molly could run from the hawk."

She spoke a great deal more, beginning slowly and reflectively. A little unsure of herself, it seemed, but gradually warming to the idea and adding intensity to her words. Soon she was glowing, her eyes looking at us brightly. Beth began to catch some of her conviction.

The Hawk Is Hungry

"Oh, we haven't given up. Only the other day we were talking about renting a place down in the valley where the soil is better. We saw a place we could get at a small rental."

Hours later, as the afternoon was cooling, we started home, Anne and I. The girls, by then, seemed cheerful and full of prospects.

Anne stirred one sceptic thought, however, which has stayed in my mind ever since. She said, "I wonder—was it worth it—if that's the way the West was settled?"

I don't like to carry that question around with me, but I confess it has lodged in my mind and I can't get rid of it.

Responding to the Selection

Questions for Discussion

1. How do the Brown sisters' lives as farmers in Montana differ from their former lives as schoolteachers in New York City? Which way of life do the sisters seem to prefer? Why?

2. How does the incident with Molly reflect the central conflict in the Brown sisters' lives? In what ways are the Brown sisters like Molly? What do you think will happen to them?

3. Do you regard the Brown sisters as pathetic or heroic? Give reasons for your answer.

4. What contrasting views of the West do you gain from this story? Which view do you think is more accurate? Why?

5. At the end of the story, Anne asks the question, "I wonder—was it worth it—if that's the way the West was settled?" How would you answer Anne's question?

6. Which would you prefer—living in a large city or living in a remote rural area? Why?

Activity

Writing an Article

1. Research the real estate and population boom that began in Montana in the 1990s as celebrities and others who wanted to flee urban life moved to the state. Write a feature article describing how these newcomers have changed Montana.

Creating a Skit

2. Work with a partner to create a skit in which you portray what the Brown sisters are doing ten years later.

Before You Read

Somewhere Out There

William Least Heat-Moon
Born 1939

" . . . to know a place in any real and lasting way is sooner or later to dream it."

About Heat-Moon

Of English, Irish, and Osage descent, William Trogdon acquired his pen name at the age of thirteen. His father used the Native name Heat Moon, his older brother was known as Little Heat Moon, and William became Least Heat Moon.

After serving in the navy, Heat-Moon wanted to become a photojournalist. He earned several college degrees and eventually became a college professor himself. But a crisis in his personal life lead to his becoming a writer. He has gone on to write three best-selling, highly praised books on his travels through the United States. In his second book, *PrairyErth,* he focused on the history and landscape of a single county in Kansas. The third, *River Horse,* describes Heat-Moon's journey across the country by river. The following excerpt comes from his first book, *Blue Highways.*

Blue Highways

In 1978, Heat-Moon's marriage broke up and he lost his job. In this unhappy time he thought to himself, as he later wrote, "A man who couldn't make things go right could at least go." He bought an inexpensive van and converted it for eating and sleeping; he named it "Ghost Dancing" in honor of the Native American spiritual movement of the 1890s. Then he set out to travel around the United States. In search of the country's true nature, he decided to stick to rural roads, away from the interstates and superhighways. The maps he was using indicated such less-traveled roads as blue lines. When *Blue Highways* finally came out in 1983, after years of revision, Heat-Moon was acclaimed as a brilliant new voice in American literature.

Somewhere Out There

— *William Least Heat-Moon*

Somewhere out there was the Colorado River perfectly hidden in the openness. The river wasn't more than a mile away, but I couldn't make out the slightest indication of it in the desert stretching level and unbroken for twenty or thirty miles west, although I was only fifty miles above where it enters Grand Canyon. This side of the Colorado gorge was once an important Hopi trail south, and, some say, the route Hopi guides took when they first led white men to the canyon. While the arid path followed the river cleft, water was an inaccessible four hundred feet down. Typically, the flexible Hopi solved the desert: women buried gourds of water at strategic points on the outward journey for use on the return.

The highway made an unexpected jog toward Navajo Bridge, a melding of silvery girders and rock cliffs. Suddenly, there it was, far below in the deep and scary canyon of sides so sheer they might have been cut with a stone saw, the naturally silted water turned an unnatural green (*colorado* means "reddish") by the big settling basin a few miles upriver called Glen Canyon Dam. Navajo Bridge, built in 1929 when paved roads began opening the area, is the only crossing over the Colorado between Glen Canyon and Hoover Dam several hundred river miles downstream.

West of the gorge lay verdant rangeland, much of it given to a buffalo herd maintained by the Arizona Game Commission; the great beasts lifted their heads to watch me pass, their dark, wet eyes catching the late sun. To the north rose the thousand foot butt end of the Vermillion Cliffs; the cliffs weren't truly vermillion, but contrasting with the green valley in the orange afternoon light, they seemed so.

In 1776, a few months after white-stockinged men in Philadelphia had declared independence, a Spanish expedition led by missionaries Francisco Silvestre Velez de Escalante and Francisco Atanasio Dominguez, returning from an unsuccessful search for a good northern route to the California missions, wandered dispiritedly along the Vermillion Cliffs as they tried to find in the maze of the Colorado a point to cross the river chasm. They looked

Somewhere Out There

for ten days and were forced to eat boiled cactus and two of their horses before finding a place to ford; even then, they had to chop out steps to get down and back up the four-hundred-foot perpendicular walls. My crossing, accomplished sitting down, took twenty seconds. What I saw as a remarkable sight, the Spaniards saw as a terror that nearly did them in.

Escalante's struggles gave perspective to the easy passage I'd enjoyed across six thousand miles of America. Other than weather, some bad road, and a few zealous police, my difficulties had been only those of mind. In light of what was about to happen, my guilt over easy transit proved ironic.

I went up an enormous geologic upheaval called the Kaibab Plateau; with startling swiftness, the small desert bushes changed to immense conifers as the Kaibab forest deepened: ponderosa, fir, spruce. At six thousand feet, the temperature was sixty: a drop of thirty degrees in ten miles. On the north edge of the forest, the highway made a long gliding descent off the plateau into Utah. Here lay Kane and Garfield counties, a place of multicolored rock and baroque stone columns and, under it all, the largest unexploited coalfield in the country. A land certain one day to be fought over.

At dusk I considered going into the Coral Sand Dunes for the night, but I'd had enough warmth and desert for a while, so I pushed north toward Cedar Breaks in the severe and beautiful Markagunt Plateau. The cool would refresh me. Sporadic splats of rain, not enough to pay attention to, hit the windshield. I turned onto Utah 14, the cross-mountain road to Cedar City. In the dim light of a mountainous sky, I could just make out a large sign:

ELEVATION 10,000 FEET
ROAD MAY BE IMPASSABLE
DURING WINTER MONTHS.

So? It was nearly May. The rain popped, then stopped, popped and stopped. The incline became steeper and light rain fell steadily, rolling red desert dust off the roof; I hadn't hit showers since east Texas. It was good. The pleasant cool turned to cold, and I switched on the heater. The headlights glared off snowbanks edging closer to the highway as it climbed, and the rain became sleet. That's when I began thinking I might have made a little miscalculation. I looked for a place to turn around, but there was only narrow, twisted, road. The sleet got heavier, and the headlights were cutting only thirty feet into it. Maybe I could drive above and out of the storm. At eight thousand feet, the wind came up—a rough, nasty wind that bullied me about the slick road. Lear, daring the storm to "strike flat the thick rotundity

166 William Least Heat-Moon

of the world," cries, "Blow, winds, and crack your cheeks! Rage! Blow!" And that's just what they did. A loud, sulphurous blast of thunder rattled the little truck, then another, and one more. Never had I seen lightning or heard thunder in a snowstorm. Although there were no signs, the map showed a camp ground near the summit. It would be suicide to stop, and maybe the same to go on. The wind pushed on Ghost Dancing so, I was afraid of getting blown over the invisible edge. Had not the falling snow taken away my vision, I might have needed a blindfold like the ones medieval travelers wore to blunt their terror of crossing the Alps. A rule of the blue road: Be careful going in search of adventure—it's ridiculously easy to find.

Then I was on the top, ten thousand feet up. UP. The wind was horrendous. Utah 14 now cut through snowbanks higher than the truck. At the junction with route 143, a sign pointed north toward Cedar Breaks campground. I relaxed. I was going to live. I puffed up at having beaten the mountain.

Two hundred yards up 143, 1 couldn't believe what I saw. I got out and walked to it as the raving wind whipped my pantlegs and pulled my hair on end. I couldn't believe it. There it was, the striped centerline, glowing through the sleet, disappearing under a seven-foot snowbank. Blocked. Back to the truck. My heart dropped like a stone through new snow. There had to be a mistake. I mean, this wasn't 1776. The days of Escalante were gone. But the only mistake was my judgment. I was stopped on state 143, and 143 lay under winter ice.

I turned up the heater to blast level, went to the back, and wrapped a blanket around the sleeping bag. I undressed fast and got into a sweatsuit, two pairs of socks, my old Navy-issue watch cap, a pair of gloves. When I cut the engine, snow already had covered the windshield. Only a quarter tank of gas. While the warmth lasted, I hurried into the bag and pulled back the curtain to watch the fulminous clouds blast the mountain. That sky was bent on having a storm, and I was in for a drubbing.

At any particular moment in a man's life, he can say that everything he has done and not done, that has been done and not been done to him, has brought him to that moment. If he's being installed as Chieftain or receiving a Nobel Prize, that's a fulfilling notion. But if he's in a sleeping bag at ten thousand feet in a snowstorm, parked in the middle of a highway and waiting to freeze to death, the idea can make him feel calamitously stupid.

A loud racketing of hail fell on the steel box, and the wind seemed to have hands, it shook the Ghost so relentlessly. Lightning tried to outdo thunder in scaring me. So did those things scare me? No. Not *those* things. It was something else. I was certain of a bear attack. That's what scared me.

Somewhere Out There

Lightning strikes the earth about eight million times each day and kills a hundred and fifty Americans every year. I don't know how many die from exposure and hypothermia, but it must be at least a comparable number. As for bears eating people who sleep inside steel trucks, I haven't been able to find that figure. It made no sense to fear a bear coming out of hibernation in such weather to attack a truck. Yet I lay a long time, waiting for the beast, shaggy and immense, to claw through the metal, its hot breath on my head, to devour me like a gumdrop and roll the van over the edge.

Perhaps fatigue or strain prevented me from worrying about the real fear; perhaps some mechanism of mind hid the true and inescapable threat. Whatever it was, it finally came to me that I was crazy. Maybe I was already freezing to death. Maybe this was the way it happened. Black Elk prays for the Grandfather Spirit to help him face the winds and walk the good road to the day of quiet. Whitman too:

> O to be self-balanced for contingencies,
> To confront night, storms, hunger, ridicule,
> accidents, rebuffs, as the trees and animals do.

I wondered how long I might have to stay in the Breaks before I could drive down. The cold didn't worry me much: I had insulated the rig myself and slept in it once when the windchill was thirty-six below. I figured to survive if I didn't have to stay on top too long. Why hadn't I listened to friends who advised carrying a CB? The headline showed darkly: FROZEN MAN FOUND IN AVALANCHE. The whole night I slept and woke, slept and woke, while the hail fell like iron shot, and thunder slammed around, and lightning seared the ice.

❖

Responding to the Selection

Questions for Discussion

1. How does Heat-Moon use personal details in this selection? What purpose do they serve? What detail did you find most effective?

2. How does the author use historical information in his writing? How does this information affect the narrative?

3. How does Heat-Moon describe the landscape he is traveling through and the storm he encounters? How does he give you a sense of the natural wonders he encounters?

4. How does the author react to the situation he encounters? How do you think you might have reacted?

5. Heat-Moon once wrote, "There are two kinds of adventurers: those who go truly hoping to find adventure and those who go secretly hoping they won't." Based on this selection, which type do you think the author is?

Activities

Writing a Diary Entry

1. Imagine you are a traveler caught in a severe storm. Write a diary entry recording your experiences.

Researching a Report

2. Using library or online resources, research and write a report on one of the natural features mentioned in this selection, such as the Colorado River or the Kaibab Plateau.

Navajo Germantown Rug, c. 1880–1885. Artist unknown. The Heard Museum, Phoenix, AZ.

Theme Four

Other
Worlds

The Great Spirit has made
us all, but . . .

— Red Jacket

Before You Read

The Cattle Thief

Emily Pauline Johnson
1861–1913

*"My aim, my joy, my pride
is to sing the glories
of my own people."*

About Johnson

Emily Pauline Johnson grew up in a mansion that her father built on the Six Nations Indian Reserve in Ontario, Canada. Her father was a Mohawk chief, and her mother was a wealthy English woman. Johnson received most of her education at home, where her mother inspired in her a love of literature. Johnson started writing poetry as a teenager. At the age of thirty-one, she began touring Canada performing readings of her poems. Her dramatic presentation and vibrant personality thrilled audiences, and soon Johnson became a popular

stage entertainer throughout Canada. Johnson was one of the few women writers of her time to make a living from writing and performing. Generations of Canadian school children have read and memorized her most famous poem, "The Song My Paddle Sings." Johnson also wrote fiction and travel articles.

The Cree and the Buffalo

"The Cattle Thief" is a narrative poem about the conflict between the European settlers and the Cree, the largest Indian tribe in Canada. At the time the poem describes, most Cree were plains dwellers. They lived in small groups and hunted buffalo, moving with the migrations of the buffalo herds. Up until the 1870s, the buffalo were numerous on the Canadian prairies. But as Europeans began to settle and farm on Cree hunting grounds, the buffalo herds dwindled. By the 1880s, the buffalo were almost wiped out, and the Plains Cree faced starvation. Between 1860 and 1899, their population dropped from about 12,500 to about 6,800.

The Cattle Thief

— Emily Pauline Johnson

They were coming across the prairie, they were galloping hard
    and fast;
For the eyes of those desperate riders had sighted their man at last—
Sighted him off to Eastward, where the Cree encampment lay,
Where the cotton woods fringed the river, miles and miles away.
5   Mistake him? Never! Mistake him? the famous Eagle Chief!
That terror to all the settlers, that desperate Cattle Thief—
That monstrous, fearless Indian, who lorded it over the plain,
Who thieved and raided, and scouted, who rode like a hurricane!
But they've tracked him across the prairie; they've followed him hard
    and fast;
10   For those desperate English settlers have sighted their man at last.
Up they wheeled to the tepees, all their British blood aflame,
Bent on bullets and bloodshed, bent on bringing down their game;
But they searched in vain for the Cattle Thief: that lion had left
    his lair,
And they cursed like a troop of demons—for the women alone were
    there.
15   "The sneaking Indian coward," they hissed; "he hides while yet
    he can;
He'll come in the night for cattle, but he's scared to face a *man*."
"Never!" and up from the cotton woods rang the voice of Eagle Chief;
And right out into the open stepped, unarmed, the Cattle Thief.
Was that the game they had coveted? Scarce fifty years had rolled
20   Over that fleshless, hungry frame, starved to the bone and old;
Over that wrinkled, tawny skin, unfed by the warmth of blood.
Over those hungry, hollow eyes that glared for the sight of food.

He turned, like a hunted lion: "I know not fear," said he;
And the words outleapt from his shrunken lips in the language of
    the Cree.
25   "I'll fight you, white-skins, one by one, till I kill you *all*," he said;
But the threat was scarcely uttered, ere a dozen balls of lead
Whizzed through the air about him like a shower of metal rain.
And the gaunt old Indian Cattle Thief dropped dead on the open
    plain.
And that band of cursing settlers gave one triumphant yell,
30   And rushed like a pack of demons on the body that writhed and fell.
"Cut the fiend up into inches, throw his carcass on the plain;
Let the wolves eat the cursed Indian, he'd have treated us the same."
A dozen hands responded, a dozen knives gleamed high,
But the first stroke was arrested by a woman's strange, wild cry.
35   And out into the open, with a courage past belief,
She dashed, and spread her blanket o'er the corpse of the Cattle
    Thief;
And the words outleapt from her shrunken lips in the language of
    the Cree,
"If you mean to touch that body, you must cut your way through *me*."
And that band of cursing settlers dropped backward one by one,
40   For they knew that an Indian woman roused, was a woman to let
    alone.
And then she raved in a frenzy that they scarcely understood,
Raved of the wrongs she had suffered since her earliest babyhood:
"Stand back, stand back, you white-skins, touch that dead man to
    your shame;
You have stolen my father's spirit, but his body I only claim.
45   You have killed him, but you shall not dare to touch him now
    he's dead.
You have cursed, and called him a Cattle Thief, though you robbed
    him first of bread—
Robbed him and robbed my people—look there, at that shrunken face,
Starved with a hollow hunger, we owe to you and your race.
What have you left to us of land, what have you left of game,
50   What have you brought but evil, and curses since you came?
How have you paid us for our game? how paid us for our land?
By a *book*, to save our souls from the sins *you* brought in your other
    hand.
Go back with your new religion, we never have understood
Your robbing an Indian's *body*, and mocking his *soul* with food.

55   Go back with your new religion, and find—if find you can—
         The *honest* man you have ever made from out a *starving* man.
         You say your cattle are not ours, your meat is not our meat;
         When *you* pay for the land you live in, *we'll* pay for the meat we eat.
         Give back our land and our country, give back our herds of game;
60   Give back the furs and the forests that were ours before you came;
         Give back the peace and the plenty. Then come with your new
            belief,
         And blame, if you dare, the hunger that *drove* him to be a thief."

Responding to the Selection

Questions for Discussion

1. What happens in the poem? How are the various characters depicted?

2. What is the conflict in the poem? How else could the conflict have been resolved?

3. What message do you think the poem conveys? How do you feel about this message?

4. This poem, first published in 1895, is written in the style of its time. How does it compare to more modern poems you have read? Do you think its use of rhyme and meter makes it more or less effective?

5. A critic in Johnson's own time described her as a poet "who spoke loud and bold . . . for the whole red race, and sang of its glories and its wrongs in strains of poetic fire." How does "The Cattle Thief" fit this description?

Activities

Writing a News Article

1. Imagine that you are a reporter writing an article on the events in this poem. In your account, include interviews with Eagle Chief's daughter and one of the settlers.

Giving a Dramatic Reading

2. Work in a small group to prepare a dramatic performance of this poem. Students might take the roles of the narrator, Eagle Chief, and Eagle Chief's daughter. Give your dramatic reading before the class.

Focus on . . .
Reel Indians

Film and television have played an important role in creating images of the "typical" Native American. These images—changing over the course of time—have in turn helped to determine how Native Americans are perceived by others and, even to some extent, by themselves. Some critics have said that films in the 1990s began to break away from long-standing ethnic stereotypes. Others have questioned whether these perceived gains were truly positive or significant.

In the early days, silent films often made an effort to portray Native American lifeways with some accuracy. Native Americans both acted in and created silent films. They included such actors as Lillian Red Wing St. Cyr (Winnebago), who starred in a series of films in the 1910s, and Daniel Yowlatchie (Yakima), who appeared in over fifty films during his career. James Young Deer (Winnebago) was an early producer and director. But over the following decades, roles for Native American actors tended to diminish in importance, although there were exceptions.

For example, Chief Dan George (Salish/Suquamish) was widely admired for his dignified and realistic performances—as in *Little Big Man,* for which he received an Academy Award nomination in 1970.

Over time, however, portrayals of Native Americans tended to become stereotyped. Spokane/Coeur d'Alene filmmaker Sherman Alexie comments that audiences were trained to expect only two kinds of Native American in films: "the noble savage or the ignoble savage." Alexie helped break that pattern of stereotypes with his own work. Of his highly praised film *Smoke Signals* (1998), he said, "I just wanted to get away from some white person's interpretation of us, and show us the way we really are: people, like any other people in any other movie—funny, sad, strange, interesting." Many hoped that *Smoke Signals* indicated a trend in which Native Americans would participate in all aspects of filmmaking, enabling them to craft their own images.

In 1992, American Indian Movement activist Russell Means (Lakota) began an acting career by playing the title role in *The Last of the Mohicans*. While Means did criticize some elements of the film, he called it "historically and culturally reliable," commenting, "I see the film as an extension of the path I've been on for 25 years—another avenue to eliminating racism."

Other films of the late twentieth century that some viewed as defying old stereotypes included 1990's *Dances with Wolves* and 1995's *Pocahontas*. Some praised the former for its portrayal of a positive relationship between Native Americans and a U.S. Cavalry officer. Others felt that, with its portrayal of the Sioux as entirely admirable and of their opponents the Pawnee as entirely evil, the film simply exploited two stereotypes at once. Many people felt that *Pocahontas*, an animated feature, made Native American beliefs and traditions accessible to a wide audience. However, others criticized it as superficial. Clearly, film viewers, creators, and critics at the turn of the twenty-first century continued to disagree as to the way films should portray Native Americans.

CELEBRATE THE COMEDY THAT HAD AUDIENCES AND CRITICS CHEERING!

"TWO BIG THUMBS UP!"
—SISKEL & EBERT

"ONE OF THE BEST FILMS OF THE YEAR!"
—ROLLING STONE

"VERY FUNNY!"
—GOOD MORNING AMERICA

SMOKE SIGNALS

Linking to . . .
- Think about how the information you have just read applies to movies you have seen and literature you have read that portray Native Americans.

Before You Read

Speech in Reply to an Emissary of the Boston Missionary Society

Red Jacket
c. *1758–1830*

> *"We believe that forms of worship are indifferent to the Great Spirit—it is the offering of a sincere heart that pleases him."*

About Red Jacket

Red Jacket was a Seneca chief who became known as a great orator. Because of his skill in public speaking, he gained the name Sagoyewatha, which means "He Keeps Them Awake."

After the Revolutionary War, Red Jacket became a leading negotiator for the Seneca in dealings with the newly formed U.S. government. In 1792 he visited the U.S. capital at the invitation of George Washington and addressed the Senate. During the War of 1812, he fought for the United States against the British. Throughout his life, he defended the Seneca's way of life and resisted attempts to change their traditional customs and values.

The Background of This Speech

In 1805, the Evangelical Missionary Society of Massachusetts sent a missionary to the Buffalo Creek Reservation in New York to persuade the Seneca to accept Christian missionaries in their villages.

The missionary addressed a council of the Seneca chiefs. In his address, he said, "There is but one religion, and but one way to serve God, and if you do not embrace the right way you cannot be happy hereafter. You have never worshipped the Great Spirit in a manner acceptable to him; but have all your lives been in great errors and darkness."

The chiefs consulted, and then Red Jacket gave the speech that follows. William L. Stone, who collected many speeches by Red Jacket, wrote that the missionary received Red Jacket's reply "with manifest displeasure—a displeasure which a wiser man, even if he had felt it, would have concealed."

Speech in Reply to an Emissary of the Boston Missionary Society

— Red Jacket

Translated by William L. Stone

Friend and Brother: It was the will of the Great Spirit that we should meet together this day. He orders all things, and has given us a fine day for our Council. He has taken his garment from before the sun, and caused it to shine with brightness upon us. Our eyes are opened, that we see clearly; our ears are unstopped, that we have been able to hear distinctly the words you have spoken. For all these favors we thank the Great Spirit; and Him *only*.

Brother: This council fire was kindled by you. It was at your request that we came together at this time. We have listened with attention to what you have said. You requested us to speak our minds freely. This gives us great joy; for we now consider that we stand upright before you, and can speak what we think. All have heard your voice, and all speak to you now as one man. Our minds are agreed.

Brother: You say you want an answer to your talk before you leave this place. It is right you should have one, as you are a great distance from home, and we do not wish to detain you. But we will first look back a little, and tell you what our fathers have told us, and what we have heard from the white people.

Brother: Listen to what we say. There was a time when our forefathers owned this great island. Their seats extended from the rising to the setting sun. The Great Spirit had made it for the use of Indians. He had created the buffalo, the deer, and other animals for food. He had made the bear and the beaver. Their skins served us for clothing. He had scattered them over the country, and taught us how to take them. He had caused the earth to produce corn for bread. All this He had done for his red children, because He loved them. If we had some disputes about our hunting ground, they were generally settled without the shedding of much blood. But an evil day came upon us. Your forefathers crossed the great water and landed on this island. Their numbers were small. They found friends and not enemies. They told us they had fled from their own country for fear of wicked men, and had come here to enjoy their religion. They asked for a small seat. We took pity on them, granted their request; and they sat down amongst us. We gave them corn and meat; they gave us poison in return.

The white people, Brother, had now found our country. Tidings were carried back, and more came amongst us. Yet we did not fear them. We took them to be friends. They called us brothers. We believed them and gave them a larger seat. At length their numbers had greatly increased. They wanted more land; they wanted our country. Our eyes were opened, and our minds became uneasy. Wars took place. Indians were hired to fight against Indians, and many of our people were destroyed. They also brought strong liquor amongst us. It was strong and powerful, and has slain thousands.

Brother: Our seats were once large and yours were small. You have now become a great people, and we have scarcely a place left to spread our blankets. You have got our country, but are not satisfied; you want to force your religion upon us.

Brother: Continue to listen. You say that you are sent to instruct us how to worship the Great Spirit agreeably to his mind, and, if we do not take hold of the religion which you white people teach, we shall be unhappy hereafter. You say that you are right and we are lost. How do we know this to be true? We understand that your religion is written in a book. If it was intended for us as well as you, why has not the Great Spirit given to us, and not only to us, but why did he not give to our forefathers, the knowledge of that book, with the means of understanding it rightly? We only know what you tell us about it. How shall we know when to believe, being so often deceived by the white people?

Brother: You say there is but one way to worship and serve the Great Spirit. If there is but one religion, why do you white people differ so much about it? Why not all agreed, as you can all read the book?

Brother: We do not understand these things. We are told that your religion was given to your forefathers, and has been handed down from father to son. We also have a religion, which was given to our forefathers, and has been handed down to us their children. We worship in that way. It teaches us to be thankful for all the favors we receive; to love each other, and to be united. We never quarrel about religion.

Brother: The Great Spirit has made us all, but He has made a great difference between his white and red children. He has given us different complexions and different customs. To you He has given the arts. To these He has not opened our eyes. We know these things to be true. Since He has made so great a difference between us in other things, why may we not conclude that he has given us a different religion according to our understanding? The Great Spirit does right. He knows what is best for his children; we are satisfied.

Brother: We do not wish to destroy your religion, or take it from you. We only want to enjoy our own.

Brother: You say you have not come to get our land or our money, but to enlighten our minds. I will now tell you that I have been at your meetings, and saw you collect money from the meeting. I cannot tell what this money was intended for, but suppose that it was for your minister, and if we should conform to your way of thinking, perhaps you may want some from us.

Brother: We are told that you have been preaching to the white people in this place. These people are our neighbors. We are acquainted with them. We will wait a little while, and see what effect your preaching has upon them. If we find it does them good, makes them honest and less disposed to cheat Indians, we will then consider again of what you have said.

Brother: You have now heard our answer to your talk, and this is all we have to say at present. As we are going to part, we will come and take you by the hand, and hope the Great Spirit will protect you on your journey, and return you safe to your friends.

Responding to the Selection

Questions for Discussion

1. How does Red Jacket's version of the settling of North America compare with other versions you have encountered?
2. Summarize Red Jacket's main arguments against the missionary's address. Which argument do you find the most persuasive? Do you agree with Red Jacket? Why or why not?
3. What is your opinion of Red Jacket's skill as an orator? What gives his speech its power?
4. Missionaries of various faiths have worked around the world to spread their beliefs among peoples who, like the Native Americans, already had belief systems of their own. Do you think Red Jacket's arguments could apply to the situations of such peoples as well?
5. Red Jacket says that his religion teaches people "to be thankful for all the favors we receive; to love each other, and to be united." How does this teaching compare with those of other belief systems you know of?

Activities

Writing a Speech

1. Imagine that some group wants to persuade you to adopt a new way of life. Write a speech defending your own beliefs and way of life.

Creating a Poster

2. Research the religion of the Seneca and create a poster that describes their beliefs and spiritual practices.

Before You Read

An Indian Teacher Among Indians

Zitkala-Ša
1876–1938

> **"I was as free as the wind that blew my hair, and no less spirited than a bounding deer. These were my mother's pride—my wild freedom and overflowing spirit."**

About Zitkala-Ša

Zitkala-Ša chose to leave her home in South Dakota when she was only eight years old to be educated at a Quaker missionary school in Indiana. After finishing school and attending college for two years, she became a teacher at the Carlisle Indian School in Pennsylvania. Originally named Gertrude Simmons, she adopted the Sioux pen name Zitkala-Ša (meaning "Red Bird") when she began publishing autobiographical stories criticizing the way in which Carlisle taught young Native Americans. The articles, published in the *Atlantic Monthly,* gained her a contract to publish a book of traditional Sioux stories, *Old Indian Legends.*

After moving to Washington, D.C., she became the editor of the *American Indian Magazine* and published *American Indian Stories,* a collection of her autobiographical stories and short fiction. In 1926 she founded the National Council of American Indians and served as president until her death.

Writing and Teaching

"An Indian Teacher Among Indians" was the third in a series of three autobiographical essays that Zitkala-Ša published in the *Atlantic Monthly* in 1900 while she was a teacher at Carlisle Indian School in Pennsylvania. In the first essay, "Impressions of an Indian Childhood," she told about growing up with her mother on the Yankton Sioux reservation in South Dakota. In the second essay, "The School Days of an Indian Girl," she described her experiences at a missionary school in Indiana.

An Indian Teacher Among Indians

— Zitkala-Ša

My First Day

Though an illness left me unable to continue my college course, my pride kept me from returning to my mother. Had she known of my worn condition, she would have said the white man's papers were not worth the freedom and health I had lost by them. Such a rebuke from my mother would have been unbearable, and as I felt then it would be far too true to be comfortable.

Since the winter when I had my first dreams about red apples I had been traveling slowly toward the morning horizon. There had been no doubt about the direction in which I wished to go to spend my energies in a work for the Indian race. Thus I had written my mother briefly, saying my plan for the year was to teach in an Eastern Indian school. Sending this message to her in the West, I started at once eastward.

Thus I found myself, tired and hot, in a black veiling of car smoke, as I stood wearily on a street corner of an old-fashioned town, waiting for a car. In a few moments more I should be on the school grounds, where a new work was ready for my inexperienced hands.

Upon entering the school campus, I was surprised at the thickly clustered buildings which made it a quaint little village, much more interesting than the town itself. The large trees among the houses gave the place a cool, refreshing shade, and the grass a deeper green. Within this large court of grass and trees stood a low green pump. The queer boxlike case had a revolving handle on its side, which clanked and creaked constantly.

I made myself known and was shown to my room,—a small, carpeted room, with ghastly walls and ceiling. The two windows, both on the same side, were curtained with heavy muslin yellowed with age. A clean white bed was in one corner of the room, and opposite it was a square pine table covered with a black woolen blanket.

Without removing my hat from my head, I seated myself in one of the two stiff-backed chairs that were placed beside the table. For several heart throbs I sat still, looking from ceiling to floor, from wall to wall, trying hard to imagine years of contentment there. Even while I was wondering if my exhausted strength would sustain me through this undertaking, I heard a heavy tread stop at my door. Opening it, I met the imposing figure of a stately gray-haired man. With a light straw hat in one hand, and the right hand extended for greeting, he smiled kindly upon me. For some reason I was awed by his wondrous height and his strong square shoulders, which I felt were a finger's length above my head.

I was always slight, and my serious illness in the early spring had made me look rather frail and languid. His quick eye measured my height and breadth. Then he looked into my face. I imagined that a visible shadow flitted across his countenance as he let my hand fall. I knew he was no other than my employer.

"Ah ha! so you are the little Indian girl who created the excitement among the college orators!" he said, more to himself than to me. I thought I heard a subtle note of disappointment in his voice. Looking in from where he stood, with one sweeping glance, he asked if I lacked anything for my room.

After he turned to go, I listened to his step until it grew faint and was lost in the distance. I was aware that my car-smoked appearance had not concealed the lines of pain on my face.

For a short moment my spirit laughed at my ill fortune, and I entertained the idea of exerting myself to make an improvement. But as I tossed my hat off a leaden weakness came over me, and I felt as if years of weariness lay like water-soaked logs upon me. I threw myself upon the bed, and, closing my eyes, forgot my good intention.

A Trip Westward

One sultry month I sat at a desk heaped up with work. Now, as I recall it, I wonder how I could have dared to disregard nature's warning with such recklessness. Fortunately, my inheritance of a marvelous endurance enabled me to bend without breaking.

Though I had gone to and fro, from my room to the office, in an unhappy silence, I was watched by those around me. On an early morning I was summoned to the superintendent's office. For a half hour I listened to his words, and when I returned to my room I remembered one sentence above the rest. It was this: "I am going to turn you loose to pasture!" He was sending me West to gather Indian pupils for the school, and this was his way of expressing it.

An Indian Teacher Among Indians

I needed nourishment, but the mid-summer's travel across the continent to search the hot prairies for overconfident parents who would intrust their children to strangers was a lean pasturage. However, I dwelt on the hope of seeing my mother. I tried to reason that a change was a rest. Within a couple of days I started toward my mother's home.

The intense heat and the sticky car smoke that followed my homeward trail did not noticeably restore my vitality. Hour after hour I gazed upon the country which was receding rapidly from me. I noticed the gradual expansion of the horizon as we emerged out of the forests into the plains. The great high buildings, whose towers overlooked the dense woodlands, and whose gigantic clusters formed large cities, diminished, together with the groves, until only little log cabins lay snugly in the bosom of the vast prairie. The cloud shadows which drifted about on the waving yellow of long-dried grasses thrilled me like the meeting of old friends.

At a small station, consisting of a single frame house with a rickety board walk around it, I alighted from the iron horse, just thirty miles from my mother and my brother Dawee. A strong hot wind seemed determined to blow my hat off, and return me to olden days when I roamed bareheaded over the hills. After the puffing engine of my train was gone, I stood on the platform in deep solitude. In the distance I saw the gently rolling land leap up into bare hills. At their bases a broad gray road was winding itself round about them until it came by the station. Among these hills I rode in a light conveyance, with a trusty driver, whose unkempt flaxen hair hung shaggy about his ears and his leather neck of reddish tan. From accident or decay he had lost one of his long front teeth.

Though I call him a paleface, his cheeks were of a brick red. His moist blue eyes, blurred and bloodshot, twitched involuntarily. For a long time he had driven through grass and snow from this solitary station to the Indian village. His weather-stained clothes fitted badly his warped shoulders. He was stooped, and his protruding chin, with its tuft of dry flax, nodded as monotonously as did the head of his faithful beast.

All the morning I looked about me, recognizing old familiar sky lines of rugged bluffs and round-topped hills. By the roadside I caught glimpses of various plants whose sweet roots were delicacies among my people. When I saw the first cone-shaped wigwam, I could not help uttering an exclamation which caused my driver a sudden jump out of his drowsy nodding.

At noon, as we drove through the eastern edge of the reservation, I grew very impatient and restless. Constantly I wondered what my mother would say upon seeing her little daughter grown tall. I had not written her the day of my arrival, thinking I would surprise her. Crossing a ravine thicketed with low shrubs and plum bushes, we approached a large yellow acre of wild sunflowers. Just beyond this nature's garden we drew near to my mother's cottage. Close by the log cabin stood a little canvas-covered wigwam. The driver stopped in front of the open door, and in a long moment my mother appeared at the threshold.

I had expected her to run out to greet me, but she stood still, all the while staring at the weather-beaten man at my side. At length, when her loftiness became unbearable, I called to her, "Mother, why do you stop?"

This seemed to break the evil moment, and she hastened to hold my head against her cheek.

"My daughter, what madness possessed you to bring home such a fellow?" she asked, pointing at the driver, who was fumbling in his pockets for change while he held the bill I gave him between his jagged teeth.

"Bring him! Why, no, mother, he has brought me! He is a driver!" I exclaimed.

Upon this revelation, my mother threw her arms about me and apologized for her mistaken inference. We laughed away the momentary hurt. Then she built a brisk fire on the ground in the tepee, and hung a blackened coffeepot on one of the prongs of a forked pole which leaned over the flames. Placing a pan on a heap of red embers, she baked some unleavened bread. This light luncheon she brought into the cabin, and arranged on a table covered with a checkered oilcloth.

My mother had never gone to school, and though she meant always to give up her own customs for such of the white man's ways as pleased her, she made only compromises. Her two windows, directly opposite each other, she curtained with a pink-flowered print. The naked logs were unstained, and rudely carved with the axe so as to fit into one another. The sod roof was trying to boast of tiny sunflowers, the seeds of which had probably been planted by the constant wind. As I leaned my head against the logs, I discovered the peculiar odor that I could not forget. The rains had soaked the earth and roof so that the smell of damp clay was but the natural breath of such a dwelling.

"Mother, why is not your house cemented? Do you have no interest in a more comfortable shelter?" I asked, when the apparent inconveniences of her home seemed to suggest indifference on her part.

"You forget, my child, that I am now old, and I do not work with beads any more. Your brother Dawee, too, has lost his position, and we are left without means to buy even a morsel of food," she replied.

Dawee was a government clerk in our reservation when I last heard from him. I was surprised upon hearing what my mother said concerning his lack of employment. Seeing the puzzled expression on my face, she continued: "Dawee! Oh, has he not told you that the Great Father at

Washington sent a white son to take your brother's pen from him? Since then Dawee has not been able to make use of the education the Eastern school has given him."

I found no words with which to answer satisfactorily. I found no reason with which to cool my inflamed feelings.

Dawee was a whole day's journey off on the prairie, and my mother did not expect him until the next day. We were silent.

When, at length, I raised my head to hear more clearly the moaning of the wind in the corner logs, I noticed the daylight streaming into the dingy room through several places where the logs fitted unevenly. Turning to my mother, I urged her to tell me more about Dawee's trouble, but she only said: "Well, my daughter, this village has been these many winters a refuge for white robbers. The Indian cannot complain to the Great Father in Washington without suffering outrage for it here. Dawee tried to secure justice for our tribe in a small matter, and today you see the folly of it."

Again, though she stopped to hear what I might say, I was silent.

"My child, there is only one source of justice, and I have been praying steadfastly to the Great Spirit to avenge our wrongs," she said, seeing I did not move my lips.

My shattered energy was unable to hold longer any faith, and I cried out desperately: "Mother, don't pray again! The Great Spirit does not care if we live or die! Let us not look for good or justice: then we shall not be disappointed!"

"Sh! my child, do not talk so madly. There is Taku Iyotan Wasaka, to which I pray," she answered, as she stroked my head again as she used to do when I was a smaller child.

My Mother's Curse upon White Settlers

One black night mother and I sat alone in the dim starlight, in front of our wigwam. We were facing the river, as we talked about the shrinking limits of the village. She told me about the poverty-stricken white settlers, who lived in caves dug in the long ravines of the high hills across the river.

A whole tribe of broad-footed white beggars had rushed hither to make claims on those wild lands. Even as she was telling this I spied a small glimmering light in the bluffs.

"That is a white man's lodge where you see the burning fire," she said. Then, a short distance from it, only a little lower than the first, was another light. As I became accustomed to the night, I saw more and more twinkling lights, here and there, scattered all along the wide black margin of the river.

An Indian Teacher Among Indians

Still looking toward the distant firelight, my mother continued: "My daughter, beware of the paleface. It was the cruel paleface who caused the death of your sister and your uncle, my brave brother. It is this same paleface who offers in one palm the holy papers, and with the other gives a holy baptism of firewater. He is the hypocrite who reads with one eye, 'Thou shalt not kill,' and with the other gloats upon the sufferings of the Indian race." Then suddenly discovering a new fire in the bluffs, she exclaimed, "Well, well, my daughter, there is the light of another white rascal!"

She sprang to her feet, and, standing firm beside her wigwam, she sent a curse upon those who sat around the hated white man's light. Raising her right arm forcibly into line with her eye, she threw her whole might into her doubled fist as she shot it vehemently at the strangers. Long she held her outstretched fingers toward the settler's lodge, as if an invisible power passed from them to the evil at which she aimed.

Retrospection

Leaving my mother, I returned to the school in the East. As months passed over me, I slowly comprehended that the large army of white teachers in Indian schools had a larger missionary creed than I had suspected.

It was one which included self-preservation quite as much as Indian education. When I saw an opium-eater holding a position as teacher of Indians, I did not understand what good was expected, until a Christian in power replied that this pumpkin-colored creature had a feeble mother to support. An inebriate paleface sat stupid in a doctor's chair, while Indian patients carried their ailments to untimely graves, because his fair wife was dependent upon him for her daily food.

I find it hard to count that white man a teacher who tortured an ambitious Indian youth by frequently reminding the brave changeling that he was nothing but a "government pauper."

Though I burned with indignation upon discovering on every side instances no less shameful than those I have mentioned, there was no present help. Even the few rare ones who have worked nobly for my race were powerless to choose workmen like themselves. To be sure, a man was sent from the Great Father to inspect Indian schools, but what he saw was usually the students' sample work *made* for exhibition. I was nettled by this sly cunning of the workmen who hoodwinked the Indian's pale Father at Washington.

My illness, which prevented the conclusion of my college course, together with my mother's stories of the encroaching frontier settlers, left me in no mood to strain my eyes in searching for latent good in my white co-workers.

An Indian Teacher Among Indians

At this stage of my own evolution, I was ready to curse men of small capacity for being the dwarfs their God had made them. In the process of my education I had lost all consciousness of the nature world about me. Thus, when a hidden rage took me to the small white-walled prison which I then called my room, I unknowingly turned away from my one salvation.

Alone in my room, I sat like the petrified Indian woman of whom my mother used to tell me. I wished my heart's burdens would turn me to unfeeling stone. But alive, in my tomb, I was destitute!

For the white man's papers I had given up my faith in the Great Spirit. For these same papers I had forgotten the healing in trees and brooks. On account of my mother's simple view of life, and my lack of any, I gave her up, also. I made no friends among the race of people I loathed. Like a slender tree, I had been uprooted from my mother, nature, and God. I was shorn of my branches, which had waved in sympathy and love for home and friends. The natural coat of bark which had protected my oversensitive nature was scraped off to the very quick.

Now a cold bare pole I seemed to be, planted in a strange earth. Still, I seemed to hope a day would come when my mute aching head, reared upward to the sky, would flash a zigzag lightning across the heavens. With this dream of vent for a long-pent consciousness, I walked again amid the crowds.

At last, one weary day in the school-room, a new idea presented itself to me. It was a new way of solving the problem of my inner self. I liked it. Thus I resigned my position as teacher; and now I am in an Eastern city, following the long course of study I have set for myself. Now, as I look back upon the recent past, I see it from a distance, as a whole. I remember how, from morning till evening, many specimens of civilized peoples visited the Indian school. The city folks with canes and eyeglasses, the countrymen with sunburnt cheeks and clumsy feet, forgot their relative social ranks in an ignorant curiosity. Both sorts of these Christian palefaces were alike astounded at seeing the children of savage warriors so docile and industrious.

As answers to their shallow inquiries they received the students' sample work to look upon. Examining the neatly figured pages, and gazing upon the Indian girls and boys bending over their books, the white visitors walked out of the schoolhouse well satisfied: they were educating the children of the red man! They were paying a liberal fee to the government employees in whose able hands lay the small forest of Indian timber.

In this fashion many have passed idly through the Indian schools during the last decade, afterward to boast of their charity to the North American Indian. But few there are who have paused to question whether real life or long-lasting death lies beneath this semblance of civilization.

Responding to the Selection

Questions for Discussion

1. What is the mood of this selection? How is it achieved?
2. What does the author experience in this selection? How does she react?
3. What is the writer's mother's attitude toward the settlers? How does the selection explain her attitude?
4. What effect do you think the experiences in this selection might have had on the author's later life?
5. How do you think you would have reacted in the author's place?

Activities

Writing a Research Paper

1. Research the Indian boarding schools of the late 1800s and early 1900s. How did they try to "assimilate" Native American students, and how successful were they? Write a report on your findings.

Presenting a Dramatic Reading

2. With a group, select one scene from this selection, and present it as a dramatic reading.

Before You Read

By Any Other Name

Santha Rama Rau
Born 1923

"The only thing that can make you a writer is the person that you are, the intensity of your feeling, the honesty of your vision, the unsentimental acknowledgment of the endless interest of the life around and within you."

About Rau

Santha Rama Rau was born in Madras, India. Her father was a high-ranking government official, and because of his work, the family traveled extensively. Rau attended schools in India, England, and the United States. Shortly after graduating from Wellesley College in Massachusetts, she published the autobiography *Home to India* (1945), which became a best-seller. She subsequently published other books of autobiography, travel writing, and fiction.

Rau frequently writes about interactions among people of different cultures. Noting that "a formidable screen of fantasy and half-truths has grown up between India and the Western world," Rau has worked to open the doors to cultural understanding.

Schools in India

The events in "By Any Other Name" take place during the late 1920s, when India was a British colony. During their rule of India, the British introduced Western education into the country, primarily in the cities and towns and among people in the high Indian castes (hereditary social classes). The British goal was to create a Western-educated class of Indians, fluent in English, who could help interpret British policies to the rest of the population. Many Western-educated Indians became government administrators, political leaders, and professionals, both before and after India became independent in 1947.

By Any Other Name

— *Santha Rama Rau*

At the Anglo-Indian day school in Zorinabad to which my sister and I were sent when she was eight and I was five and a half, they changed our names. On the first day of school, a hot, windless morning of a north Indian September, we stood in the headmistress's study and she said, "Now you're the new girls. What are your names?"

My sister answered for us. "I am Premila, and she"—nodding in my direction—"is Santha."

The headmistress had been in India, I suppose, fifteen years or so, but she still smiled her helpless inability to cope with Indian names. Her rimless half-glasses glittered, and the precarious bun on the top of her head trembled as she shook her head. "Oh, my dears, those are much too hard for me. Suppose we give you pretty English names. Wouldn't that be more jolly? Let's see, now—Pamela for you, I think." She shrugged in a baffled way at my sister. "That's as close as I can get. And for *you*," she said to me, "how about Cynthia? Isn't that nice?"

My sister was always less easily intimidated than I was, and while she kept a stubborn silence, I said, "Thank you," in a very tiny voice.

We had been sent to that school because my father, among his responsibilities as an officer of the civil service, had a tour of duty to perform in the villages around that steamy little provincial town, where he had his headquarters at that time. He used to make his shorter inspection tours on horseback, and a week before, in the stale heat of a typically postmonsoon day, we had waved good-bye to him and a little procession—an assistant, a secretary, two bearers, and the man to look after the bedding rolls and luggage. They rode away through our large garden, still bright green from the rains, and we turned back into the twilight of the house and the sound of fans whispering in every room.

By Any Other Name

Up to then, my mother had refused to send Premila to school in the British-run establishments of that time, because, she used to say, "you can bury a dog's tail for seven years and it still comes out curly, and you can take a Britisher away from his home for a lifetime and he still remains insular." The examinations and degrees from entirely Indian schools were not, in those days, considered valid. In my case, the question had never come up, and probably never would have come up if Mother's extraordinary good health had not broken down. For the first time in my life, she was not able to continue the lessons she had been giving us every morning. So our Hindi books were put away, the stories of the Lord Krishna as a little boy were left in midair, and we were sent to the Anglo-Indian school.

That first day at school is still, when I think of it, a remarkable one. At that age, if one's name is changed, one develops a curious form of dual personality. I remember having a certain detached and disbelieving concern in the actions of "Cynthia," but certainly no responsibility. Accordingly, I followed the thin, erect back of the headmistress down the veranda to my classroom feeling, at most, a passing interest in what was going to happen to me in this strange, new atmosphere of School.

The building was Indian in design, with wide verandas opening onto a central courtyard, but Indian verandas are usually whitewashed, with stone floors. These, in the tradition of British schools, were painted dark brown and had matting on the floors. It gave a feeling of extra intensity to the heat.

I suppose there were about a dozen Indian children in the school—which contained perhaps forty children in all—and four of them were in my class. They were all sitting at the back of the room, and I went to join them. I sat next to a small, solemn girl who didn't smile at me. She had long, glossy-black braids and wore a cotton dress, but she still kept on her Indian jewelry—a gold chain around her neck, thin gold bracelets, and tiny ruby studs in her ears. Like most Indian children, she had a rim of black kohl around her eyes. The cotton dress should have looked strange, but all I could think of was that I should ask my mother if I couldn't wear a dress to school, too, instead of my Indian clothes.

I can't remember too much about the proceedings in class that day, except for the beginning. The teacher pointed to me and asked me to stand up. "Now, dear, tell the class your name."

I said nothing.

"Come along," she said, frowning slightly. "What's your name, dear?"

"I don't know," I said, finally.

The English children in the front of the class—there were about eight or ten of them—giggled and twisted around in their chairs to look at me.

By Any Other Name

I sat down quickly and opened my eyes very wide, hoping in that way to dry them off. The little girl with the braids put out her hand and very lightly touched my arm. She still didn't smile.

Most of that morning I was rather bored. I looked briefly at the children's drawings pinned to the wall, and then concentrated on a lizard clinging to the ledge of the high, barred window behind the teacher's head. Occasionally it would shoot out its long yellow tongue for a fly, and then it would rest, with its eyes closed and its belly palpitating, as though it were swallowing several times quickly. The lessons were mostly concerned with reading and writing and simple numbers—things that my mother had already taught me—and I paid very little attention. The teacher wrote on the easel blackboard words like "bat" and "cat," which seemed babyish to me; only "apple" was new and incomprehensible.

When it was time for the lunch recess, I followed the girl with braids out onto the veranda. There the children from the other classes were assembled. I saw Premila at once and ran over to her, as she had charge of our lunchbox. The children were all opening packages and sitting down to eat sandwiches. Premila and I were the only ones who had Indian food—thin wheat chapatties, some vegetable curry, and a bottle of buttermilk. Premila thrust half of it into my hand and whispered fiercely that I should go and sit with my class, because that was what the others seemed to be doing.

The enormous black eyes of the little Indian girl from my class looked at my food longingly, so I offered her some. But she only shook her head and plowed her way solemnly through her sandwiches.

I was very sleepy after lunch, because at home we always took a siesta. It was usually a pleasant time of day, with the bedroom darkened against the harsh afternoon sun, the drifting off into sleep with the sound of Mother's voice reading a story in one's mind, and, finally, the shrill, fussy voice of the ayah[1] waking one for tea.

At school, we rested for a short time on low, folding cots on the veranda, and then we were expected to play games. During the hot part of the afternoon we played indoors, and after the shadows had begun to lengthen and the slight breeze of the evening had come up we moved outside to the wide courtyard.

I had never really grasped the system of competitive games. At home, whenever we played tag or guessing games, I was always allowed to "win"—"because," Mother used to tell Premila, "she is the youngest, and we have to allow for that." I had often heard her say it, and it seemed quite reasonable to me, but the result was that I had no clear idea of what "winning" meant.

---

1. An *ayah* is a nursemaid.

By Any Other Name

When we played twos-and-threes that afternoon at school, in accordance with my training, I let one of the small English boys catch me, but was naturally rather puzzled when the other children did not return the courtesy. I ran about for what seemed like hours without ever catching anyone, until it was time for school to close. Much later I learned that my attitude was called "not being a good sport," and I stopped allowing myself to be caught, but it was not for years that I really learned the spirit of the thing.

When I saw our car come up to the school gate, I broke away from my classmates and rushed toward it yelling, "Ayah! Ayah!" It seemed like an eternity since I had seen her that morning—a wizened, affectionate figure in her white cotton sari, giving me dozens of urgent and useless instructions on how to be a good girl at school. Premila followed more sedately, and she told me on the way home never to do that again in front of the other children.

When we got home we went straight to Mother's high, white room to have tea with her, and I immediately climbed onto the bed and bounced gently up and down on the springs. Mother asked how we had liked our first day in school. I was so pleased to be home and to have left that peculiar Cynthia behind that I had nothing whatever to say about school, except to ask what "apple" meant. But Premila told Mother about the classes, and added that in her class they had weekly tests to see if they had learned their lessons well.

I asked, "What's a test?"

Premila said, "You're too small to have them. You won't have them in your class for donkey's years." She had learned the expression that day and was using it for the first time. We all laughed enormously at her wit. She also told Mother, in an aside, that we should take sandwiches to school the next day. Not, she said, that *she* minded. But they would be simpler for me to handle.

That whole lovely evening I didn't think about school at all. I sprinted barefoot across the lawns with my favorite playmate, the cook's son, to the stream at the end of the garden. We quarreled in our usual way, waded in the tepid water under the lime trees, and waited for the night to bring out the smell of the jasmine. I listened with fascination to his stories of ghosts and demons, until I was too frightened to cross the garden alone in the semidarkness. The ayah found me, shouted at the cook's son, scolded me, hurried me in to supper—it was an entirely usual, wonderful evening.

It was a week later, the day of Premila's first test, that our lives changed rather abruptly. I was sitting at the back of my class, in my usual inattentive way, only half listening to the teacher. I had started a rather guarded friendship with the girl with the braids, whose name turned out to be Nalini (Nancy, in school). The three other Indian children were already fast friends. Even at that age it was apparent to all of us that friendship with the English or Anglo-Indian children was out of the question. Occasionally, during the class, my new friend and I would draw pictures and show them to each other secretly.

The door opened sharply and Premila marched in. At first, the teacher smiled at her in a kindly and encouraging way and said, "Now, you're little Cynthia's sister?"

Premila didn't even look at her. She stood with her feet planted firmly apart and her shoulders rigid, and addressed herself directly to me. "Get up," she said. "We're going home."

I didn't know what had happened, but I was aware that it was a crisis of some sort. I rose obediently and started to walk toward my sister.

"Bring your pencils and your notebook," she said.

I went back for them, and together we left the room. The teacher started to say something just as Premila closed the door, but we didn't wait to hear what it was.

In complete silence we left the school grounds and started to walk home. Then I asked Premila what the matter was. All she would say was "We're going home for good."

It was a very tiring walk for a child of five and a half, and I dragged along behind Premila with my pencils growing sticky in my hand. I can still remember looking at the dusty hedges, and the tangles of thorns in the ditches by the side of the road, smelling the faint fragrance from the eucalyptus trees and wondering whether we would ever reach home. Occasionally a horse-drawn tonga² passed us, and the women, in their pink or green silks, stared at Premila and me trudging along on the side of the road. A few coolies and a line of women carrying baskets of vegetables on their heads smiled at us. But it was nearing the hottest time of day, and the road was almost deserted. I walked more and more slowly, and shouted to Premila, from time to time, "Wait for me!" with increasing peevishness. She spoke to me only once, and that was to tell me to carry my notebook on my head, because of the sun.

When we got to our house the ayah was just taking a tray of lunch into Mother's room. She immediately started a long, worried questioning about what are you children doing back here at this hour of the day.

Mother looked very startled and very concerned, and asked Premila what had happened.

Premila said, "We had our test today, and she made me and the other Indians sit at the back of the room, with a desk between each one."

Mother said, "Why was that, darling?"

---

2. A *tonga* is a two-wheeled cart.

"She said it was because Indians cheat," Premila added. "So I don't think we should go back to that school."

Mother looked very distant, and was silent a long time. At last she said, "Of course not, darling." She sounded displeased.

We all shared the curry she was having for lunch, and afterward I was sent off to the beautifully familiar bedroom for my siesta. I could hear Mother and Premila talking through the open door.

Mother said, "Do you suppose she understood all that?"

Premila said, "I shouldn't think so. She's a baby."

Mother said, "Well, I hope it won't bother her."

Of course, they were both wrong. I understood it perfectly, and I remember it all very clearly. But I put it happily away, because it had all happened to a girl called Cynthia, and I never was really particularly interested in her.

Responding to the Selection

Questions for Discussion

1. In "By Any Other Name," how does the author portray British attitudes toward Indians? What incidents illustrate these attitudes?

2. Think about how Premila reacts to school until the day of the test. How are her reactions similar to Zitkala-Ša's initial reactions to the dominant culture in which she finds herself?

3. Premila, Santha, and Zitkala-Ša all feel a conflict between the two cultures in which they are raised. How would you describe their reactions to this conflict?

4. What aspects of your own culture are most important to you? Why?

Activities

Creating a List

1. Write a list of valuable things you have learned from cultures other than your own.

Staging a Scene

2. Select a scene from either Rau's or Zitkala-Ša's story and stage it as a dramatic reading.

Before You Read

The Snakeman

Luci Tapahonso
Born 1953

> *"I write every day, and
> it's like eating and sleeping.
> I can't not do it."*

About Tapahonso

Luci Tapahonso grew up in a large Navajo family in Shiprock, New Mexico, on the Navajo reservation. She learned Navajo before she learned English. As an adult, she continues to write in both languages.

Tapahonso earned a master's degree in creative writing and English from the University of New Mexico and is an associate professor of English at the University of Kansas. Although she now lives in Kansas, she often visits her family in New Mexico. Tapahonso says that her writing "becomes a prayer of sorts back to the land, the people, and the families from whence we came originally."

The Old Stories

With a love for stories, the Navajo tradition includes many tales that explain events and people's reactions to them. "The Snakeman" works as such a tale on two levels. First, it captures the boarding school setting many Navajo (and other Native American) children encountered during a period when educators sponsored by the United States government sought to assimilate these children by removing them from their home cultures. Second, it recalls a traditional abduction story from the Navajo tradition. In that story, two young women were kidnapped by their people's enemy. Isolated from one another, each finds herself the next day with a spirit keeper. The Snakeman, one of these spirit keepers, takes one woman to live among the spirits, where she never quite fits in. In time, however, she becomes a link between the spirits and her people, just as in this story the young protagonist links her isolated schoolmates to their Navajo traditions.

The Snakeman

— *Luci Tapahonso*

The child slid down silently and caught herself at the end of the fire escape. She eased herself down until she felt the cold, hard sidewalk through her slippers—then she let go.

The night was clear and quiet. The only noise that could be heard was the echo of the child's footsteps in the moonlit alley behind the old, brick buildings.

The little girls, watching her from the top floor of the dorm, swung the window screen in and out, catching it before it struck the window frame. They always talked about what would happen if the top hinges suddenly gave way but they hadn't yet.

"Good thing—it's spring," one of them said.

"She could freeze her toes off for sure," another hissed.

"SHHH-H," the biggest one hissed.

They whispered in lispy voices and someone on the other side of the room would only hear "s . . . sss," hissing and an occasional "shut-up!" The room was large with windows on three sides. The fire escape the child slid down was in the center of the north windows, which faced a big, dark hill, its slope covered with huge, round rocks and dry tumbleweeds. Opposite the fire escape was the door to the hall.

Sometimes the dorm mother, who lived at the other end of the hall, heard them giggling or running around. She would walk down the dark, shiny hall so fast her housecoat would fly behind her in billows. The girls would scurry to their beds, tripping over their long nightgowns, finally faking snores as she turned on the harsh, bright lights in each room. After she went back to her room, the children jumped up and laughed silently with wide, open mouths and pounded their fists into their beds.

One of the girls whispered loudly, "She's coming back." They all ran noiselessly to the window and watched the small figure coming. The little girl walked briskly with her hands in her housecoat pockets. She wore the soft, wool slippers all the little girls made for their sister or mother at Christmastime. But she had neither, so she wore them herself.

"Seems like she floats," one girl commented.

"How could she? Can't you hear her walking?" the biggest retorted.

The girls went back to their beds and the ones that were closest to the fire escape window opened the window and held it up until she was in. Then they all gathered at one bed and sat in the moonlight telling ghost stories or about how the end of the world was REALLY going to be. Except for the girl who left, she always went to sleep and wasn't noisy like the rest.

Sometimes late in the night or towards morning when the sun hadn't come up completely and everything was quiet and the room filled with the soft, even breathing of the children—one of them might stand at the window facing east and think of home far away and tears would stream down her face. Late in the night someone always cried and if the others heard her—they would pretend not to notice. They understood how it was with all of them . . . if only they could go to public school and eat at home everyday.

When they got up in the morning before they went downstairs to dress, two of them emptied their pockets of small, torn pieces of paper and scattered them under the beds. The beds had white ruffled bottoms that reached the floor and the bits of paper weren't visible unless one lifted the ruffles. This was the way they tested the girl that cleaned their room. When they returned to their bedroom in the evenings, they checked under their beds to see if the paper was gone. If it wasn't, they immediately reported it to the dorm mother, who never asked why they were so sure their room hadn't been cleaned.

The building was divided into three floors and an attic. The little girls who were in grade school occupied the bottom and top floors and the junior high girls had the middle floor. The top floor was used only for bedrooms and all daytime activity was on the bottom level. The building was old, like all the other buildings on campus, and the students were sure it was haunted. Besides, there was a graveyard a little ways away. How could it not be? they asked among themselves.

This was especially true for those little girls in the east end of the dorm, since they were so close to the attic door. There was a man in there, they always said in hushed voices, he always kept the attic door open just a little, enough to throw evil powder on anyone that walked by. For this reason, they all stayed out of the hallway at night. Once they had even heard him coming down the attic stairs to the door and the smaller girls started crying. They all slept two-to-a-bed, and the big girls made sure all the little girls had someone bigger with them. They stayed up later than usual, crying and praying, so that no one woke early enough to get everyone back into their right beds. The dorm mother spanked each of them but at least, they said, that night nothing happened to any of them.

Once when the little girl went on one of her walks at night, the other children were waiting for her as they usually did. Two of them were by the hall door trying to figure how to get to the bathroom two doors down the hall when they heard a scratching noise outside on the sidewalk.

The Snakeman

"You guys! come here! he's over here!!" they whispered loudly.

They ran to the east window and saw a dark figure go around the corner and the biggest girl took control.

"You two get over by that window. You on that side. Someone get on the fire escape in case he tries to get up here."

They watched the man below and tried to get a description of him, in case someone asked them. They couldn't see him very well because he was on the shady side of the building. Some of the girls started crying, and some crawled quietly back into bed. Two of them, the bigger ones, waited to open the window for the other girl when she got back. When she came back, they all huddled around her and told her and started crying again. She said it was probably someone's father trying to see his daughter. Probably the mother won't let him see her, she said. So the girls calmed down and tried to figure out whose parents were divorced or fought a lot. They finally decided that he was the boyfriend of a junior high girl downstairs.

When a new girl came, she asked why the girl always walked at night, and the biggest one had said:

"Wouldn't you if you could see your mother every night, dummy?"

"Well, where's her mom? Can't she see her on weekends like us? That's not fair."

"Fair? FAIR??" they had all yelled in disbelief.

Then the girl who walked explained that her parents had died years before, when she was six, and they were buried at the school cemetery. So that's why she went to see them. Just her mother, mostly, though.

"How is she? Does she talk?"

"Can you REALLY see her?" the new girl asked.

"Yeah," she answered patiently. "She calls me and she waits at the edge of the cemetery by those small, fat trees. She's real pretty. When she died, they put a blue outfit on her. A Navajo skirt that's real long and a shiny, soft, light blue blouse. She waves at me like this: 'Come here, shi yashil, my little baby.' She always calls me that. She's soft and smells so good."

The little girls all nodded, each remembering their own mothers.

"When it's cold or snowing, she lets me stand inside the blanket with her. We talk about when I was a baby, and what I'll do when I get big. She always worries if I'm being good or not."

"Mine, too," someone murmured.

"Why do mothers always want their girls to be goody-good?"

"So you won't die at the end of the world, dummy."

"Dying isn't *that* bad. You can still visit people like her mother does."

The Snakeman

"But at the end of the world, all the dinosaurs and monsters that are sleeping in the mountains will bust out and eat the bad people. No one can escape, either," said the biggest girl with confidence.

Then the little girl who talked to her mother every night said quietly:

"No one can be that bad." She went to her bed and lay there looking at the ceiling until she fell asleep.

The other girls gathered on two beds and sat in a little circle and talked in tight, little voices about the snakeman who stole jewelry from some of the girls.

"You can't really see him," one said, "cause he's sort of like a blur, moves real fast and all you can see is a black thing go by."

"He has a silver bracelet that shines and if he shines it on you, you're a goner cause it paralyzes."

They talked about him until they began looking around to make sure he wasn't in the room.

The bigger girls slept with the littler ones, and they prayed that God wouldn't let that man in the attic or the snakeman come to them, and that the world wouldn't end until after their moms came to visit.

As the room got quiet and the breathing became even and soft, the little girl got up, put on her housecoat and slid soundlessly down the fire escape.

Responding to the Selection

Questions for Discussion

1. Where does this story take place? Who are the main characters?

2. What does one young girl do each night? Why?

3. How do the girls feel about being at school? How do you think the girl's speaking with her mother makes the other girls feel about their homes? Do you think that being educated away from home will change the girls' feelings about their Navajo culture?

4. What frightens the young girls? Who do they think this man is? How does the story present the spirit world?

5. What does the story suggest about Luci Tapahonso's attitude toward her Navajo heritage?

Activities

Writing a Dialogue

1. The young girl in this story misses her family and home very much. What do you think she and her mother say to one another? How, if at all, do you think her mother is able to soothe the young girl's fears and loneliness? Write a dialogue between the girl and her mother. If possible, perform your dialogue with a classmate or on your own as a dramatic reading.

Researching Traditions

2. Using online or library sources, locate and read some other traditional Navajo stories. Share these stories with classmates and discuss common themes that emerge. How do the stories reflect Luci Tapahonso's take on to Navajo culture, in which storytelling is a precious and important tool?

Before You Read

Early Reservation Days

John Stands In Timber
1884–1967

"It is important . . . to remember some of the things that made the Cheyennes a great and strong people."

About Stands In Timber

When he was in his seventies, John Stands In Timber decided to write a book telling the history of his people, the Cheyenne. From the time he was a young boy, he had listened to the stories of the old men and women of his tribe. He had memorized some of the stories, and as an adult, he went back to the old-timers to ask about details he had forgotten. He became known as a tribal historian of the Cheyenne; and with the help of anthropologist Margot Liberty, he published *Cheyenne Memories,* which relates the stories of the Cheyenne from legendary times to the early 1900s.

The Cheyenne

The following excerpt from *Cheyenne Memories* takes place in the 1880s, as the Northern Cheyenne were first experiencing life on the reservation.

The Montana reservation of the Northern Cheyenne was next to one belonging to their traditional enemies, the Crow. By the 1880s, some white ranchers also lived in the area of the reservations. By this time, few buffalo remained, and the Cheyenne depended on the U.S. government for rations of food on the reservation. Although many Native American peoples, especially in the South and Southeast, had practiced farming for centuries, it was an alien lifestyle for the Plains tribes, whose lands were generally not well suited for agriculture. Conflicts sometimes arose with settlers when the Cheyenne butchered cattle that strayed onto their lands, and the government stationed soldiers on the reservation in case of trouble.

The Cheyenne also came into conflict with the Piegans, who sometimes raided the Cheyenne to steal their horses.

Early

Reservation

Days

— *John Stands In Timber*

The last Piegan raid was in 1885, and it was the last fighting of the Cheyennes against other tribes. For the next few years things were pretty quiet. The Cheyennes were learning to settle down, but it took quite a while, especially among the young men. In the past they had always been able to go out and win war honors, but now there was no way for them to show the women how brave they were unless they got into trouble with white people, or at least got away with stealing some beef. Most of the Indians stayed home and minded their own business, but the settlers were angry about the killing of white men that happened sometimes, as well as the butchering, and they were always afraid of an Indian uprising.

One scare started over on the Crow Reservation. A medicine man there had gone up into the Big Horn Mountains and fasted, and he dreamed that he had received power which would keep him from being killed. The Crows were usually friendly to the white man. That was why they got such a big reservation. But this fellow thought they should fight the soldiers and drive them out of the country. He organized some other Crows against them, and I suppose he wanted to kill the settlers too. He rode a black bobtailed horse that he painted with a crooked lightning line, and he used to paint himself black, with white stripes and spots on his body and face. He tied his hair together in front of his head, so it fell down over his face. It made him strange looking, all right. Austin Texas was there when he rode through a Crow village one time dressed that way, and up onto a high hill. He faced east and south and west, and then clouds came up and a big storm came and blew a lot of tepees down.

This Crow succeeded in doing that much. It scared them and they tried to make him stop. But he started making trouble at Crow Agency. He said if anyone hurt him that he would harm all the people. But they were not all afraid of him. Big Medicine was the chief of police at Crow Agency then, and he finally shot this man and killed him.

The Cheyennes had nothing to do with it, but the white settlers on Tongue River all thought the Cheyennes and Crows were going together in an uprising, and would try to kill all the white people. They began to organize posses to fight the Indians, and that scared the Indians. They had had enough of being shot up in their villages at places like Sand Creek. It was the one thing they always feared when trouble started, that the white people would come in and attack the villages. But this time nothing came of it.

They built a second camp for soldiers in the winter of 1890, near the present Lame Deer campground. It happened after two young men, Head Chief and Young Mule, were shot by the troops after they killed a white man.

This young fellow Head Chief was a troublemaker. He had been mixed up in the murders of two other people, though the white men did not know that. He was around twenty-five years old—one of those who had not had a chance to prove himself in warfare, and he was bitter about it. His father used to talk to him like a child, telling him he could do this or that later, "when he was a man." He talked as if it was an easy thing to go out and count coups. Of course it was not.

Head Chief liked a daughter of the chief American Horse, and he used to hang around their camp. Much of the time he was followed by an orphan boy of thirteen or fourteen named John Young Mule. He was with Head Chief a lot. That was how they happened to die together.

The day before they went out to get meat this American Horse girl, Goa, took Head Chief some coffee and fry bread, and told him, "This is all we have had to eat for a long time." They were getting rations then, every two weeks, but the Indians could not make them last until the next ration day. Anyway, Head Chief laughed and told her he would get something better. And the next day he and Young Mule went hunting.

They might have tried to get a deer first, but they wound up with a cow. It belonged to old man Gaffney, a settler who homesteaded not far from Lame Deer. Head Chief shot it and they had just finished butchering and loading the meat, when they met Gaffney's nephew, Hugh Boyle, riding out after the milk cows on an old white horse. The Indians claim he rode up to them and said, "I see a hungry dog has snapped up one of our cows." Head Chief could not talk any English, but Young Mule had been to school for a year or two—he even had a haircut—and he translated, "He calls us dogs." Head Chief got mad, and grabbed his rifle out from under the load of meat on his pack horse. When the white boy saw it he turned to run, but Head Chief shot him once and knocked him off his horse, and then galloped by him and blew the top of his head off. They found most of his brains afterward in the red cap he was wearing.

Early Reservation Days

The two Cheyennes threw the cap under some rosebushes and unloaded the meat. They packed Boyle on the horse and went up into the hills. It stormed that night and they got lost, but they scratched him out a shallow grave in some shale rocks, and covered his face with his handkerchief before burying him—"so he won't get his face dirty," said Head Chief. The Indians remembered that story for years. It was around noon the next day when they got back down to the American Horse camp. Already soldiers had been there searching. The horse had been found, and a bloodstain where the boy was shot. I remember about that myself, though I was just six years old. I was traveling to Lame Deer with my grandparents to get there by Friday, the next ration day, and our team shied and snorted at that bloody place on the side of the road.

The Indians were all afraid their camp would be attacked. When Head Chief heard that, he told American Horse what he had done. "Go in and tell them at the agency I am guilty," he said. "But I will not come in and be hung like a dog. Tell them I will play with the soldiers on ration day outside the town. I will die like a man."

He rode back to his parents' camp near Ashland the same afternoon, to get his war clothes and to say goodbye. We saw him galloping up a little draw on a sorrel horse, though I did not know till later who the rider was. He got to their camp and told them all what he had done, and that he was going to fight the soldiers on the next ration day. "When I am gone, sing me a victory song, Father," he said. "Be a man." He got his war clothes then and left, going back to the agency.

The members of his military society guarded him in camp. They did not want him to be arrested before his time. On Thursday night they all sat up late, feasting and telling stories. Then he went to talk to Goa for the last time. They all went up on a high hill above Lame Deer before daylight. Young Mule wanted to go with him. He had nobody else. "When you are dead I will have nothing," he said. "I will die too."

They sat up there and talked until sunrise—the place is called Squaw Hill today. Then the chiefs made all the rest of the young men come down. They were afraid that if they stayed, they would start shooting too, and it might end up in a battle or a massacre, because the whole tribe was there picking up rations. While the two on the hill were performing their last ceremonies, the soldiers were getting ready to meet them, and the valley below was full of people. Everyone knew what was going to happen, and criers kept riding back and forth telling them not to sing or make any excitement when the boys came down.

My family had gotten their meat and other stuff. Most of the families had. It was about noon. Many were eating their noon meal. The tepee poles where they were camped were already full of drying meat from the beef ration. We saw the soldiers, cavalry and infantry, moving into place around the hill where the boys were. We heard shots as they galloped down. They had come from the top to a bench on the hill below, and they circled at a run out there, drawing the soldiers' fire. The trail to the top was very steep, and Head Chief made it to the top again all right, but Young Mule's horse was hit before he got to safety out of range, and the boy had to lead him up the rest of the way. He barely made it.

After that it did not take long. Head Chief put on a war-bonnet he had gotten from his grandfather, and he got on his horse and galloped down off the end of the butte across Alderson Gulch, to meet the soldiers. They were dismounted and ready in a firing line to meet him. He had told everyone he wanted to ride through the soldiers' line. And he made it. He was hit several times but he did not fall until he passed through them. Then an officer ran up and shot him in the head.

Young Mule's horse was crippled so badly he could not ride, so he had to come down afoot, off the steep southern face of the butte, running zigzag to dodge the soldiers' fire. He stopped once in a shallow gully to shoot, and then ran down to take cover in some brush, where they finally killed him. The brush has grown up today, but they say bullet scars are still there. I have looked and they are hard to tell from natural scars in the bark.

After the boys were dead their bodies were brought to the American Horse camp. Everyone came to see them. They looked as if they were sleeping. I remember Head Chief's war-bonnet was hanging outside. A feather had fallen from it where he was shot, and someone fastened it to a rock there marking the place, until the wind and rain finally tore it away.

Responding to the Selection ———————————

Questions for Discussion

1. What is your opinion of Head Chief? Do you think he got what he deserved? Do you agree with his decision to "die like a man"?

2. How would you describe the reasons for the conflict between the white settlers and the Cheyenne from a white settler's point of view? How would you describe the reasons from a Cheyenne's point of view? How could these points of view be reconciled?

3. Imagine yourself as a Cheyenne man who has been raised to be a warrior and to respect bravery. Your people formerly roamed freely, hunting buffalo and providing for their own needs. How would you adjust to living on a reservation and accepting rations to survive?

4. Margot Liberty, who helped John Stands In Timber produce *Cheyenne Memories,* wrote, "There is no bitterness in this book." Judging from this excerpt, do you agree? What do you think of Stands In Timber's perspective on events?

Activities

Writing a Diary Entry

1. Imagine yourself as the daughter of American Horse. Write a diary entry describing your reactions to the way in which Head Chief died.

Creating a Poster

2. Create a movie poster advertising a film based on one of the stories in this selection.

Before You Read

The Truth Teller

Diane Glancy
Born 1941

> *"I see theater as a tipi with an open smoke-hole where many voices tell stories of war."*

About Glancy

Diane Glancy was born in Kansas City, Missouri. Her father was descended from a Cherokee family that had walked the Trail of Tears to what is now the state of Oklahoma. Her mother was of English and German heritage. Glancy grew up a silent child and teenager who found her voice through writing. She studied literature in college, married and began raising a family. When the Glancys moved to Oklahoma, a mere hundred miles from her great grandfather's birthplace, she developed a new interest in learning about her Native American heritage.

Glancy has been repeatedly honored for her writing, receiving prizes, awards, and grants such as the American Book Award she won for *Claiming Breath.* In 1996, Glancy wrote her first novel, *Pushing the Bear,* which tells a story about the Trail of Tears her ancestors walked long ago.

Between Two Worlds

Diane Glancy has struggled to balance two heritages and two cultures. She remembers her mother being ashamed of Diane's Native American heritage and even her father abandoning it. Glancy felt that she never wholly fit into either of her worlds. Many of her characters don't fit either, as Glancy often highlights the tensions between traditional Native American lifeways and modern American culture. In *The Truth Teller,* Glancy presents a main character like herself—of mixed blood—and explores his divided loyalties. She also weaves into her story the real changes, both positive and negative, that white settlement brought to Native Americans around 1800. Not unlike the tricksters of Native American legend, the newcomers brought changes with little or no regard for the consequences.

The Truth Teller

— Diane Glancy

*Because to go forward
we must first go back—*

CHARACTERS

HALFBREED MAN

INDIAN WOMAN

SETTING: *Circa 1800.*

Pine Country in the North Woods, an Indian village on the Upper Mississippi near a Trading Post.

The stage is a maple sugar camp in spring (Part I), a drying rack for fish in the summer (Part II), a ricing camp during the fall (Part III), and a teepee for winter camp (Part IV).

The main prop is a tripod of some sort, which can serve as a tree, a drying rack, a canoe, and a teepee.

Other props are the accoutrements needed for the four seasons: birchbark basket for collecting and boiling maple sugar, poles, rawhide ties, winnowing basket, wild rice sticks, blanket, cradle-board, moss, twigs, deer antler rake, hide-stretcher, birchbark scroll, snow shoes, lure and spear, canoe paddle, masks, leg bands, stick antlers and drum for the dances.

With special thanks to Fred Benjamin, Mille Lacs Museum, Mille Lacs, Minnesota; Walter Caribou, Grand Portage, Minnesota; and Mary and Maggie Magiskan, Old Fort William, Canada, who told their stories.

Also special gratitude to Kristi Wheeler and Doug Birk, research assistants.

I.

[*Maple sugar season (spring). The* WOMAN *puts a wood peg in the tree and ties her birchbark basket below it. Later she takes the bucket, ties it over the fire. Stirs until the syrup becomes sugar. The cradle board is always near her.*]

INDIAN WOMAN. [*Sings to her baby as an* INDIAN *appears from offstage.*] Mey mey mey mey.

INDIAN. The Great Spirit wanted to fly. So He asked a bird to tell Him how. Just where to put the feathers on. Just how to move the arms. Flap. Flap. It wasn't easy. Now faster You. Hey Great Spirit. Said the bird. Flap faster. And the Great Spirit flapped faster and finally got It off the ground. Now hey when You are above. The Indian people will call You. The bird said. Now don't look down. Hey. Don't look anywhere but to the sky before You. Now the Great Spirit practiced flying and flapping. Out there in the trees before anyone is looking. Just snorting and flapping feathers and getting out of breath flapping. Yeah. Until He got It going. Yeah. He got It off the ground. The beavers clapped their hands. Yo. The otter. Yeah. The muskrats. Ho. All of creation got to clapping. The Great Spirit is flying. Well He got to going so high and fast and the Indian people got to calling Him and He had to look down because He was the Great Spirit you know. And He had to listen. Had to answer. And He got so busy looking at the ground that He crashed. Yes He fell right to earth. Thud. [*He looks at her.*] Thud. [*He tries to put his arms around her and pull her down with him.*]

INDIAN WOMAN. My eyes are shut. My ears are closed.

INDIAN. I've been gone since last summer. Now it's spring. I'm returned like the sun. Aren't you glad to see me?

INDIAN WOMAN. The seasons change. The trees shed. The snow falls. The trees get their leaves again. Do they ask your help? How can you guide those white soldiers? It's like leading a storm to our door.

INDIAN. Because I know the river and the way north to the headwaters.

INDIAN WOMAN. You know what I mean.

INDIAN. Because my father was white and I speak their language. They paid me well. I bought a steel trap. [*He demonstrates and it snaps shut.*] And see what I brought you—these garters. [*He gives her two red leg-bands.*]

INDIAN WOMAN. [*She looks at them.*] Where do you wear them? [*She tries to tie one on as a headband.*]

INDIAN. They go on your leg. [*She ties it at her knee.*] No, like this. [*He tries to tie it higher.*]

The Truth Teller

INDIAN WOMAN.   Do white women wear these?

INDIAN.   They wear them higher—like this—

INDIAN WOMAN.   I would rather you chop fire-wood. Kill a deer. Make me another deer antler rake. Find some chokecherry. Dream a name for the child. Draw a birchbark scroll for his life's path. Paddle the boat while I gather rice with my cedar rice-beaters. Trample the rice once it's gathered. Repair my bear-paw snow shoe. Find some pine-pitch. Bear-grease. Spruce-gum so my birchbark basket won't leak maple syrup. You could bring me an iron kettle from the fur traders instead of their garters. But no. You lead the white man north along a river. They'll take our way of life. The elders say so. I feel it also in my heart. Sometimes they call you a half-breed traitor.

INDIAN.   Then why do you want me to name the child?

INDIAN WOMAN.   Because I do. A name is the pine-pitch that holds you together. Otherwise your arm would fall off when you lifted the bow. Your knees would turn when you wanted to go straight. It's like knowing your history. It's knowing who you are.

INDIAN.   The Northwest Company Post had a door. To hold it closed there were lead musket-balls in a sock tied on a string as a weight. The door swings. [*He has trouble explaining this.*] Well like the deer-hide flap on the teepee door, but it swings inward.

INDIAN WOMAN.   What's a sock?

INDIAN.   An over-the-foot. [*He puts his hand over his foot trying to explain this too.*] A thin moccasin. [*Lifts her foot into the air and puts his hand over it to make the motion of putting on a sock.*] But under the moccasin—

INDIAN WOMAN.   Soon it will be black-fly season. I could use a door with a weight. In the meantime I'll smoke moss over the fire and keep them away. [*She fans the fire.*]

INDIAN.   They have guns that can kill anything—man or animal—if they can hit it. [*Pantomime of horned animal being stalked by white hunter but escaping.*] They have a bigger gun that sounds like thunder. They have stamina. Ideas come to them. They have a way of telling how cold it is. They have numbers for the cold. And numbers for how far they've gone. All day the leader kept taking notes in his book—[*Scribbles in an imaginary book.*] They tell the directions by a needle under a glass. They make doors close by a weight. A sock is something that goes under the moccasin and over the foot. A between-them. The way the moon looks in the day sky. An image almost. A ghost moccasin. That's a sock.

INDIAN WOMAN.   What is the purpose of this ghost moccasin? Other than to hold doors closed?

The Truth Teller

INDIAN. No it holds the foot closed. It keeps the boot from rubbing a sore on the toes and heel. It keeps the foot warm so they don't get sick.

INDIAN WOMAN. Our people die from their diseases.

INDIAN. The white man doesn't know how to hunt, yet he endures a winter with courage. He doesn't seem to have many stories to tell.

INDIAN WOMAN. How can anyone survive without stories?

INDIAN. They have stories written in a book. But not stories like we tell.

INDIAN WOMAN. They can't be stories then.

INDIAN. They are. I've heard some of them. A man in a boat and another man on a cross.

INDIAN WOMAN. We have a cross on our birchbark scrolls that tell our sacred stories.

INDIAN. But it stands for the four directions. It's not the kind of cross in their book. My father wanted me to study it, but I would rather stay in the woods. [*He tickles her.*]

INDIAN WOMAN. Our stories carry us like a canoe. That's what stories do. I tell stories to myself when you're gone.

INDIAN. When I was a boy my mother and father died within two days of each other. My father died of a hunting accident. My mother died in childbirth. I went into the woods. I didn't want to live. I had nothing but water for seven days, and a man and woman came to me. They said your grandmother is crying for you. What are you doing here? They asked. Then they changed into bears and walked away. I must have gone to sleep then and had a dream. A wind came and brought the sound of a drum. I saw the drum in my dream. It was painted red and blue. I saw that the red was for the rising sun. But the blue was for the land still left in darkness. It was that darkness from which a storm came. I sang my song and said storm you go around the other way. You don't run over me. I said hey storm. Hey you storm. Go the other way. Afterwards, I went home and lived with my grandmother. I sing that song now and beat my drum. I tell the story of how I got my song. Sometimes the storm goes away.

INDIAN WOMAN. They won't go away. Nothing will stop them. We'll be broken forever like ice on the creek where a tomahawk falls.

INDIAN. I will sing my song.

INDIAN WOMAN. I will sing mine as I stir the maple syrup. Mey mey mey mey. I make my song the way cottonwood leaves rise and fall with the wind. My baby hears my voice and knows I am near. Mey mey mey mey.

The Truth Teller

Once the maple syrup fell like rain. But Wenebojo, our trickster, decided that was too easy. The Indian had to work. We had to make an offering of tobacco. We had to put a small piece of wood into the tree so the sap would run out. Catch it in a birchbark basket. We had to cut wood. Boil sap for a long time. Boil it until it is maple syrup. Boil some of the syrup longer until it is maple sugar.

[*Sound of thunder.*]

II.

[*Fish spearing season (summer). The* INDIAN MAN *and* WOMAN *sit in the teepee for cover during the thunderstorm. Later, during the dialogue, the* MAN *paddles the canoe with his lure and spear. The* WOMAN *cuts the fish into strips and dries them. She also rakes the ground and gathers wild onions, walnuts and berries.*]

INDIAN WOMAN.   The thunder sounds to me now like the white man. Will they buy the blades of grass? How much for the clouds?

INDIAN.   Listen to the thunderstorm. Forget the people moving into our land.

INDIAN WOMAN.   All we have is rain. And the thunder of their guns. Do you have a name for the baby yet? [*She uses moss for the baby's diaper.*]

INDIAN.   I haven't dreamed of one. What's your hurry?

INDIAN WOMAN.   Then tell a story.

INDIAN.   You know how we always move from one place to another. From maple-sugar camp to fishing camp to ricing and berry-picking camp to hunting camp. Sometimes just moving. Here and there. [*He marks on the ground.*] HO. Here. Then ho ho. There. We never stayed just one place like the white man. No. The Indian is always moving. Well, the land got to feeling the Indian moving all over it. Just squirming like a trail of ants always walking. Like a swarm of bees always buzzing in its ear. [*The* INDIAN *tickles the* WOMAN's *ear.*] The land decided it wanted to move too. It said I will just rearrange myself. One night a thunderstorm happened. A giant thunderstorm. It parted the darkness until the sky was white with lightning. They watched the thunderstorm jump up and down over the land. It jumped and snorted and tossed away the darkness until. Thud. The Indians saw some of the land get up and walk off. Yes the land rearranged itself. It decided to move too. So a part moved away. Just like that. No one knows where it went.

INDIAN WOMAN.   Your story worries me. I don't want part of the land to leave. The others will hear your story and be afraid. Stop the storm, if you want to do something. Take your arrow and shoot the clouds. Make the sun come back. Make the summer come. [*He shoots into the sky.*] Where will we go when they take the land? [*She talks while the MAN clicks rocks to start a fire.*]

INDIAN. We won't go anywhere. We belong with the animals and trees and rivers. We'll be here as long as the land is.

INDIAN WOMAN. What do their Grandfathers say about them coming?

INDIAN. They don't talk to their Ancestors.

INDIAN WOMAN. They don't talk to their Grandfathers?

INDIAN. They don't see ghosts.

INDIAN WOMAN. What drives them up the river to make marks of land on their map? To set up villages behind walls? There's a new fort just across the river. [*She scrapes the ground with her deer antler rake.*]

INDIAN. The map makes them feel less a stranger to the land. They change the names of rivers and lakes from our words to theirs. There were nights I was guiding the white man upriver that I dreamed of him standing mid-air. Trying to find a place to put his feet. The land didn't feel like home to him and he dug and looked and smelled and poked, trying to make a place he felt was his. He doesn't know where he's walking. It's because he wears hard boots and doesn't know the land is his mother.

INDIAN WOMAN. He won't hear the voice of the earth. He doesn't know it's part of us. He won't have dreams.

INDIAN. Maybe there are men who can live without vision.

INDIAN WOMAN. Who can live without dreams? Remember those people in your dream when you were a boy? You said they turned into bears. They were your parents talking to you after their death. They wanted you to live. Where would you be without their dream? [*Here the INDIAN turns away from her and fishes.*] Mey mey mey mey. [*She sings to her baby and soon ties a fish to the drying poles.*]

[*Here there is music in preparation for the bear dance. The musician is in a mask. He beats the drum and acts like a bear. He jumps around the INDIAN MAN as he fishes. The WOMAN joins him as the other bear. They motion for the INDIAN MAN to follow. They show him where to fish. One of them carries the sun.*]

III.

[*Wild rice season (fall). First, the dance. Later, the WOMAN sits in the canoe while the MAN paddles. She gathers rice into the canoe with the rice sticks. They dry the rice on the ground, parch it in a kettle to loosen the husks, fan it, trample or jig it, fan again and trample.*]

The Truth Teller

INDIAN. [*In his red & blue mask.*] I am a Spirit person. I have walked over the boundary. I'm in the Spirit world. I dance. I talk to the earth. Which plants can I use for healing? Where are the fish? When is the rice ready for harvest? I listen and it tells me. The eagle drops his feather for me. I hear the voice of the bird. The voice of the bear blesses my lure and spear. I give thanks to the fish for his life. I give thanks to the river for the wild rice. I talk to the wind and rain. I say rain go around us. Rain you stay over there. Over the walled fort—make mud up to their knees. Ho ho. Ha ha. Sink their boats. Stop their forward going. Make the rain to rise above their ears. [*The three dancers make a comic act of rowing and drowning.*]

INDIAN WOMAN. This is the dancing we do. On my bird face is the rising sun and the land still in darkness where the winds rise. Go around me I say. What are you doing here? Go around me I say. Tell me bird. How to fly? Flap. Flap. How to fall to earth? Thud. [*The two other dancers blow on her. She falls over, then gets up.*] How to survive the fall? [*After dancing.*] Tell me. What is the truth of those who come?

INDIAN. I don't know.

INDIAN WOMAN. You traveled with the white man for a summer and winter. You know about his Bible and you don't know his truth? I think they say they have one truth, and anyone who doesn't believe it, doesn't have truth.

INDIAN. What is truth to you?

INDIAN WOMAN. Why do you ask me?

INDIAN. Because you think there's just one truth.

INDIAN WOMAN. The elders say that truth is written on our birchbark scrolls.

INDIAN. The white men have a truth too. Something that makes them go on. I've seen them cough up blood from carrying their heavy barrels and canoes. I've seen them hungry. Sometimes their feet were so swollen they could hardly walk.

INDIAN WOMAN. I thought you said they have a sock.

INDIAN. They had a truth they live by. In one camp, a chief offered a squaw to the white man who was the leader and he refused, saying he already had a wife. The chief said many men had many wives, even during one winter. But he still refused.

INDIAN WOMAN. Truth is what the birchbark scrolls say. Our Elders and Grandfathers speak truth. The earth speaks truth. Truth is what we hear in our stories.

The Truth Teller

INDIAN. But our stories have different voices. We tell stories in our own way. I have stories. The Elders have stories.

INDIAN WOMAN. They aren't that different. I hear truth when you speak. I hear truth in the Elder's stories. Truth is like water through a gorge.

INDIAN. The white men have a way to live too that carries them like a canoe.

INDIAN WOMAN. I won't hear it. They kill the game we hunt for food. They say they buy our land. But the land was given to us. How can something like truth be changeable?

INDIAN. Because it's the core of our lives. Life is changeable like the seasons. I think it must change form to meet different needs at different times. The white man searches for the source of the Mississippi. The river may have several sources. Could truth have several headwaters also? Yet flowing into one stream? Could the blood of red and white mix like rivers yet flow together in one Great River?

INDIAN WOMAN. That can't be.

INDIAN. Yet truth is lasting. It's like the change that the birch tree makes before it becomes our scrolls. Sometimes it's invisible. When it's in the seed. Then it's a sapling. Then a tree. You peel the bark when it's easy to peel. Then it's in a different form. You sew it with cedar root. And it has another shape. You draw on it with lines from a pointed stick dipped in red ochre. The birchbark scrolls have many shapes. They tell many stories. Yet they are always birchbark. They are the one thing we carry with us from the Elders. From camp to camp.

INDIAN WOMAN. When I see the white man, I see a beaver damming one little creek until the backed-up water spills into the woods and kills the trees.

INDIAN. You worry for nothing.

INDIAN WOMAN. Your eyes are closed with buffalo robes. Your ears are blocked with beaver dams.

INDIAN. Only the Great Spirit knows the truth. He's the all-knowing Truth Teller. Our way is covered by a blanket. Slowly I feel the darkness more each day. But there is truth in the end. We may not see it at the moment.

INDIAN WOMAN. They're a people who won't hear, won't speak to the spirit world to know things. They push on like the stories of the glacier. The glaciers pushed and our people moved. This is the trail of my mother, the trail of my grandmother. What trail will the baby have? I don't want to lose the land. I feel like an animal in the trap. Gnawing my hind foot off.

[*She does beading work.*] Mey mey mey. [*She sings to the baby. Ties a small fir bough to the cradle board.*] The baby watches this and counts the Ancestors in the needles.

INDIAN.   Our birchbark scrolls say that from our first home along the eastern sea. We wear the seashell to remember our home. Our Grandfathers moved westward by the coming of the white man. Farther and farther across the Great Lakes to the Great River Mississippi. Our path is sometimes blocked by evil spirits who appear as horned serpents or great fish. But our helpers are there too.

INDIAN WOMAN.   You're so hopeful.

INDIAN.   Maybe the Great Spirit and their God are one. The good times are under a blanket for a while but they return. The Great Spirit calls all men together in the smoke of the peace pipe.

INDIAN WOMAN.   All lakes and rivers now will run with our tears. The wolf, fox, buffalo, prairie mole, goose, duck. All the animals will go away. The earth will cry. It can't get along without the animals. My heart curls like smoke from the fire.

INDIAN.   Our scrolls tell about our power. Our vision quests. We see the Ancestors who cheer us on and protect our path. We are young faces of the old faces. [*He puts on a mask and takes it off.*]

IV.

[*Winter camp season (winter). The* WOMAN *wraps the blanket over the tripod with the lodge poles sticking up at the top for a teepee. She hangs up the hide-stretcher and snow shoes.*]

INDIAN WOMAN.   What will happen to us? I see more of them all the time. I see them with eyes like maple sugar. Some of them have hair yellow as the tamaracks in fall. I see their stars on their flag at the new fort. I remember when I was a girl. We belonged to the whole earth.

INDIAN.   The part of it we knew anyway.

INDIAN WOMAN.   The women didn't hurry to the river for water. They talked and laughed. No men groaned in their sleep. Our children didn't know fear unless a bear sniffed at the teepee at night. Or the wolf howled at the flap. I feel something inside me. My skin grows cold. My heart is a hard pellet. Like buckshot from muskets that hangs on doors. There's something that won't go away.

INDIAN.   When we smoke the peace pipe, we have communion with the Great Spirit and all living creatures. [*They lie beside one another as he talks. His arm is under her head. Her ankle is over his leg. Their left hands hold at the* *thumbs.*] There's a story of men who would come to take the earth away from us. Even the stars. I look at the night sky and think, how can that be? Yet I know our legends are true.

INDIAN WOMAN. But the Great Spirit saved some stars for the Indian— inside the twig of the cottonwood. Maybe it will be all right. While you were gone, a trader at the new fort cut an apple crosswise for me. I saw the star inside the apple too. Just like in the twig of the cottonwood. I gave him the sparrow-bone bracelet for it. I didn't like the bracelet anyway. Sleep a while and I will pray for you. [*She sits up and he rests his head in her lap.*] When he sleeps I hear him snore. I think of his wolf-growl when he plays with the children. I think of the children as they die from the white man's diseases. I hear them cough in their teepees. My sister's two children have already died. I look at my baby. Then I feel the cold place inside me again. There's another kind of darkness out there now.

[*The* INDIAN MAN *dreams. A deer dancer enters beating a drum. Motioning to follow.*]

INDIAN MAN. [*He wakes.*] I dreamed a name for the baby. He-who-sees-the-way.

INDIAN WOMAN. What does it mean?

INDIAN. I don't know. Am I the Truth Teller for his life also? He will have to discover what it means. He's the one who follows the new ways. Maybe he's the one who can walk where we can't. Maybe he will show us a way when our life comes to a close.

INDIAN WOMAN. How would you draw the scroll for his life's walk?

INDIAN. I would mark four stages for his life on the birchbark. Before each one are obstacles. But there are guardian bear spirits, and beaver spirits guiding him, and elders protecting him, and the four winds and four directions to help him, and the birds to carry his prayers. [*Pause.*]

INDIAN WOMAN. You are thinking of the obstacles?

INDIAN. Yes. I'm thinking of what's coming for him—I don't want you going to the new fort anymore.

INDIAN WOMAN. It seems to me I should learn to go to the fort. I want their calico. And the-bird-beak-that-cuts-through-cloth. [*She makes scissor-motions with her fingers.*] I want to make their quilts and bead their flower-patterns. I want to see a door close with a sock. I want to know how they survive their sickness. The spots-on-the-face. The coughing-up disease. The no-strength-sleep of our children. I will have to walk in a place where there's no path. That's what our lives will be.

INDIAN. [*He stands and takes the snow shoes.*] I remember the story of the Great Spirit's flying lesson. He flew and crashed. Maybe it will be that way for us also. The Great Spirit of the white man fell to earth also. They put him on a cross. Maybe our thud is coming. If the Great Spirit thuds and survives, then we can too.

INDIAN WOMAN. Where are you going?

INDIAN. To see if anything is in the trap.

INDIAN WOMAN. Don't go yet.

INDIAN. We need the meat and skins. [*He exits to the edge of the stage.*]

INDIAN WOMAN. Sometimes I'm afraid he won't come back. But I remember our stories. In the winter, the evil spirit, Windigo, comes bringing sickness and death. One winter, when the men were out hunting, there was no one strong or brave enough to go out and face Windigo. So a small girl walked out on the lake carrying two sumac sticks. As she walked, she grew stronger, and the sticks of sumac froze hard as stone. She attacked the Windigo monster, crushing his skull. [*After the story, the INDIAN WOMAN sits rocking the cradle board for a moment. Then she talks to the baby.*] I name you He-who-sees-the-way. You're the one who will lead. I mark you with bravery. I say there is a way where none is. I say you are a Truth Teller. And I say it to the children who come after you. You'll see in your own way. You will see a way.

INDIAN. I hear you, earth. You are myself. A part of you is leaving. I saw it in my dream. I am leaving too. I don't know how to walk in more than one world.

INDIAN WOMAN. Do I not have two feet? One for the path of each world. [*Here the INDIAN attempts to fly, and in falling, exits. The INDIAN WOMAN talks to the baby.*] In time you'll have a birchbark scroll which will help you with your walk. Maybe you will make new stories. Because with stories we will know the way. [*She sings.*] Mey mey mey mey.

Responding to the Selection

Questions for Discussion

1. How are the main characters in the play related to one another?

2. What is unique about the Indian's heritage? Briefly retell his story. How does the Indian's heritage affect his outlook on the world?

3. What concerns the Indian Woman? How does the Indian reassure her?

4. In her epigraph to this story, Diane Glancy says, "Because to go forward / we must first go back—" How do her characters reflect these words? In what ways do you agree with them?

5. At the end of the story, how have the two characters changed their attitudes?

Activities

Writing an Essay

1. The two characters in this play engage in a debate over the relative values of the old and new ways and over the possibility for successful merger between the two. Use the information of the play and your own knowledge and views to write a persuasive essay supporting one or the other position.

Performing a Scene

2. With a classmate, rehearse and perform a scene from the play. Develop mannerisms and speech styles, determine movements, and think of ways to convey the characters' emotions.

Web Site

Many Native Americans have fought with courage and resourcefulness in defense of the United States. This Web site entry gives one example.

The Navajo Code Talkers

By Gerald Knowles

Lying in the hot black sands of Iwo Jima, the marine extended his hand into the sand. He felt cold steel several inches below the surface. He froze with intense fear. He knew that few of his fellow marines had survived the blast of the dreaded Japanese land mines. Corporal Teddy Draper, a Navajo from the towering red canyons of Chinle, Arizona, was a long way from home. Yet, his presence and that of other Navajo Americans on Iwo Jima and many other islands on the road to Japan played a key role in the ultimate victory of the U.S. forces in the Pacific theater of the war.

Every communications code set up by the marines was eventually broken by the Japanese. It was only a matter of time. Most of the radio communications, essential to the direction of critical combat operations, were being intercepted by the Japanese, many of whom could both understand English and sound like an American marine.

In early 1942 Philip Johnson met with high ranking marines at Camp Eliot in San Diego and presented the idea of using the Navajo language as a code. The American officers gave the project a skeptical go-ahead. It seemed too simple and vulnerable to have two soldiers talking back and forth to each other.

While the agility, endurance, and courage of the Navajo soldier in the Pacific campaigns are legendary, only a passing notion of the use of Navajo as code is understood. It was mistakenly seen as a simple process of two Navajos talking to each other. On the contrary, the major contribution of the Navajo marine was cerebral. The Navajo marines had literally created an alternative Navajo language. They changed around and substituted words. Not

even native Navajo speakers tested with the new code talk knew what these Navajo marines were talking about. "That's crazy Navajo," one remarked. In addition, none of the Navajo code was written down. It was all committed to memory!

Code Talker Teddy Draper Sr. relates the Code Talker role on the front lines in the battle of Iwo Jima, which he calls "Hell Island." The thirty-six-day ordeal was characterized by hand-to-hand combat and a constant stream of hand grenades, mortars, bayonet duels, and deployment of flame throwers by American forces. Comrades had to be left dead in the hot tropic sun because rescue often meant death to those who tried. Major Howard Connor was to remark after the war that "without the Navajo

(Code Talker), the marines would never have taken Iwo Jima."

General Setzo Avisue, head of Japanese intelligence, when told after the war about the Code Talkers sighed, "Thank you, that is a puzzle I thought would never be solved." The Navajo Code Talk may have been the only unbreakable code in the history of warfare.

The tenacity of the Japanese soldier, the torturous terrain and climate and the defenses of the enemy could have well combined to stop the essential U.S. capture of the Pacific Islands. Many believe that it was the Navajo Code Talker weapon that tipped the balance and brought victory for the American forces.

Questions for Discussion

1. What about this story did you find most interesting?
2. What do you think might have happened on Iwo Jima if the code talkers had not been there?

Before You Read

Windmills and Crazy Papers

Gerald Vizenor
Born 1934

"The tricksters in all my work, everywhere, and, in one character or another, disrupt the ambitions of people, contradict, unsettle, and unglue the creeds . . ."

About Vizenor

Gerald Vizenor writes to dispel common stereotypes of Indians, which he says "have nothing to do with real Indians." He is driven, he once wrote, "to change the way in which people think about the rich and complex and contradictory experience of being Native American."

Vizenor's life has been as varied as his writing. A native of Minnesota, Vizenor had a very unstable childhood. At the age of eighteen, Vizenor dropped out of high school and joined the army. While stationed in Japan, he became fascinated with Japanese culture. After his discharge from the army, he earned a bachelor's degree in child development, worked as a social worker, and published a collection of haiku. He continued his studies and became first a journalist and then a college professor. He has taught Native American literature at a number of universities, including the University of Minnesota and the University of California at Berkeley.

Tricksters of Today

In Vizenor's novels and stories, one or more of the characters is often a mixed-blood "trickster," modeled loosely after the legendary animal characters in Native American oral literature. A trickster typically escapes difficult situations or upsets the status quo by outwitting others, often in a humorous way. Trickster figures are found in many cultures around the world. Many modern Native American writers have used this figure in their writings, either creating new stories in the traditional style or reinterpreting the Trickster in modern terms.

Windmills and Crazy Papers

— *Gerald Vizenor*

Tulip Browne is obsessed with wind and natural power; she builds miniature windmills in her new condominium in the hills. She throws open the windows and listens to the ocean wind over the copper blades of seventeen windmills; at dawn she attends a palace of whirs and secret twitters.

Once a week she wanders on the lower streets to encounter poor and destitute people; to brush with contention and common pleasures. The rude misconnections, wild separations, and blame shouted on the streets remind her of natural power and her untamed relatives in woodland reservation dreams. "Those down and out people," she told her mother, "are overlooked thunder storms in the cities, and we need their storms and stories to remember we are alive."

Tulip reveals no secrets and she bears no confessions from the baronage or her mixedblood identities; her sensitive moves are secluded, but she haunts memories with her personal power. She invites street people to dinner at the best restaurants and challenges them to a "persona grata rencounter."

"Do you know what that means?"

"Listen," he sighed behind his shopping cart.

"What is your name?"

"No," he shouted and waved his arms. His wild voice aroused two white cats in a cardboard box lashed to the top of his cart.

"No what?"

"No I don't know what you mean," he said.

"How about dinner?"

"When?"

"Down the block at the Krakow on the Vistula."

"You name it, you got it, you pay it," he said and pushed his cart down the sidewalk at her side. He parked under a bright red canopy at the entrance to the restaurant and covered the white cats with a broken parasol. "This place never leaves any garbage out, did you know that?"

"Have you ever eaten here?"

"Persona grata, what does that mean?" he asked and folded a thick slice of black bread over three butter cones. He lowered his head and leaned closer to the table, an animal over bread and butter.

"Persona grata means one is acceptable and welcome," she said, "and rencounter means to meet, an unplanned meeting, that's what I'm doing with you."

"Chance, you mean?"

"Yes, you could put it that way."

"Ronin Bloom," he mumbled over his bread.

"What?"

"Ronin Bloom," he shouted, "that's my name, not my real name, but my name, persona nongrata in the uppity hills where you come from sister." He finished the sentence and the black bread at the same time.

"Sir, could you leave your rope outside," said the black waiter. His forehead wrinkled when he spoke; he pinched his nose. "The rope, man, the rope, out, out, now."

Ronin wore a blue leather necktie, a paisley shirt, an oversized matted wool coat, threadbare wide-ribbed corduroy trousers, black boots with no heels, and thick canvas knee pads. He had not violated the liberal dress code in the restaurant, but the rope and his pungent odor would have been enough to remove him with reasonable cause.

"The rope, man, now."

"My cart's on the end of this," he said with the rope in his hands. One end of the thin orange tether was tied to two shopping carts parked under the canopy, and the other end encircled his waist in the belt loops.

"Could he bring his carts inside?" asked Tulip. She cocked her head and folded her hands on the rim of the table.

"I'm afraid not."

"Give me one good reason."

"Well, the stench is enough," said the waiter, his hand over his nose. He moved back from the table and summoned the owner of the restaurant.

"The shopping carts block the entrance, which in case of fire is very dangerous, but that's not the real problem," said the stout owner in rapid speech. "The cats are in violation of the city health code."

Ronin pushed his chair back in preparation to defend the honor of his two shorthairs, but the chair was on rollers and the gesture was lost in a collision with another table. "Man," he said to the owner, "I'm a street-wiser and nobody talks about my family like that, but nobody. Whistle and Black Duck were born on my carts."

"Perish the thought," the owner smirked.

Windmills and Crazy Papers

"The carts are their home and my place too, our place, the carts are a sovereign place, we got everything we need on eight wheels," he shouted at the owner.

Ronin moved around the restaurant, from table to table, and repeated his stories about his sovereign carts. The customers were overwhelmed and covered their noses with monogrammed napkins when he landed too close to their tables. One woman covered her head and whimpered. "Sure, you can sit there with your keys to a house in the hills. Well, this rope is my key, man," he said to the shrouded woman. "So, who's crazy around here, me and my rope or you under that dumb napkin?"

"Please, sir," said the owner.

"Ronin is my name."

"Mister Ronin, sir, would you please step outside with us now?" The owner and three waiters surrounded the streetwiser, pushed him down into a chair, and rolled him out of the restaurant. The owner tripped on the orange rope and cursed street people; he hated the destitute and even denied them garbage from the restaurant.

Tulip paid for the two meals; the owner delivered the food outside in decorative cartons embossed with an imperial seal and Krakow on the Vistula. The cartons were tied with cotton braids. She cocked her head and assured the owner that she would return soon, but her gestures were lost in the confusion. The owner and three waiters rushed to the back of the restaurant to block the streetwiser and his carts.

Ronin Bloom had pushed his tandem shopping carts through the restaurant and parked between two tables at the rear. There he presented his collection of lost shoes and told stories about Black Duck and Whistle to seven customers. The waiters rushed the streetwiser and pushed his carts out the back door onto the trash landing.

"Whistle does but Black Duck is white . . . listen, I've got my crazy papers, you can't treat me this way," were his last words when the owner cursed him once more and slammed the steel door closed.

Ronin and Tulip pushed the carts down the main street to a park bench between a hotel and a bank. He ate with his fingers from the embossed carton and repeated his best lost shoe stories. Tulip listened and fed the cats on a thick golden napkin.

"My uncle has a shoe collection," she said.

"So, what's his name?" he asked and wiped his mouth on his matted sleeve. He wiped his hands on the shorthairs.

"Mouse Proof Martin."

"Never heard of him," he mumbled.

Windmills and Crazy Papers

"No one has a better lost shoe collection," she boasted. "He even travels around and shows his shoes at colleges and museums."

"Maybe so," he shouted over the roar of a diesel bus, "but no one has a better lost shoe collection in a shopping cart, you can believe that."

"What got you started?"

"Sylvan Goldman."

"Relative?"

"Better than that, he was a grocer," he sighed and teased the shorthairs on their tethers. "Goldman's invention changed the world."

"Plastic clothes?" she teased in response.

"Heck no, he invented the shopping cart, the nesting cart, my tandem wheels, my mobile home where the urban buffalo roam," he chanted and waved his hands.

"Nice tune. Still hungry?"

"No, that crack on the river place was too much," he said and then turned his hands over and over on his knees. "Street people eat faster than the uppity hill people, you know."

"Why do you wear knee pads?"

"Balance," he shouted.

"You mean weights?" she said and ducked his breath.

"No, no, you know," he hesitated, "like two gloves, same shoes, balance like that, balance on the run, because I only have to wear one."

"Tell me, which one?"

"Look at this knee," he said and raised his right trouser leg. He wore no socks and his ankles were marbled black. "See, the patella is gone, broken and removed. The doc said wear a pad or lose my leg, so, two pads for me, balance."

"Ronin, you have nice legs."

"No woman ever said that to me before," he mumbled and covered his knee. "You got nice legs too. Do you live in the hills or something?"

"Yes, with a mongrel."

"What's his name?"

"White Lies."

"Shoot, is that a real name?"

"Reservation name."

"You heard about crazy papers?"

"No, but you said something about that back at the Krakow on the Vistula," she said. "Should I have crazy papers?"

"Definitely. With a dog named White Lies, you definitely need your own crazy papers," he said and laughed. His teeth were stained and marked with caries. "Did you ever take your hound to a black hangout and call his name?"

Windmills and Crazy Papers

"Never."

"Then you need crazy papers," he said and stretched his hands. Ronin opened a blue folder and removed an official certificate. He touched a pencil stub to his tongue and asked, "So, what's your real name?"

"Tulip Browne."

"Twolips and White Lies," he repeated and printed it on the document. "Now, with this, you can hangdog the street, wander into restaurants and search for food, and stay out of jail because the cops will know you're a wacko lodge member and not a case from Club Mental."

"Do I get a cart with crazy papers?"

"You ever heard about Terry Wilson?" he asked and propped his boots on the back of the carts. Black Duck pawed the holes in his soles.

"Does he have crazy papers?"

"He wrote *The Cart That Changed the World: The Career of Sylvan Goldman*, and that book and the cart changed my world," he said. "Goldman invented the nest cart, and I declared the tandem cart a sovereign state on low wheels.

"Sylvan made a seven-minute movie about how to use his invention because men would not be seen behind a cart. Well," he said and scratched his ear, "my mother saw that movie when I was born and it changed our lives, she decided that the cart was a perfect baby nest. She was the first person to buy her own cart to keep me in. So here I am, over twice as many wheels now."

Ronin unloaded a down sleeping bag, pushed several bundles of soiled clothes aside, and revealed his library and personal files wrapped in black plastic at the bottom of one cart.

"Here's my mother with me and our first nest cart," he said and selected several other photographs from a cigar box. "This one was my first elevator ride in my cart, the sides were decorated with crepe paper."

"Wait a minute."

"What?"

"Who's that with the beaded belt buckle?" she asked. Tulip pointed to an enormous stomach at the side of the photograph.

"Rainbow, that's my uncle, he lived with us for a time," he said and turned the photograph to read the inscription on the back. "Mogul's Department Store, October 23, 1939, with Rainbow, the day he said we're going to Oklahoma."

"You traveled in your cart," she mocked.

"Right, on the train," he said and passed her several photographs of his mother and various new carts painted in bright colors. "Rainbow got a job at the Folding Carrier Corporation in Oklahoma City because Sylvan Goldman owned the company and he liked to hire Indians way back then."

"Where is his face?"

"Who?"

"Rainbow, nothing but his stomach here."

"Well, somehow, he never got his face into a picture," he said and sorted through a stack of irregular shaped photographs, "nothing but his gut, you're right, and that beaded belt, except this one where you can see his boots and the brim of his cowboy hat. He always wore that hat, even to bed."

"Rainbow with no head."

"Listen," he said as he closed the cigar box, "you're a really nice person, you can borrow my cart book to change your world too." The book was covered with plastic, an unmarked treasure. "This is the only book that really counts, the only one I ever read cover to cover."

"Ronin, do you like windmills?"

"You got a windmill book that changed your world?"

"I build miniature windmills."

"No kidding, where?"

"Meet me here on this bench in one week," she said. Tulip leaned forward and buttoned her coat. "I'll return your book then and give you one of my windmills. You can mount it on the front of your cart."

"Whistle loves the wind."

"Next week then?"

"Tulip, what a name for a streetwiser, and she even makes little windmills," he shouted as she crossed the street.

"Who cares? I got my crazy papers right here," she shouted back and then disappeared behind a bus at the intersection.

Responding to the Selection

Questions for Discussion

1. Tulip Browne meets with street people because they "remind her of natural power and her untamed relatives in woodland reservation dreams." This is an example of Vizenor's use of **irony** to poke fun at stereotypes of Indians. Give another example of irony from the selection.

2. What do you think Tulip Browne hopes to accomplish by taking street people to dinner at expensive restaurants? Is she successful?

3. What qualities of a typical trickster does Tulip Browne have? How are she and Ronin alike?

4. Ronin says that the invention of the shopping cart changed his world and his life. Do you think he regards the change as positive or negative? What makes you think so? What do you think he likes or dislikes about his life?

5. Besides being known for combining the trickster tradition with contemporary literary techniques, Vizenor frequently coins new words in his works. "Streetwiser" is an example. How is the connotation of the term different from that of the more common term "street people"?

Activities

Writing a Story

1. Write a contemporary trickster story using a setting that is familiar to you. Try to coin at least one new word in your story.

Acting Out a Scene

2. Work in a small group to create and present a pantomime of the restaurant scene from this selection.

Beauty All Around Me. Larry Yazzie. Bronze, 28½ in. The Turquoise Tortoise, Sedona, AZ.

Theme Five

Change and Continuity

And he dreamed of another light . . .

— Mark Turcotte

Focus on . . .
The Past and
the Future

Native Americans at the close of the twentieth century faced many challenges. How could they balance the goal of economic advancement with the preservation of a vital traditional culture? With more than 30 percent of Native Americans living in poverty as of 1990, tribal leaders knew they needed a road toward economic self-sufficiency. Unfortunately, many reservations lay in areas with limited economic potential.

A number of tribes began to take a lead from the increasingly popularity of state lotteries and began to establish gaming facilities. This helped them meet at least the first goal of increasing economic stability. Such gaming quickly became very successful, at least for those establishments near urban areas. The industry grew rapidly, producing a number of new jobs at each site. As Native Americans worked at well-paying casino jobs, tax revenues rose sharply. In addition, reservation governments, which provide basic services to residents, began to have budgets for economic development. They built housing and civil infrastructure such as roads and sewers. They funded new schools and the programs to run them. They developed health-care systems and focused on broadening tribal economic bases.

Revenues were also used to preserve tradition. For example, the Mashantucket Pequot Indians used gaming revenues to build a highly regarded museum and research center. As families visited the museum and scholars used its library, the history of Native Americans came alive.

During these same years, many Native Americans practiced the rituals of their traditional lifeways. They held scores of powwows, or ceremonial dances, throughout the year all around the U.S. and in parts of Canada. They developed programs to protect and preserve Native American languages. The traditional sweat lodge and its ceremonies became more common, even spreading outside the Indian community. From early tribal times, the sweat lodge held an important place in many traditional cultures, providing both physical and spiritual cleansing. The lodge is treated with reverence, as a place of spiritual

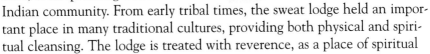

healing and renewal. Bathers may sit in silence, or they may be led in prayer by a medicine man or spiritual leader. The sweat lodge became at least one symbol of a growing cultural revival among Native Americans at the close of the twentieth century, as places like the Mashantucket museum became symbols of growing economic prosperity.

Linking to . . .
- Think about the past and the future of Native Americans as you read the selections that follow.

The Past and the Future **237**

Before You Read

Trusting the Words

Michael Dorris
1945–1997

*"Growing up mixed-blood is,
for too many of us and
for too long in our lives,
growing up mixed up."*

About Dorris

Born in 1945 in Louisville, Kentucky, Dorris was raised mostly by his mother and an aunt (his father had passed away earlier). The family had little money and moved often. For Dorris, the thread holding his many homes together was his love of books. He kept this love of books while studying at Yale and Georgetown Universities. Later he wrote both fiction and nonfiction for adults and children, much of it focused on Native American concerns. He and his wife Louise Erdrich worked closely together on several books. His nonfiction book *The Broken Cord* received a National Book Critics Circle Award and brought him national attention. Dorris also founded and taught at the Native American Studies program at Dartmouth College.

The Mixed-Blood Struggle

Michael Dorris spoke eloquently about his difficulty finding an identity as a person with mixed-blood heritage. He recalled feeling excluded at Native American gatherings—identified as an outsider by his light complexion. At the same time, he faced unknowing discrimination from white schoolmates who told jokes about stereotypical Native Americans. And though he read and read, he seldom encountered characters who reflected his own experience or heritage. Nonetheless, he developed his character by "nurturing . . . a self-image strong enough to stand up to all challengers." As a writer, he later spoke out for those of mixed-blood, developing several characters who proudly announced their mixed heritage.

Trusting
the
Words

— *Michael Dorris*

On the Banks of Plum Creek was the first brand-new hardback book I ever
bought for myself. It was not a casual or impulse purchase—such a luxury
was beyond a family of our economic level—but a considered acquisition.
Two summers before, during my daily browse in the small neighborhood
library a short walk from where I lived, I had stumbled upon the shelf of
Laura Ingalls Wilder novels. With their pastel covers, gentle illustrations,
large type, and homey titles, they were appealing, inviting, but which one
to try first? In the manner of Goldilocks, I decided that *Farmer Boy* looked
too long, *Little House in the Big Woods* too short. *Plum Creek*, though, was
just right. More than just right: by an amazing coincidence I had just an
hour before consumed a plum for lunch!

Naturally, like thousands of other readers over the past fifty years, I was
captured from page one. The snug little dwelling dug into the side of a creek
bank was as irresistible to me at age eight as Bilbo Baggins's similar den
proved to be some ten years later. The ever-mobile Ingalls family—adaptable,
affectionate Pa; conventional, resourceful Ma; pretty, good-girl Mary; baby
Carrie—were the Swiss Family Robinson next door, the us-against-the-
world American ideal of underdogs who, through grit and wit and optimism,
prevailed over every natural disaster and took advantage of every available
resource in their inexorable path toward increased creature comforts and
status. As linchpin and leading protagonist, second child Laura was full-swing
into the adventure of growing up, and as such she was not just like me, but
like me the way I aspired to be: plucky and brave, composed of equal parts
good will and self-interest. Her life was a constantly unfolding tapestry, its
events intricately connected and stitched with affectionate detail. The cast
of human and animal players auxiliary to the central family was limited and
manageable enough for a reader to grasp as distinct individuals, and within
the balanced, safe context of ultimate parental protection, even a week-long
blizzard was the occasion for a chapter titled "A Day of Games."

Trusting the Words

I doubt if any of today's powerful publishing marketing committees would project the young me as a likely target audience for the Wilder books. Superficially, Laura and I had so little in common, so few intersections of experience with which I should logically have been able to identify. Those experts would probably conclude that I—as a mixed-blood, male, only child of a single-parent, mostly urban, fixed-income family—would prefer novels more reflective of myself. True, I wasn't immune to "boy books." I dutifully followed every scrape that Frank and Joe Hardy fell into, worked my way through James Fenimore Cooper, Charles Dickens, and Alexandre Dumas, and had a stack of *D.C. Comics* in which both Superman and Batman figured prominently. But when the time came to buy a real book, to receive the first volume in what has become an extensive personal collection of literature, I didn't hesitate: *On the Banks of Plum Creek* was an old friend I was sure I'd want to read many more times in the years to come, as indeed I have.

The nine Little House books—*Little House in the Big Woods, Little House on the Prairie, On the Banks of Plum Creek, By the Shores of Silver Lake, The Long Winter, Farmer Boy, Little Town on the Prairie, These Happy Golden Years,* and *The First Four Years*—together with two subsequent collections of Laura Ingalls Wilder's diary entries (*On the Way Home*) and letters (*West from Home*), supplemented by related songbooks and cookbooks, chronicle and particularize like no other source the mythic American frontier journey from precarious adversity into middle-class security. If, as it appears from *The Ghost in the Little House,* William Holtz's new and convincing life of Rose Wilder Lane (Laura's only child, who grew up to be a thoroughly modern woman and one of the most far-flung and daring journalists of the 1920s and 1930s), the novels are more collaborative biography than homespun autobiography, their power is in no way diminished. That the characters are crafted verisimilitudes rather than drawn word-for-word upon fact only contributes to the readability of the series. The belated discovery that the generous, self-taught, talented, and complicated daughter shaped the rough yet keenly precise recollections of her farmer mother into art is an intriguing surprise—but certainly does not undermine either the historical or the humanistic value of a saga that at its heart depicts the universal struggle of a child growing to adulthood and independence.

Far more problematic, at least for me, were the issues raised when, with the enthusiasm of a father who had long looked forward to sharing a favorite tale, I set down last year to begin reading the books to my two daughters, ages seven and eight. Not one page into *Little House in the Big Woods,* I heard my own voice saying, "As far as a man could go to the north in a day, or a week, or a whole month, there was nothing but

Trusting the Words

woods. There were no houses. There were no roads. There were no people. There were only trees and the wild animals who had their homes among them."

Say what? Excuse me, but weren't we forgetting the Chippewa branch of my daughters' immediate ancestry, not to mention the thousands of resident Menominees, Potawatomis, Sauks, Foxes, Winnebagos, and Ottawas who inhabited mid-nineteenth-century Wisconsin, as they had for many hundreds of years? Exactly upon whose indigenous land was Grandma and Grandpa's cozy house constructed? Had they paid for the bountiful property, teeming with wild game and fish? This fun-filled world of extended Ingallses was curiously empty, a pristine wilderness in which only white folks toiled and cavorted, ate and harvested, celebrated and were kind to each other.

My dilemma, as raconteur, was clear. My little girls looked up to me with trusting eyes, eager to hear me continue with the first of these books I had promised with such anticipation. I had made "an event" out of their reading, an intergenerational gift, and now in the cold light of an adult perspective I realized that I was, in my reluctance to dilute the pleasure of a good story with the sober stuff of history, in the process of perpetuating a Eurocentric attitude that was still very much alive. One had only to peruse newspaper accounts of contemporary Wisconsin controversies over tribal fishing rights, bingo emporia, and legal and tax jurisdiction to realize that many of Grandpa and Grandma's descendants remained determined that there could be "no people" except those who were just like them.

Okay, I admit it. I closed the book rather than be politically correct at 8 P.M. in my daughters' bedroom. I'd save the cold water of reality for the light of day, and anyway, I seemed to remember that once Ma and Pa pushed west they had encountered native people.

"Let's start instead tomorrow with *Little House on the Prairie*," I suggested. This idea went over well, since it evoked in my girls the visual image of the pretty, if often saccharine, TV series of the same name.

Fast forward to the next evening, paragraph two: "*They were going to the Indian country.*"

Good sign! The packing up and the journey west were lovingly and minutely related. The sense of space and sky found on the plains was gloriously rendered. The pages turned, my daughters' eyes stayed bright long past their usual bedtime, the book was everything I remembered—realistic, lyrical, exciting in all the right ways. And then, page 46.

> Laura chewed and swallowed, and she said, "I want to see a papoose."
> "Mercy on us!" Ma said. "Whatever makes you want to see Indians? We will see enough of them. More than we want to, I wouldn't wonder."

Trusting the Words

"They wouldn't hurt us, would they?" Mary asked. Mary was always good; she never spoke with her mouth full.

"No!" Ma said. "Don't get such an idea into your head."

"Why don't you like Indians, Ma?" Laura asked, and she caught a drip of molasses with her tongue.

"I just don't like them, and don't lick your fingers, Laura," said Ma.

"This is Indian country, isn't it?" Laura said. "What did we come to their country for, if you don't like them?"

Ma said she didn't know whether this was Indian country or not. She didn't know where the Kansas line was. But whether or no, the Indians would not be here long. Pa had word from a man in Washington that the Indian Territory would be open to settlement soon.

What was a responsible father to do? Stop the narrative, explain that Ma was a know-nothing racist? Describe the bitter injustice of unilateral treaty abridgment? Break into a chorus of "Oklahoma!" and then point out how American popular culture has long covered up the shame of the Dawes Act by glossing it over with Sooner folklore?

This time, I simply invented an extra line of dialogue.

"That's awful, Ma," I had Laura say. "I'm ashamed to hear such a thing."

But the fantasy of the 1990s-enlightened Laura evaporated not ten pages later.

That night by the fire Laura asked again when she would see a papoose, but Pa didn't know. He said you never saw Indians unless they wanted you to see them. He had seen Indians when he was a boy in New York State, but Laura never had. She knew they were wild men with red skins, and their hatchets were called tomahawks.

Pa knew all about wild animals, so he must know about wild men, too. Laura thought he would show her a papoose some day, just as he had shown her fawns, and little bears, and wolves.

That part, I confess, I simply skipped, edited right out, blipped. In no time flat Pa was back to his fiddle, Ma was doing something deft and culinary with cornmeal. Nature was nature.

Only the wind rustled in the prairie grasses. The big, yellow moon was sailing high overhead. The sky was so full of light that not one star twinkled in it, and all the prairie was a shadowy mellowness.

And there were no Indians, no cholera-ridden, starving reservations, no prohibitions to the practice of native religion, no Wounded Knee a few hundred miles to the north, no Sand Creek an equal distance to the west.

Trusting the Words

Manifest Destiny protected its own, and family values prevailed, staunchly Calvinist and oblivious to any ethical messiness that might interfere with the romance.

The next chapter, "Moving In," was heralded by a drawing of tipis. I closed the book and kissed the girls goodnight, then retreated to my office to preview on my own. For a while, beyond Ma's offhand disparaging comments about not wanting to "live like Indians," the Ingalls family contented itself with building a house and fending off a wolf pack. Good clean fun, character-building hard work, the grist that made this country great.

Until . . .

> suddenly [Jack, the bulldog] stood up and growled a fierce, deep growl. The hair on his neck stood straight up and his eyes glared red.
>
> Laura was frightened. Jack had never growled at her before. Then she looked over her shoulder where Jack was looking, and she saw two naked wild men coming, one behind the other, on the Indian trail.
>
> "Mary! Look!" she cried. Mary looked and saw them, too.
>
> They were tall, thin, fierce-looking men. Their skin was brownish-red. Their head seemed to go up to a peak, and the peak was a tuft of hair that stood straight up and ended in feathers. Their eyes were black and still and glittering, like snake's eyes.
>
> The Indians went into the new house and Laura worried for the safety of Ma and baby Carrie. "I'm going to let Jack loose," Laura whispered, hoarsely. "Jack will kill them."

But no, the Indians only wanted some of Ma's cornbread and Pa's tobacco. They were wearing skunk skins, which didn't smell good, and their eyes glittered some more, but otherwise they were perfectly benign. When Pa came home he at first dealt with news of the visit with laudable equanimity, but then went on, before stopping himself, to add, "The main thing is to be on good terms with the Indians. We don't want to wake up some night with a band of the screeching dev—."

The concluding chapters of *Little House on the Prairie* are full of Indians—some threatening, some noble. The settlers worry over the possibility of being attacked and driven out, but it doesn't transpire. Instead, inevitably, the Indians are forced to evacuate in an endless line that trails past the family home. Pa takes this banishment as a given.

> "When white settlers come into a country, the Indians have to move on. The government is going to move these Indians farther west, any time now. That's why we're here, Laura. White people are going to settle

Trusting the Words

all this country, and we get the best land because we get here first and take our pick. Now do you understand?"

"Yes, Pa," Laura said. "But, Pa, I thought this was Indian Territory. Won't it make the Indians mad to have to—"

"No more questions, Laura," Pa said firmly. "Go to sleep."

Pa never felt as guilty as I would have liked him to, though he did disagree with his friend Mr. Scott who maintained that "the only good Indian is a dead Indian." Ma, on the other hand, remained an unreconstructed bigot—as late as *The Long Winter*, three novels and many years later, the very mention of even friendly, helpful Indians set her off.

> "What Indian?" Ma asked [Pa]. She looked as if she were smelling the smell of an Indian whenever she said the word. Ma despised Indians. She was afraid of them, too.
>
> For her part, Laura seemed typically open-minded, wanting at one point to adopt an Indian baby.
>
> "Its eyes are so black," Laura sobbed. She could not say what she meant.

At last, the Ingalls family, emblematic of all those like them who went west with the blithe assumption that resident tribes had no title rights to the country they had occupied from time immemorial, witnessed the realization of their dream: a vanishing native population. Surprisingly, it was not a jubilant moment.

> It was dinner-time, and no one thought of dinner. Indian ponies were still going by, carrying bunches of skins and tent-poles and dangling baskets and cooking pots. There were a few more women and a few more naked Indian children and Laura and Mary still stayed in the doorway, looking, till that long line of Indians slowly pulled itself over the western edge of the world. And nothing was left but silence and emptiness. All the world seemed very quiet and lonely.

As it turned out, I didn't read aloud the Little House books to my daughters because, quite frankly, I realized I couldn't have kept my mouth shut at the objectionable parts. I would have felt compelled to interrupt the story constantly with editorial asides, history lessons, thought questions, critiques of the racism or sexism embedded in the text. I would have studiously purified those novels, treated them as sociology or fixed them up to suit a contemporary and, I firmly believe, more enlightened sensibility.

Trusting the Words

Certainly they could be used that way, but, I wonder, would my daughters then grow up with the selective fond memories of each volume that I myself carried? Or would they learn from me that every page of a book had to pass a test in order for the whole to entertain? Would reading with me become a chore, a "learning experience," a tension, and not the pleasure I wished it?

Laura Ingalls Wilder and her daughter, Rose Wilder Lane, created a series peopled by characters who were, for better or worse, true to the prevailing attitudes of their day. Resisting the temptation to stereotype or sensationalize beyond the often ill-informed opinions of both adults and children, the actual incidents that involve Indians are portrayed as invariably anticlimactic—more ordinary and less dramatic than anyone, even Pa, expects them to be. Distilled from the aura of mystery and danger, the Indians on the periphery of the Ingalls family's vision are thin, unfortunate, and determinedly honest. Their journey is the sad underside of the bright pioneer coin, and their defeat and expulsion brings no one any glory. Ma and Pa's self-serving lack of compassion was probably no worse than most and much better than that of those who filed claims west of the Mississippi 150 years ago, and to create them otherwise and still present them as "typical" would be wishful thinking.

Ruminating on my own various interactions with the Little House books, I remembered that I had never much cared for Ma—even when I was a young boy she had struck me as prudish and cautious and uptight, with untested prejudices and unexamined rules that fairly cried out for rebellion. I remembered that I had Ma to thank, possibly more than anyone else in real life or in literature, for my first startling awareness that an adult authority figure could actually be dense and narrow minded. I remembered that those nagging, unanswered questions about what *did* happen to Indians in the nineteenth century (and why) had engendered an indignant pride in the Modoc part of my ethnic heritage. They had sent me to elderly relatives and to the history section of the library and that in turn had led to school research projects and maps, activism in the 1960s, and support of the American Indian Movement and, ultimately, no doubt, contributed heavily to my founding of the Native American Studies Program at Dartmouth College in 1972 and teaching there for the next fifteen years. Take that, Ma!

Books, important as they can and should be, are after all but a part of the much larger context that informs them. They illuminate our experience but at the same time our experience sheds light back upon their ideas and theories. A book converts less than it nudges us toward what we otherwise already think. The existence of characters who are distasteful or complicated merely reflects the world as it is.

Trusting the Words

I placed the Little House novels on the top shelf of the bookcase and told my daughters I thought it would be better if they read them, when and if they wanted to, to themselves. I trust that they will not be corrupted into Indianophobes even as they thrill to description of a runaway buggy or warm to the first blush of young love when Laura and Almanzo go courting. I trust that they will be able to differentiate courage from pettiness, justice from exploitation. I'll bide my time, and when, eventually, each of my girls bursts through a door, eyes ablaze with outrage, waving a book in her hand, furious . . . then we'll talk about it.

Responding to the Selection ───────

Questions for Discussion

1. Who is the narrator of this selection? Who is he addressing?
2. Why does the narrator remember the Laura Ingalls Wilder books with such fondness? How are his feelings changed by an adult perspective?
3. Briefly summarize the narrator's **main idea** and **point of view.** Do you agree with that view? Why or why not?
4. How does the author relate his heritage to the selection topic? After reading this selection, how do you think Michael Dorris regards that heritage?
5. In the end, how do you think Dorris feels about the Little House books?

Activities

Writing an Essay

1. Read a section of a Laura Ingalls Wilder book in which Native Americans feature. Then write your own **critical essay** about Wilder's treatment of Native Americans.

Writing an Advice Column

2. Imagine that you are an advice columnist and that Michael Dorris wrote to you requesting guidance on how to present the Wilder books to his children. What would you say in response? Draft an **advice column** or **open letter** giving your solution.

Before You Read

Two Poems

Joy Harjo
Born 1951

"The word, warrior, it applies to women just as well."

About Harjo

Born in Tulsa, Oklahoma, into a family of Muskogee Creek heritage, Joy Harjo has spent nearly all her life in the Southwest, close to her Native American roots. She studied creative writing at the Institute of American Indian Arts and at the Universities of New Mexico and Iowa. Planning at first to be a painter, Harjo often writes highly visual poetry that draws from the Southwestern landscape. She also expresses herself through other media, writing film screenplays, giving poetry readings, and playing saxophone with her band, Poetic Justice. While teaching creative writing at the university level, Harjo also published a number of books of poetry, including *The Woman Who Fell from the Sky*, *Secrets from the Center of the World*, and *In Mad Love and War*, which includes "Transformations" and "Summer Night" and which received an American Book Award.

Harjo's Poetic Forms and Themes

Not all poetry is written in rhyme, nor even in verse. In "Transformations," Harjo writes in a prose format but makes choices in sentence structure, language, and punctuation that turn this prose into poetry. With those choices, she inspires an emotional reaction about the struggle to survive hatred. In this way, "Transformations" represents a major theme in Harjo's work: many of her poems focus on struggles for survival, whether emotional or literal, and on the trials that these struggles present. "Summer Night," on the other hand, is written in long lines of free verse. Its references to music from a variety of cultures reflect Harjo's own interest in exploring musical possibilities.

Two Poems

— *Joy Harjo*

Transformations

This poem is a letter to tell you that I have smelled the hatred you have
tried to find me with; you would like to destroy me. Bone splintered in the
eye of one you choose to name your enemy won't make it better for you to
see. It could take a thousand years if you name it that way, but then, to see
after all that time, never could anything be so clear. Memory has many
forms. When I think of early winter I think of a blackbird laughing in the
frozen air; guards a piece of light. (I saw the whole world caught in that
sound, the sun stopped for a moment because of tough belief.) I don't
know what that has to do with what I am trying to tell you except that
I know you can turn a poem into something else. This poem could be a
bear treading the far northern tundra, smelling the air for sweet alive
meat. Or a piece of seaweed stumbling in the sea. Or a blackbird, laughing.
What I mean is that hatred can be turned into something else, if you have
the right words, the right meanings, buried in that tender place in your
heart where the most precious animals live. Down the street an ambulance
has come to rescue an old man who is slowly losing his life. Not many can
see that he is already becoming the backyard tree he has tended for years,
before he moves on. He is not sad, but compassionate for the fears moving
around him.

That's what I mean to tell you. On the other side of the place you live stands
a dark woman. She has been trying to talk to you for years.
You have called the same name in the middle of a nightmare,
from the center of miracles. She is beautiful.
This is your hatred back. She loves you.

Summer Night

The moon is nearly full,
              the humid air sweet like melon.
Flowers that have cupped the sun all day
                   dream of iridescent wings
under the long dark sleep.
              Children's invisible voices call out
in the glimmering moonlight.
               Their parents play worn-out records
of the cumbia. Behind the screen door

5   their soft laughter swells
into the rhythm of a smooth guitar.
              I watch the world shimmer
inside this globe of a summer night,
             listen to the wobble of her
spin and dive. It happens all the time, waiting for you
                 to come home.
There is an ache that begins
           in the sound of an old blues song.
It becomes a house where all the lights have gone out

10   but one.
And it burns and burns
          until there is only the blue smoke of dawn
and everyone is sleeping in someone's arms
             even the flowers
even the sound of a thousand silences.
         And the arms of night
in the arms of day.
      Everyone except me.

15 But then the smell of damp honeysuckle twisted on the vine.
And the turn of the shoulder
         of the ordinary spirit who keeps watch
over this ordinary street.
      And there you are, the secret
of your own flower of light
      blooming in the miraculous dark.

Responding to the Selection

Questions for Discussion

1. What feeling is "Transformations" mostly about? What two powers does the speaker associate with that feeling? How does the speaker use that feeling?

2. What memories does the speaker recall in "Transformations"? Why do you think the memories are of these natural elements?

3. Describe the **setting** of "Summer Night."

4. How does the speaker in "Summer Night" feel? What do you think happens at the end of the poem to change the speaker's feelings?

5. Both poems refer to Harjo's Native American heritage in their views about the life cycle, the value of memory, and the power of landscape. Use examples from each poem to explain how.

Activities

Performing a Dramatic Reading

1. Reread one of the poems until you know it well. Then create and present a **dramatic reading** of it. Use gestures, tone of voice, and facial expression— as you think appropriate—to capture the poem's emotions. If you wish, locate music to accompany your reading.

Writing an Essay

2. Write an **essay** on dealing with hatred or prejudice, using the ideas in "Transformations" as your starting point.

Before You Read

Men on the Moon

Simon J. Ortiz
Born 1941

> *"There have always been the songs, the prayers, the stories. There have always been the voices. There have always been the people."*

About Ortiz

Simon J. Ortiz grew up in the Acoma Pueblo in New Mexico. The Acoma reservation is centered on an ancient, still-inhabited village at the top of a high mesa; the village is often referred to as Sky City. Ortiz's family belonged to the Eagle clan *(Dyaani hanoh)*, whose members played an active role in his childhood. He grew up speaking Acoma; later he attended the U.S. government school in his area, which required students to learn and speak English. Ortiz's early interest in writing led to regular journal keeping throughout high school. After high school, he entered the mining industry and then served in the army. Later he went to college where he wrote and taught. He has since written a number of books, both prose and poetry, as well as edited several important collections of Native American writing. He has also served as lieutenant governor of the Acoma Pueblo.

Moon Voyages

This story takes place in the late 1960s or early 1970s, when the U.S. space program had finally achieved its goal of putting humans on the Moon. Astronaut Neil Armstrong became the first man on the Moon in July 1969. People all over the world watched the landing on television. Although television was first invented in the 1920s, decades elapsed before it became widely available. It may seem strange that even as late as this story, Faustin, living in a remote area, regards television as a novelty. Unlike today's cable or satellite systems, early televisions used antennae to receive signals. "Snow," or static, resulted from poor reception.

M⍷n on the Moon

— *Simon J. Ortiz*

I.

Joselita brought her father, Faustin, the TV on Father's Day. She brought it over after Sunday mass and she had her son hook up the antenna. She plugged the TV into the wall socket.

Faustin sat on a worn couch. He was covered with an old coat. He had worn that coat for twenty years.

It's ready. Turn it on and I'll adjust the antenna. Amarosho told his mother. The TV warmed up and then it flickered into dull light. It was snowing. Amarosho tuned it a bit. It snowed less and then a picture formed.

Look, Naishtiya, Joselita said. She touched her father's hand and pointed at the TV.

I'll turn the antenna a bit and you tell me when the picture is clear, Amarosho said. He climbed on the roof again.

After a while the picture turned clearer. It's better, his mother shouted. There was only the tiniest bit of snow falling.

That's about the best it can get I guess, Amarosho said. Maybe it'll clear up on the other channels. He turned the selector. It was clearer on another.

There were two men struggling with each other. Wrestling, Amarosho said. Do you want to watch wrestling? Two men are fighting, Nana. One of them is Apache Red. Chiseh tsah, he told his grandfather.

The old man stirred. He had been staring intently into the TV. He wondered why there was so much snow at first. Now there were two men fighting. One of them was a Chiseh, an Apache, and the other was a Mericano. There were people shouting excitedly and clapping hands within the TV.

The two men backed away from each other once in a while and then they clenched. They wheeled mightily and suddenly one threw the other. The old man smiled. He wondered why they were fighting.

Something else showed on the TV screen. A bottle of wine was being poured. The old man liked the pouring sound and he moved his mouth. Someone was selling wine.

The two fighting men came back on the TV. They struggled with each other and after a while one of them didn't get up and then another person came and held up the hand of the Apache who was dancing around in a feathered headdress.

It's over, Amarosho announced. Apache Red won the fight, Nana.

The Chisheh won. Faustin watched the other one, a lighthaired man who looked totally exhausted and angry with himself. He didn't like the Apache too much. He wanted them to fight again.

After a few moments something else appeared on the TV.

What is that? Faustin asked. There was an object with smoke coming from it. It was standing upright.

Men are going to the moon, Nana, his grandson said. It's Apollo. It's going to fly three men to the moon.

That thing is going to fly to the moon?

Yes, Nana.

What is it called again?

Apollo, a spaceship rocket, Joselita told her father.

The Apollo spaceship stood on the ground emitting clouds of something that looked like smoke.

A man was talking, telling about the plans for the flight, what would happen, that it was almost time. Faustin could not understand the man very well because he didn't know many words in Mericano.

He must be talking about that thing flying in the air? he said.

Yes. It's about ready to fly away to the moon.

Faustin remembered that the evening before he had looked at the sky and seen that the moon was almost in the middle phase. He wondered if it was important that the men get to the moon.

Are those men looking for something on the moon, Nana? he asked his grandson.

They're trying to find out what's on the moon, Nana, what kind of dirt and rocks there are, to see if there's any water. Scientist men don't believe there is any life on the moon. The men are looking for knowledge, Amarosho told him.

Faustin wondered if the men had run out of places to look for knowledge on the earth. Do they know if they'll find knowledge? he asked.

They have some information already. They've gone before and come back. They're going again.

Did they bring any back?

They brought back some rocks.

Rocks. Faustin laughed quietly. The scientist men went to search for knowledge on the moon and they brought back rocks. He thought that perhaps Amarosho was joking with him. The grandson had gone to Indian School for a number of years and sometimes he would tell his grandfather some strange and funny things.

The old man was suspicious. They joked around a lot. Rocks—you sure that's all they brought back?

That's right, Nana, only rocks and some dirt and pictures they made of what it looks like on the moon.

The TV picture was filled with the rocket, closeup now. Men were sitting and moving around by some machinery and the voice had become more urgent. The old man watched the activity in the picture intently but with a slight smile on his face.

Suddenly it became very quiet, and the voice was firm and commanding and curiously pleading. Ten, nine, eight, seven, six, five, four, three, two, liftoff. The white smoke became furious and a muted rumble shook through the TV. The rocket was trembling and the voice was trembling.

It was really happening, the old man marvelled. Somewhere inside of that cylinder with a point at its top and long slender wings were three men who were flying to the moon.

The rocket rose from the ground. There were enormous clouds of smoke and the picture shook. Even the old man became tense and he grasped the edge of the couch. The rocket spaceship rose and rose.

There's fire coming out of the rocket, Amarosho explained. That's what makes it go.

Fire. Faustin had wondered what made it fly. He'd seen pictures of other flying machines. They had long wings and someone had explained to him that there was machinery inside which spun metal blades which made them fly. He had wondered what made this thing fly. He hoped his grandson wasn't joking him.

After a while there was nothing but the sky. The rocket Apollo had disappeared. It hadn't taken very long and the voice from the TV wasn't excited anymore. In fact the voice was very calm and almost bored.

I have to go now, Naishtiya, Joselita told her father. I have things to do.
Me too, Amarosho said.

Wait, the old man said, wait. What shall I do with this thing. What is it you call it?

TV, his daughter said. You watch it. You turn it on and you watch it.

I mean how do you stop it. Does it stop like the radio, like the mahkina? It stops?

This way, Nana, Amarosho said and showed his grandfather. He turned the dial and the picture went away. He turned the dial again and the picture flickered on again. Were you afraid this one-eye would be looking at you all the time? Amarosho laughed and gently patted the old man's shoulder.

Faustin was relieved. Joselita and her son left. He watched the TV for a while. A lot of activity was going on, a lot of men were moving among machinery, and a couple of men were talking. And then it showed the rocket again.

He watched it rise and fly away again. It disappeared again. There was nothing but the sky. He turned the dial and the picture died away. He turned it on and the picture came on again. He turned it off. He went outside and to a fence a distance from his home. When he finished he studied the sky for a while.

II.

That night, he dreamed.

Flintwing Boy was watching a Skquuyuh mahkina come down a hill. The mahkina made a humming noise. It was walking. It shone in the sunlight. Flintwing Boy moved to a better position to see. The mahkina kept on moving. It was moving towards him.

The Skquuyuh mahkina drew closer. Its metal legs stepped upon trees and crushed growing flowers and grass. A deer bounded away frightened. Tshushki came running to Flintwing Boy.

Anaweh, he cried, trying to catch his breath.

What is it, Anaweh? You've been running, Flintwing Boy said.

The coyote was staring at the thing which was coming towards them. There was wild fear in his eyes.

What is that, Anaweh? What is that thing? he gasped.

It looks like a mahkina, but I've never seen one like it before. It must be some kind of Skquuyuh mahkina.

Where did it come from?

I'm not sure yet, Anaweh, Flintwing Boy said. When he saw that Tshushki was trembling with fear, he said gently, Sit down, Anaweh. Rest yourself. We'll find out soon enough.

The Skquuyuh mahkina was undeterred. It walked over and through everything. It splashed through a stream of clear water. The water boiled and streaks of oil flowed downstream. It split a juniper tree in half with a terrible crash. It crushed a boulder into dust with a sound of heavy metal. Nothing stopped the Skquuyuh mahkina. It hummed.

Anaweh, Tshushki cried, what shall we do? What can we do?

Flintwing Boy reached into the bag at his side. He took out an object. It was a flint arrowhead. He took out some cornfood.

Come over here, Anaweh. Come over here. Be calm, he motioned to the frightened coyote. He touched the coyote in several places of his body with the arrowhead and put cornfood in the palm of his hand.

This way, Flintwing Boy said and closed Tshushki's fingers over the cornfood gently. And they faced east. Flintwing Boy said, We humble ourselves again. We look in your direction for guidance. We ask for your protection. We humble our poor bodies and spirits because only you are the power and the source and the knowledge. Help us then—that is all we ask.

They breathed on the cornfood and took in the breath of all directions and gave the cornfood unto the ground.

Now the ground trembled with the awesome power of the Skquuyuh mahkina. Its humming vibrated against everything. Flintwing Boy reached behind him and took several arrows from his quiver. He inspected them carefully and without any rush he fit one to his bowstring.

And now, Anaweh, you must go and tell everyone. Describe what you have seen. The people must talk among themselves and decide what it is about and what they will do. You must hurry but you must not alarm the people. Tell them I am here to meet it. I will give them my report when I find out.

Coyote turned and began to run. He stopped several yards away. Hahtrudzaimeh, he called. Like a man of courage, Anaweh, like a man.

The old man stirred in his sleep. A dog was barking. He awoke and got out of his bed and went outside. The moon was past the midpoint and it would be morning light in a few hours.

III.

Later, the spaceship reached the moon.

Amarosho was with his grandfather. They watched a replay of two men walking on the moon.

So that's the men on the moon, Faustin said.

Yes, Nana, that's it.

There were two men inside of heavy clothing and equipment. The TV picture showed a closeup of one of them and indeed there was a man's face inside of glass. The face moved its mouth and smiled and spoke but the voice seemed to be separate from the face.

It must be cold. They have heavy clothing on, Faustin said.

It's supposed to be very cold and very hot. They wear the clothes and other things for protection from the cold and heat, Amarosho said.

The men on the moon were moving slowly. One of them skipped and he floated alongside the other.

The old man wondered if they were underwater. They seem to be able to float, he said.

The information I have heard is that a man weighs less than he does on earth, much less, and he floats. There is no air either to breathe. Those boxes on their backs contain air for them to breathe, Amarosho told his grandfather.

He weighs less, the old man wondered, and there is no air except for the boxes on their backs. He looked at Amarosho but his grandson didn't seem to be joking with him.

The land on the moon looked very dry. It looked like it had not rained for a long, long time. There were no trees, no plants, no grass. Nothing but dirt and rocks, a desert.

Amarosho had told him that men on earth—the scientists—believed there was no life on the moon. Yet those men were trying to find knowledge on the moon. He wondered if perhaps they had special tools with which they could find knowledge even if they believed there was no life on the moon desert.

The mahkina sat on the desert. It didn't make a sound. Its metal feet were planted flat on the ground. It looked somewhat awkward. Faustin searched vainly around the mahkina but there didn't seem to be anything except the dry land on the TV. He couldn't figure out the mahkina. He wasn't sure whether it could move and could cause fear. He didn't want to ask his grandson that question.

After a while, one of the bulky men was digging in the ground. He carried a long thin hoe with which he scooped dirt and put it into a container. He did this for a while.

Is he going to bring the dirt back to earth too? Faustin asked.

I think he is, Nana, Amarosho said. Maybe he'll get some rocks too. Watch.

Indeed several minutes later the man lumbered over to a pile of rocks and gathered several handsize ones. He held them out proudly. They looked just like rocks from around anyplace. The voice from the TV seemed to be excited about the rocks.

They will study the rocks too for knowledge?

Yes, Nana.

What will they use the knowledge for, Nana?

They say they will use it to better mankind, Nana. I've heard that. And to learn more about the universe we live in. Also some of them say that the knowledge will be useful in finding out where everything began and how everything was made.

Faustin smiled at his grandson. He said, You are telling me the true facts aren't you?

Why yes, Nana. That's what they say. I'm not just making it up, Amarosho said.

Well then—do they say why they need to know where everything began? Hasn't anyone ever told them?

I think other people have tried to tell them but they want to find out for themselves and also I think they claim they don't know enough and need to know more and for certain, Amarosho said.

The man in the bulky suit had a small pickaxe in his hand. He was striking at a boulder. The breathing of the man could clearly be heard. He seemed to be working very hard and was very tired.

Faustin had once watched a crew of Mericano drilling for water. They had brought a tall mahkina with a loud motor. The mahkina would raise a limb at its center to its very top and then drop it with a heavy and loud metal clang. The mahkina and its men sat at one spot for several days and finally they found water.

The water had bubbled out weakly, gray-looking and didn't look drinkable at all. And then they lowered the mahkina, put their equipment away and drove away. The water stopped flowing.

After a couple of days he went and checked out the place. There was nothing there except a pile of gray dirt and an indentation in the ground. The ground was already dry and there were dark spots of oil-soaked dirt.

He decided to tell Amarosho about the dream he had.

After the old man finished, Amarosho said, Old man, you're telling me the truth now? You know that you have become somewhat of a liar. He was teasing his grandfather.

Yes, Nana. I have told you the truth as it occurred to me that night. Everything happened like that except that I might not have recalled everything about it.

That's some story, Nana, but it's a dream.

It's a dream but it's the truth, Faustin said.

I believe you, Nana, his grandson said.

IV.

Sometime after that the spacemen returned to earth. Amarosho informed his grandfather that they had splashed down in the ocean.

Are they all right? Faustin asked.

Yes, Amarosho said. They have devices to keep them safe.

Are they in their homes now?

No, I think they have to be someplace where they can't contaminate anything. If they brought back something from the moon that they weren't supposed to they won't pass it on to somebody else, Amarosho said.

What would that something be?

Something harmful, Nana.

In that dry desert land there might be something harmful. I didn't see any strange insects or trees or even cactus. What would that harmful thing be, Nana?

Disease which might harm people on earth, Amarosho said.

You said there was the belief by the men that there is no life on the moon. Is there life after all? Faustin asked.

There might be the tiniest bit of life.

Yes I see now, Nana. If they find even the tiniest bit of life then they will believe, he said.

Yes. Something like that.

Faustin figured it out now. The men had taken that trip to the moon to find even the tiniest bit of life and if they found even the tiniest bit they would believe that they had found knowledge. Yes that must be the way it was.

He remembered his dream clearly now. He was relieved.

When are those two men fighting again, Nana? he asked his grandson.

What two men?

Those two men who were fighting with each other that day those other men were flying to the moon.

Oh—those men. I don't know, Nana. Maybe next Sunday. You like them?

Yes. I think that the next time I'll be cheering for the Apache. He'll win again. He'll beat the Mericano again, Faustin said, laughing.

Responding to the Selection ⸺

Questions for Discussion

1. What gift does Faustin receive for Father's Day? How does he respond to the gift?

2. What initially captures the old man's interest in the television? Why do you think this interests the old man?

3. Simon J. Ortiz greatly admired his own grandfather. How does he treat this family relationship in "Men on the Moon"? Do you find it consistent with your own family experiences?

4. What do you think Faustin's dream means?

5. Describe Faustin's view of the Moon mission. How does his Native American heritage contribute to this view? Do you think Ortiz agrees with that view? Why or why not?

Activities

Creating an Artwork

1. Create an artwork illustrating this story. You may prefer to focus on a particular episode or to combine elements from the entire story in the work.

Writing an Essay

2. Research television's role in unifying Americans of all backgrounds during moments of national importance and crisis. Write an **essay** discussing the ways television—especially live television—has changed our responses to major events.

Before You Read

The Man to Send Rain Clouds

Leslie Marmon Silko
Born 1948

*"We are together always
We are together always
There never was a time
When this
Was not so."*

About Silko

"I was fortunate to be reared by my great-grandmother and others of her generation," says Leslie Marmon Silko. "They always took an interest in us children and they were always delighted to answer our questions and to tell us stories about the old days." Born in Albuquerque, Silko grew up on the Laguna Pueblo reservation in New Mexico. Silko's writings reflect her mixed heritage. While Laguna stories and traditions figure prominently in her work, she focuses on the flexibility of Laguna culture in adapting to outside influences. Much of her work is influenced by the traditional Pueblo sense of time: "The indigenous people of the Americas see time as round, not as a long linear string. If time is round . . . then something that happened five hundred years ago may be quite immediate and real, whereas something inconsequential that happened an hour ago could be far away. Think of time as an ocean always moving."

Laguna Tradition

The Laguna are one of more than twenty groups of Pueblo Indians, most of whom live in northern New Mexico. The Laguna Pueblo reservation, the setting of the story you are about to read, is located west of Albuquerque.

In traditional Pueblo burial rites, corn-meal plays a significant role. It is associated with praying and is sprinkled on corpses and graves as a blessing, much as holy water is used in the Catholic church. Another Pueblo tradition is for dead people to be buried with food and water for their journey to their afterlife.

The Man to Send Rain Clouds

— Leslie Marmon Silko

ONE

They found him under a big cottonwood tree. His Levi jacket and pants were faded light-blue so that he had been easy to find. The big cottonwood tree stood apart from a small grove of winterbare cottonwoods which grew in the wide, sandy arroyo. He had been dead for a day or more, and the sheep had wandered and scattered up and down the arroyo. Leon and his brother-in-law, Ken, gathered the sheep and left them in the pen at the sheep camp before they returned to the cottonwood tree. Leon waited under the tree while Ken drove the truck through the deep sand to the edge of the arroyo. He squinted up at the sun and unzipped his jacket—it sure was hot for this time of year. But high and northwest the blue mountains were still deep in snow. Ken came sliding down the low, crumbling bank about fifty yards down, and he was bringing the red blanket.

Before they wrapped the old man, Leon took a piece of string out of his pocket and tied a small gray feather in the old man's long white hair. Ken gave him the paint. Across the brown wrinkled forehead he drew a streak of white and along the high cheekbones he drew a strip of blue paint. He paused and watched Ken throw pinches of corn meal and pollen into the wind that fluttered the small gray feather. Then Leon painted with yellow under the old man's broad nose, and finally, when he had painted green across the chin, he smiled.

"Send us rain clouds, Grandfather." They laid the bundle in the back of the pickup and covered it with a heavy tarp before they started back to the pueblo.

They turned off the highway onto the sandy pueblo road. Not long after they passed the store and post office they saw Father Paul's car coming toward them. When he recognized their faces he slowed his car and waved for them to stop. The young priest rolled down the car window.

"Did you find old Teofilo?" he asked loudly.

Leon stopped the truck. "Good morning, Father. We were just out to the sheep camp. Everything is O.K. now."

"Thank God for that. Teofilo is a very old man. You really shouldn't allow him to stay at the sheep camp alone."

"No, he won't do that any more now."

"Well, I'm glad you understand. I hope I'll be seeing you at Mass this week—we missed you last Sunday. See if you can get old Teofilo to come with you." The priest smiled and waved at them as they drove away.

TWO

Louise and Teresa were waiting. The table was set for lunch, and the coffee was boiling on the black iron stove. Leon looked at Louise and then at Teresa.

"We found him under a cottonwood tree in the big arroyo near sheep camp. I guess he sat down to rest in the shade and never got up again." Leon walked toward the old man's bed. The red plaid shawl had been shaken and spread carefully over the bed, and a new brown flannel shirt and pair of stiff new Levis were arranged neatly beside the pillow. Louise held the screen door open while Leon and Ken carried in the red blanket. He looked small and shriveled, and after they dressed him in the new shirt and pants he seemed more shrunken.

It was noontime now because the church bells rang the Angelus. They ate the beans with hot bread, and nobody said anything until after Teresa poured the coffee.

Ken stood up and put on his jacket. "I'll see about the gravediggers. Only the top layer of soil is frozen. I think it can be ready before dark."

Leon nodded his head and finished his coffee. After Ken had been gone for a while, the neighbors and clanspeople came quietly to embrace Teofilo's family and to leave food on the table because the gravediggers would come to eat when they were finished.

THREE

The sky in the west was full of pale-yellow light. Louise stood outside with her hands in the pockets of Leon's green army jacket that was too big for her. The funeral was over, and the old men had taken their candles and medicine bags and were gone. She waited until the body was laid into the pickup before she said anything to Leon. She touched his arm, and he noticed that her hands were still dusty from the corn meal that she had sprinkled around the old man. When she spoke, Leon could not hear her.

"What did you say? I didn't hear you."

"I said that I had been thinking about something."

The Man to Send Rain Clouds 263

"About what?"

"About the priest sprinkling holy water for Grandpa. So he won't be thirsty."

Leon stared at the new moccasins that Teofilo had made for the cere-monial dances in the summer. They were nearly hidden by the red blanket. It was getting colder, and the wind pushed gray dust down the narrow pueblo road. The sun was approaching the long mesa where it disappeared during the winter. Louise stood there shivering and watching his face. Then he zipped up his jacket and opened the truck door. "I'll see if he's there."

FOUR

Ken stopped the pickup at the church, and Leon got out; and then Ken drove down the hill to the graveyard where people were waiting. Leon knocked at the old carved door with its symbols of the Lamb. While he waited he looked up at the twin bells from the king of Spain with the last sunlight pouring around them in their tower.

The priest opened the door and smiled when he saw who it was. "Come in! What brings you here this evening?"

The priest walked toward the kitchen, and Leon stood with his cap in his hand, playing with the earflaps and examining the living room—the brown sofa, the green armchair, and the brass lamp that hung down from the ceiling by links of chain. The priest dragged a chair out of the kitchen and offered it to Leon.

"No thank you, Father. I only came to ask you if you would bring your holy water to the graveyard."

The priest turned away from Leon and looked out the window at the patio full of shadows and the dining-room windows of the nuns' cloister across the patio. The curtains were heavy, and the light from within faintly penetrated; it was impossible to see the nuns inside eating supper. "Why didn't you tell me he was dead? I could have brought the Last Rites anyway."

Leon smiled. "It wasn't necessary, Father."

The priest stared down at his scuffed brown loafers and the worn hem of his cassock. "For a Christian burial it was necessary."

His voice was distant, and Leon thought that his blue eyes looked tired.

"It's O.K. Father, we just want him to have plenty of water."

The priest sank down into the green chair and picked up a glossy missionary magazine. He turned the colored pages full of lepers and pagans without looking at them.

"You know I can't do that, Leon. There should have been the Last Rites and a funeral Mass at the very least."

The Man to Send Rain Clouds

Leon put on his green cap and pulled the flaps down over his ears. "It's getting late, Father. I've got to go."

When Leon opened the door Father Paul stood up and said, "Wait." He left the room and came back wearing a long brown overcoat. He followed Leon out the door and across the dim churchyard to the adobe steps in front of the church. They both stooped to fit through the low adobe entrance. And when they started down the hill to the graveyard only half of the sun was visible above the mesa.

The priest approached the grave slowly, wondering how they had managed to dig into the frozen ground; and then he remembered that this was New Mexico, and saw the pile of cold loose sand beside the hole. The people stood close to each other with little clouds of steam puffing from their faces. The priest looked at them and saw a pile of jackets, gloves, and scarves in the yellow, dry tumbleweeds that grew in the graveyard. He looked at the red blanket, not sure that Teofilo was so small, wondering if it wasn't some perverse Indian trick—something they did in March to ensure a good harvest—wondering if maybe old Teofilo was actually at sheep camp corraling the sheep for the night. But there he was, facing into a cold dry wind and squinting at the last sunlight, ready to bury a red wool blanket while the faces of his parishioners were in shadow with the last warmth of the sun on their backs.

His fingers were stiff, and it took him a long time to twist the lid off the holy water. Drops of water fell on the red blanket and soaked into dark icy spots. He sprinkled the grave and the water disappeared almost before it touched the dim, cold sand; it reminded him of something—he tried to remember what it was, because he thought if he could remember he might understand this. He sprinkled more water; he shook the container until it was empty, and the water fell through the light from sundown like August rain that fell while the sun was still shining, almost evaporating before it touched the wilted squash flowers.

The wind pulled at the priest's brown Franciscan robe and swirled away the corn meal and pollen that had been sprinkled on the blanket. They lowered the bundle into the ground, and they didn't bother to untie the stiff pieces of new rope that were tied around the ends of the blanket. The sun was gone, and over on the highway the eastbound lane was full of headlights. The priest walked away slowly. Leon watched him climb the hill, and when he had disappeared within the tall, thick walls, Leon turned to look up at the high blue mountains in the deep snow that reflected a faint red light from the west. He felt good because it was finished, and he was happy about the sprinkling of the holy water; now the old man could send them big thunderclouds for sure.

Responding to the Selection ——————

Questions for Discussion

1. How do Leon, Ken, Louise, and Teresa react to the death of Teofilo? How do they prepare the body for burial? How do their reactions and preparations compare with the ones you are most familiar with?

2. How does Leon behave toward Father Paul? What meaning do Leon and Louise attach to the sprinkling of holy water on a dead body? How does this differ from the Catholic interpretation of the rite? What have the Laguna done with this Catholic rite?

3. How would you describe the relationship between Father Paul and the people of the pueblo? Why does Father Paul decide to go with Leon to the grave? As he sprinkles the holy water, what do you think Father Paul is trying to remember so that he "might understand this"?

4. What attitude toward the death of an old person do the Laguna seem to have? What do they believe will happen to Teofilo after his burial? How do their attitudes and beliefs compare with yours?

5. What do you think of the way that Teofilo died and was buried?

Activities

Writing a Prayer

1. Write a **prayer** that the people of the pueblo might have said as Teofilo was buried.

Presenting a Play

2. Work in a small group to practice and present this story in the form of a short **play.**

Before You Read

The Journey

Duane Big Eagle
Born 1946

" . . . *we travel those roads black, gray and red ribbons of speed in a time not measured by the distance between two points.*"

About Big Eagle

Osage poet Duane Big Eagle lives in Petaluma, California, and has taught creative writing in the California public schools through a program called California Poets in the Schools. He also performs at tribal gatherings, specializing in the traditional Southern Straight Dance, which tells the story of a hunting or war party trailing an animal or an enemy. An award-winning poet, Big Eagle has written two books, *Bidato: ten mile river poems* and *Birthplace, Poems & Paintings,* and his works have appeared in numerous magazines and anthologies.

Traditional and Modern Healing

"The Journey" deals with traditional Native American beliefs, especially those of the Yaqui people. The Yaqui are a farming people who live in northwestern Mexico and Arizona. In this story, a young boy suffering from a mysterious illness fails to respond to treatment by medical doctors. He travels from his hometown of Mazatlan, Mexico, to Oklahoma to be treated by his aunt, who is a Yaqui medicine woman.

The use of both modern medical treatments and traditional healing methods is common among Native Americans in the Southwest, including the Yaqui. Traditionally, the Yaqui believed that a person could gain supernatural powers through animal spirits and through visions. A Yaqui healer, who was usually a woman, was considered to have such powers and treated illnesses by performing certain rites.

The Journey

— *Duane Big Eagle*

I had known the train all my life. Its wailing roar rushed through my dreams as through a tunnel and yet I had never even been on one. Now I was to take one on a two thousand kilometer journey half way into a foreign country!

This particular adventure was my fault, if you can call being sick a fault. Mama says finding fault is only a way of clouding a problem and this problem was clouded enough. It began when I was thirteen and I still have tuberculosis scars on my lungs but this illness was more than tuberculosis. The regular doctors were mystified by the fevers and delirium that accompanied a bad cough and nausea. After six months of treatment without improvement they gave up.

Papa carried me on his back as we left the doctor's office and began our walk to the barrio that was our home. Mama cried as she walked and Papa seemed weighted by more than the weight of my thinned-down frame. About half way home Papa suddenly straightened up. I was having a dizzy spell and almost slipped off his back but he caught me with one hand and shouted, "Aunt Rosalie! What a fool I am! Aunt Rosalie Stands Tall!" Papa started to laugh and to dance around and around on the dirt path in the middle of a field.

"What do you mean?" cried Mama as she rushed around with her hands out, ready to catch me if I fell. From the look on her face, the real question in her mind was more like, Have you gone mad? "Listen, woman," said Papa, "there are some people who can cure diseases the medical doctors can't. Aunt Rosalie Stands Tall is a medicine woman of the Yaqui people and one of the best! She'll be able to cure Raoul! The only problem is she's married to an Indian in the United States. But that can't be helped, we'll just have to go there. Come on, we have plans to make and work to do!"

The planning began that day. We had very little money, but with what we had and could borrow from Papa's many friends there was just enough for a child's ticket to the little town in Oklahoma where Rosalie lived. I couldn't be left alone in a foreign country so Papa decided simply to walk. "I'll take the main highway north to the old Papago trails that go across the desert. They'll also take me across the border undetected. Then I'll head east and north to Oklahoma. It should be easy to catch occasional rides once I get to the U.S. When I arrive I'll send word for Raoul to start."

268 Duane Big Eagle

Papa left one fine Spring morning, taking only a blanket, a few extra pairs of shoes, bow and arrows to catch food, and a flintstone for building fires. Secretly I believe he was happy to be travelling again. Travel had always been in his blood. As a young man, Papa got a job on a sailing ship and travelled all over the world. This must have been how he learned to speak English and also how he met Mama in the West Indies. Myself, I was still sixty kilometers from the town I was born in and even to imagine the journey I was about to take was more than my fevered brain could handle. But as Mama said, "You can do anything in the world if you take it little by little and one step at a time." This was the miraculous and trusting philosophy our family lived by, and I must admit it has usually worked.

Still, the day of departure found me filled with a dread that settled like lead in my feet. If I hadn't been so light-headed from the fevers, I'm sure I would have fallen over at any attempt to walk. Dressed in my best clothes which looked shabby the minute we got to the train station, Mama led me into the fourth-class carriage and found me a seat on a bench near the windows. Then she disappeared and came back a minute later with a thin young man with sallow skin and a drooping Zapata mustache. "This is your second cousin, Alejandro. He is a conductor on this train and will be with you till you get to Juarez; you must do whatever he says."

At that time, the conductors on trains in Mexico were required to stay with a train the entire length of its journey which perhaps accounted for Alejandro's appearance. He did little to inspire my confidence in him. In any case, he disappeared a second later and it was time for Mama to go too. Hurriedly, she reminded me that there was money in my coat to buy food from the women who came onto the train at every stop and that there was a silver bracelet sown into the cuff of my pants to bribe the guards at the border. With one last tearful kiss and hug, she was gone and I was alone. The train started with a jerk which knocked me off my bench and I began my journey upside down in a heap on top of my crumpled cardboard suitcase. I didn't even get a chance to wave goodbye.

I soon got used to the jerking starts of the train, and unsmiling Alejandro turned out to be a guardian angel which was fortunate because my illness began to get worse as the journey went along. Many times I awoke to find Alejandro shuffling some young thief away from my meager possessions or buying me food at the last stop before a long stretch of desert. He would bring me things too, fresh peaches and apples and left-over bread and pastries from the first-class carriages where he worked. Once, in the middle of the desert he brought me a small ice-cold watermelon, the most refreshing thing I'd ever tasted—who knows where he got it?

To this day, I'm not sure exactly which of the things I saw through the window of the train were real and which were not. Some of them I know

The Journey

were not real. In my delirium, a half day's journey would pass in the blink of an eye. Often I noticed only large changes in the countryside, from plains to mountains to desert. Broad valleys remain clearly in my mind and there were many of these. Small scenes, too, remain—a family sitting down to dinner at a candle-lit table in a hut by a river. And a few more sinister ones—once between two pine trees I caught a glimpse of one man raising a large club to strike another man whose back was turned. I cried out but there was nothing to be done, the train was moving too fast on a downgrade and probably couldn't have been stopped. But then, did I really see them at all? My doubt was caused by the girl in the dark red dress.

I think I began to see her about half way through the journey to Juarez. She was very beautiful, high cheekbones, long black hair and very dark skin. She was about my height and age or maybe a little older. Her eyes were very large and her mouth seemed to have a ready smile. The first time I saw her, at a small station near a lake, she smiled and waved as the train pulled away. Her sensuality embarrassed me and I didn't wave back. I regretted it immediately. But she was back again the next day at a station in the foothills of the mountains, this time dressed in the white blouse and skirt that the Huichol women wear.

She became almost a regular occurrence. Sometimes she was happy, sometimes serious and most of the time she was wearing the dark red dress. Often I would only see her in passing; she'd be working in a field and raise up to watch the train go by. Gradually, my condition grew worse. My coughing fits grew longer and I slept more so I began not to see the girl so much, but the last time I saw her really gave me a shock. The mountains of the Sierra Madre Oriental range are very rugged and are cut in places by deep gorges called barrancas. The train was in one of these gorges on a ledge above the river and was about to go around a bend. For some reason, I looked back the way we had come and there, imbedded in the mountain with her eyes closed, was the face of the girl, thirty feet high! For the first time, I noticed the small crescent-shaped scar in the middle of her lower lip.

The vision, or whatever it was, quickly disappeared as the train rounded the curve. I sank back on to the bench with a pounding heart and closed my eyes. I must have slept or perhaps I fell into a coma because I remember very little of the last part of the trip. I awoke once while Alejandro was carrying me across the border and delivering me to a friend of his on the train to Dallas. How I got from Dallas to Oklahoma I may never know because I remember nothing. But it happened. And finally, I awoke for a minute in my father's arms as he carried me off the train.

Then, there was a sharp pain in the center of my chest. And a pounding. Rhythmic pounding. A woman's voice began to sing in a very high pitch.

270 Duane Big Eagle

The Journey

My eyes opened of themselves. At first I couldn't make it out, arched crossing lines, flickering shadows. I was in the center of an oval-shaped lodge built of bent willow limbs covered with skins and lit by a small fire. A tall woman came into view; she was singing and dancing back and forth. Somehow I knew this was Rosalie Stands Tall, the medicine woman. The pain hit me again and I wanted to get away but hands held me still.

Papa's voice said in my ear, "She is calling her spirit helpers, you must try and sit up." I was sitting up facing the door of the lodge. There was a lizard there and he spoke in an old man's voice, words I couldn't understand. Rosalie sang again and there was a small hawk there. The pain rose up higher in my chest. There was a coyote in the door and his words were tinged with mocking laughter. The pain rose into my throat. There was a small brown bear in the door, his fur blew back and forth in the wind. The pain rose into the back of my mouth. I felt I needed to cough. Rosalie put two porcupine quills together and bound them with leather to make a pair of tweezers. She held my lips closed with them, painfully tight. A pair of wings beat against the top of the lodge. I needed badly to cough. There was something hot in my mouth, it was sharp, it was hurting my mouth, it needed to come out! IT WAS OUT!

I awoke in bed in a small room lit by a coal-oil lamp. There was a young woman with her back to me preparing food by the side of the bed. She had very long black hair. She put the tray down on the table beside the bed. As she turned to leave the room, I saw a small crescent-shaped scar in the middle of her lower lip. I started to call her back but there was no need. I knew who she was. An immense peacefulness settled over me. It was warm in the bed. Papa sat on the other side of the bed. He seemed very happy when I turned and looked at him. He said softly, "Raoul, you have changed completely. You're not anymore the young boy I left in Mazatlan." I wanted to tell him everything! There was so much to say! But all I could get out was, "Yes, I know, Papa, I've come on a journey out of childhood." And then I went to sleep again.

Responding to the Selection

1. What recurring vision does Raoul have on his journey? What might this vision represent?

2. What methods does the Yaqui medicine woman use to treat Raoul? What visions does he have during the treatment? What do you think the visions represent? How is he finally cured?

3. What change does Raoul experience after his treatment? How is his experience a "journey out of childhood"?

4. What does the story tell you about Raoul's illness? How is the illness treated? What effects do you think the treatments have?

Activities

Writing a Continuation

1. Write a continuation of this story in which Raoul wakes up and explains to his father what he experienced and how the experience has changed him.

Creating a Mural

2. Work in a small group to create a **mural** or **poster** portraying Raoul's visions. You might investigate Mexican mural art and model your work on that style.

Before You Read

Love Poem and *Unshadow*

Leslie Marmon Silko *Born 1948*
Mark Turcotte *Born 1958*

> *"It is time to let*
> *our shoulders rise.*
> *It is time to let*
> *our shoulders lift."*
> — Mark Turcotte

About Turcotte

As he was growing up, Turcotte lived on the Turtle Mountain Chippewa reservation in North Dakota, in migrant camps in the West, and in Lansing, Michigan. He belongs to the Chippewa, or Anishinabe, people of the Great Lakes region.

In the early 1990s, Turcotte moved to Chicago and became involved in that city's poetry and performance scene. He won several awards for his work over the next few years. Turcotte is very active in performing his poetry, conducting workshops, and speaking on Native American issues. He has published three books, all of which have been illustrated by his wife, artist Kathleen Presnell.

About Silko

A biography of Leslie Marmon Silko appears with her short story "The Man to Send Rain Clouds" on page 261.

Diverse Influences

The writing of Leslie Marmon Silko shows the influence of both her Laguna background and modern lyric poetry. Elements in "Love Poem" that reflect Silko's Laguna roots are the imagery of the landscape of the Southwest and the emphasis on water, a constant concern in that arid country. In addition, her use of repetition and the indentation and separation of words and phrases has a chant-like effect, echoing the traditional chants or songs of the Southwest Indians.

Mark Turcotte's poetry also displays such dual influences. In "Unshadow," for example, the use of repetition is a common technique in the poetry and song of many Native American peoples. This element is combined with an almost abstract subject matter, giving the poem a mood that is both modern and timeless.

Love Poem

— *Leslie Marmon Silko*

Rain smell comes with the wind
    out of the southwest.
Smell of sand dunes
        tall grass glistening
5   in the rain.
Warm raindrops that fall easy
        this woman
the summer is born.
Smell of her breathing
10   new life
small grey toads hopping on damp red sand.
This woman
    whispering to dark wide leaves
        white moon flowers
15   dripping little tracks in the sand.
Rain smell
    I am full of hunger
        deep and longing to touch
wet tall grass, green and strong beneath.
20   This woman loved a man
    and she breathed to him her damp earth
song.
    I am haunted by this story I remember it in cottonwood
        leaves
25   their fragrance in the shade.
    I remember it in the wide blue sky
    when the rain smell comes with the wind.

Unshadow

— *Mark Turcotte*

And he dreamed of another light.

Another light
that would not fall
in shafts or rays
5   but instead be
carried curved
on the wind
into all our darkest places.

A light on the wind into
10   every crack of
every street of
every house of
every room, into
every dimly known corner
15   of every heart.

A light of anger grace
and healing
curving on the wind
to unshadow all those mouths
20   filled with all those tiny whisperings,
curving on the wind
to unshadow all those eyes
filled with all those tiny visions.

A light of anger grace
25 and healing
curving on the wind
to unshadow all those rough hands
filled with every unwanted touch,
curving on the wind
30 to unshadow all those rough words
filled with every unneeded cut.

A light of anger grace
and healing
curving on the wind
35 to unshadow every muffled refusal
every defiled trust
every stony denial,
curving on the wind
to unshadow every shadow.

40 And as he dreamed
he felt,
over his shoulder,
the wind
beginning to shine.

Responding to the Selection

Questions for Discussion

1. Both of these poems describe something that the wind brings. What does the wind bring in each poem? What is the effect of what it brings?

2. How would you characterize the way in which the speaker relates to the landscape in "Love Poem"? The speaker says, "I am haunted by this story." What is the story that haunts the speaker?

3. Light is often used as a **symbol** of goodness, virtue, or truth. What does light symbolize in "Unshadow"? What is the speaker suggesting by saying that the light is curved and carried on the wind rather than falling in "shafts or rays"?

4. What is the meaning of the word *unshadow* in Turcotte's poem? What is the significance of the wind "beginning to shine" at the end of the poem?

5. Each of these poems expresses a longing in striking **imagery**. What does the speaker long for in each poem? Which line or lines from each poem express this longing most strongly, in your opinion?

Activities

Writing a Poem

1. Write a **poem** describing something that you would like the wind to bring to you.

Creating a Poster

2. Investigate Native American folktales about the weather and create a **poster** illustrating one or a group of these stories.

Web Site

In this interview, acclaimed author
N. Scott Momaday offers his insights
into writing as a way of life.

An Interview with N. Scott Momaday

Interview, June 28, 1996, Sun Valley, Idaho

I lived on the Navajo reservation when I was little, and I lived on two of the Apache reservations, and lived at the Pueblo of Jemez for the longest time. So I had a Pan-Indian experience before I knew what that term meant. And it turned out to be fortunate, I think, in terms of writing, because I had an unusual experience—and a very rich one—of the southwestern landscape, the Indian world. And that became for me a very important subject.

. . .

I tell young people often, "Don't worry about having a distinctive voice right now, it comes with experience and practice. You will develop a voice." Someone once said to me, "Don't worry about imitating someone, that's how you learn." And eventually you will verge out and go on your own. I simply kept my goal in mind, and persisted. Perseverance is a large part of writing.

. . .

Poetry is the crown of literature. I think it's the highest of the literary arts. To write a great poem is to do as much as you can do in literature. Everything has to be very precise. The poem has to be informed with motive and emotion. You're bringing to bear everything that literature is based upon when you write a poem. A poem, if it succeeds, brings together the best of your intelligence, the best of your articulation, the best of your emotion. And that is the highest goal of literature, I suppose.

. . .

I would rather be a poet than a novelist, because I think it's on a slightly higher plane. You know, poets are the people who really are the most insightful among us. They stand in the best position to enlighten us, and encourage, and inspire us, and what better thing could you be than a poet?

. . .

There's a lot of frustration in writing. I heard an interview with a writer not long ago in which the interviewer said, "Tell me is writing difficult?" And the writer said, "Oh, no . . . no, of course not." He said, "All you do is sit down at a typewriter, you put a page into it, and then you look at it until beads of blood appear on your forehead. That's all there is to it." There are days like that. But when you come away after two or three hours with a sentence, or two, or three and you understand in your heart that those are the best sentences you could have written in that time, there is a sat-

isfaction to that that is like nothing else. That justifies everything.

. . .

One of the things that amazes me is that I think the Indian is more secure than he was a half-century ago. He has a much better idea of himself and of the contribution that he can make. He's only two percent of the population, but has an influence much greater than that would indicate.

. . .

In the Plains culture, which is my ancestral culture, and a warrior culture, there are four principles. A warrior had to live by these principles: bravery, fortitude, generosity and virtue. When I learned about those principles, they have been extremely important to me, you know. I would like to live my life according to those four things.

. . .

What does the American Dream mean to [me]? It means a great deal actually, and the reason it does has something to do with my being a Native American. I belong to a race of people, a society, that has been oppressed. We, the Indians, have had a hard time, for a long time. We have had to endure a great deal, but the dream means as much to us as it does to anyone. You'll never find a greater patriot than an American Indian.

N. SCOTT MOMADAY
WINNER OF THE PULITZER PRIZE FOR FICTION

In the Bear's House

Questions for Discussion

1. What part of the interview seems most significant to you? Why?

2. What point in the interview would you like to discuss further with Momaday? What would you like to ask or say to him?

Before You Read

Four Poems

N. Scott Momaday
Born 1934

"I think that the greatest deprivation that the Native American suffers today is the theft of the sacred, that it is not reaching down to the children as it always has."

About Momaday

Kiowa author Navarro Scott Momaday sparked what critics called the Native American Renaissance when he won the Pulitzer Prize for Fiction for his first novel, *House Made of Dawn,* in 1969. Drawing on oral traditions, rituals, and sacred landscapes, his writing influenced other Native American writers who achieved widespread recognition in the following decades.

"I'm fortunate to have the heritage I have," says Momaday. "I grew up in two worlds and straddle both those worlds even now. It has made for confusion and a richness in my life." Born in Lawrence, Oklahoma, Momaday grew up on Navajo, Apache, and Pueblo reservations in the Southwest, where his parents worked as teachers. Both of his parents were talented. Momaday's father was a painter and his mother was a writer. Momaday took after both parents and has achieved acclaim for his painting as well as his writing. In both art forms, he synthesizes Native American and European American traditions. Momaday has taught at the University of California, Stanford University, and the University of Arizona.

The Gourd Dancer

The poems you are about to read come from Momaday's collection of poetry *The Gourd Dancer.* The gourd dance is a traditional dance of the Kiowa and other Southern Plains peoples; often the opening dance at intertribal gatherings, it honors the warriors who defend the people and "cleanses" the dance area.

Four Poems

— N. Scott Momaday

The Horse That Died of Shame

Once there was a man who owned a fine hunting horse. It was black and fast and afraid of nothing. When it was turned upon an enemy it charged in a straight line and struck at full speed; the man need have no hand upon the rein. But, you know, that man knew fear. Once during a charge he turned that animal from its course. That was a bad thing. The hunting horse died of shame.

from *The Way to Rainy Mountain*

In the one color of the horse there were many colors. And that evening it wheeled, riderless, and broke away into the long distance, running at full speed. And so it does again and again in my dreaming. It seems to concentrate all color and light into the final moment of its life, until it streaks the vision plane and is indefinite, and shines vaguely like the gathering of March light to a storm.

The Fear of Bo-talee

Bo-talee rode easily among his enemies, once, twice, three—and four times. And all who saw him were amazed, for he was utterly without fear; so it seemed. But afterwards he said: Certainly I was afraid. I was afraid of the fear in the eyes of my enemies.

The Delight Song of Tsoai-talee

I am a feather on the bright sky
I am the blue horse that runs in the plain
I am the fish that rolls, shining, in the water
I am the shadow that follows a child
5   I am the evening light, the lustre of meadows
I am an eagle playing with the wind
I am a cluster of bright beads
I am the farthest star
I am the cold of the dawn
10   I am the roaring of the rain
I am the glitter on the crust of the snow
I am the long track of the moon in a lake
I am a flame of four colors
I am a deer standing away in the dusk
15   I am a field of sumac and the pomme blanche
I am an angle of geese in the winter sky
I am the hunger of a young wolf
I am the whole dream of these things

You see, I am alive, I am alive
20   I stand in good relation to the earth
I stand in good relation to the gods
I stand in good relation to all that is beautiful
I stand in good relation to the daughter of Tsen-tainte
You see, I am alive, I am alive

Plainview: 3

The sun appearing: a pendant
of clear cutbeads, flashing;
a drift of pollen and glitter
lapping, and overlapping night;
a prairie fire.

Responding to the Selection

Questions for Discussion

1. The critic Kenneth Mason calls the poem "Plainview: 3" a "prayer of praise to the sun." To what is the Sun compared in the poem? In what ways does the poem resemble a haiku?

2. "The Fear of Bo-talee" is an example of Momaday's prose poems. What characteristics of prose and of poetry does the poem have? What do you think Bo-talee means by "I was afraid of the fear in the eyes of my enemies"?

3. What does "The Horse That Died of Shame" describe? What might the death of the horse **symbolize,** or represent, to the speaker in the poem?

4. What does the speaker in the poem "The Delight Song of Tsoai-talee" convey by repeating "I am" followed by a variety of images? How would you describe the feelings of the speaker? Have you ever felt this way? When?

5. What do you think is the predominant feeling in these poems?

Activities

Writing a Prose Poem

1. Write a **prose poem** of your own about a story that has made a deep impression on you, a recurring dream you have had, or a feeling you have about nature.

Creating an Artwork

2. Choose one of these poems as the inspiration for a painting, a poster, a sculpture, a mobile, or another form of art.

Before You Read

Horses

Pablo Neruda
1904–1973

"If you ask what my poetry is, I must confess that I don't know; but if you'll ask my poetry, it will tell you who I am."

About Neruda

As a boy growing up in southern Chile, Pablo Neruda immersed himself in literature. He received encouragement to write from the poet Gabriela Mistral, who taught at his school and later became the first Chilean to win a Nobel Prize for Literature. Neruda began publishing poems when he was fifteen. By his early twenties, he was already one of Chile's most popular poets.

Unable to support himself from his writing, Neruda took a series of diplomatic positions in Asia and Europe. His experiences during the Spanish civil war made him deeply committed to left-wing politics. After returning to Chile, he joined the Communist Party and won election to the Senate. However, he soon had to go abroad for several years because his harsh criticism angered the president. In 1971 he became the second Chilean to win the Nobel Prize for Literature.

A Varied Achievement

Pablo Neruda wrote about fifty volumes of poetry in a career that spanned half a century. He wrote in different styles. Some of his poems are dense, highly experimental works; others are simple and direct. Neruda wrote epic poetry in which he reinterpreted the history of Latin America. He could also narrow his scope considerably; in his book *Elementary Odes,* he wrote about common objects such as onions and scissors. Uniting the different phases of his career are his love for the people and landscape of Chile, his exuberance, and the freshness of his imagery. Many critics regard Neruda as the most important Latin American poet of the twentieth century.

Horses

— *Pablo Neruda*
Translated by Alastair Reid

It was from the window I saw the horses.

I was in Berlin, in winter. The light
was without light, the sky skyless.

The air white like a moistened loaf.

5   From my window, I could see a deserted arena,
a circle bitten out by the teeth of winter.

All at once, led out by a man,
ten horses were stepping into the snow.

Emerging, they had scarcely rippled into existence
10   like flame, than they filled the whole world of my eyes,
empty till now. Faultless, flaming,
they stepped like ten gods on broad, clean hooves,
their manes recalling a dream of pure grace.

Their rumps were globes, were oranges.

15   Their color was amber and honey, was on fire.

Their necks were towers
carved from the stone of pride,
and in their furious eyes, sheer energy
showed itself, a prisoner inside them.

Horses

20   And there, in the silence, at the midpoint of the day, in a dirty, disgruntled winter,
the horses' intense presence was blood,
was rhythm, was the beckoning Grail of being.

I saw, I saw, and, seeing, I came to life.
25   There was the unwitting fountain, the dance of gold, the sky,
the fire that sprang to life in beautiful things.

I have obliterated that gloomy Berlin winter.

I shall not forget the light from these horses.

Responding to the Selection

1. In the poem "Horses," how do the horses contrast with their surroundings? How does the sight of the horses affect the speaker in the poem?

2. Compare and contrast the theme of "Horses" with that of "The Horse That Died of Shame." What might the horses **symbolize,** or represent, to the speakers in each poem?

3. What similar feeling about horses is conveyed in "Horses" and "The Horse That Died of Shame"? How do you respond to this feeling? Explain your answer.

4. What does the theme of "Horses" have in common with the theme of "The Delight Song of Tsoai-talee"?

5. What similarities in **style** and **imagery** do you see in the poetry of Pablo Neruda and N. Scott Momaday? What do you learn about each of these poets from their poetry? What do you think they have in common?

Activities

Writing a Found Poem

1. Make a list of the imagery of horses in N. Scott Momaday's and Pablo Neruda's poems. Choose some of the images to create a **"found poem,"**—a poem formed by selecting phrases from another work of writing, then rearranging and adding to them. Credit the source or sources of the images in your found poem.

Creating a Dance

2. Working in a small group, choreograph a brief **dance** that depicts the grace, vitality, and beauty of horses. Practice and present your dance to the class.

Index of Titles and Authors

❖

Index of Titles and Authors

Acknowledgments

❖ *cont. from page ii*

"We Are Singing in the Night," "I am Running Toward the Edge of the World," "Dream Song #4," and "The Sunset," from *Papago Music*, by Frances Densmore. Bulletin 90 of the Bureau of American Ethnology, 1929.

"Trusting the Words" from *Paper Trail* by Michael Dorris. Copyright © 1994 by Michael Dorris. Reprinted by permission of HarperCollins Publishers, Inc.

"The Chickadee's Tongue," "Local Deer" and "Morning Glories and Eastern Phoebes" from *The Blue Jay's Dance* by Louise Erdrich. Copyright © 1995 by Louise Erdrich. Reprinted by permission of HarperCollins Publishers, Inc.

"The Warrior Maiden" from *American Indian Myths and Legends* by Richard Erdoes and Alfonso Ortiz, editors. Copyright © 1984 by Richard Erdoes and Alfonso Ortiz. Reprinted by permission of Pantheon Books, a Division of Random House, Inc.

"Mother of Mosquitoes" and "The Truth Teller" from *War Cries*, copyright © 1997 by Diane Glancy. Reprinted by permission of Holy Cow! Press.

"Mine" by Diane Glancy, originally appeared in *The Sycamore Review*. Reprinted by permission of the author.

"Summer Night" from *In Mad Love and War*, copyright © 1990 by Joy Harjo, Wesleyan University Press, reprinted by permission of the author and University Press of New England.

"Arrowhead," "Thanksgiving," "Man in the Moon" and "hackleberry trees" from *Calling Myself Home*, copyright © 1978 by Linda Hogan. Reprinted by permission of Sanford J. Greenburger Associates.

"Going Home," "Friendship Days at Atwesasne" and "Black River-Summer 1981" from *On Second Thought: A Compilation by Maurice Kenny*. Copyright © 1995 by Maurice Kenny. Reprinted by permission of the University of Oklahoma Press.

"The Hunter," copyright © 1983 by Larry Littlebird. Reprinted by permission of the author.

Fable XXII 'The Oaks and the Reed' from *La Fontaine: Selected Fables*, translated by James Michie (Penguin Classics, Allen Lane, 1979) Translation copyright © James Michie, 1979. Reprinted by permission of Penguin Books Ltd.

"Rock climbers, Washoe Indians clash over Cave Rock." Copyright © 1997 Los Angeles Times. Reprinted by permission.

"Eskimo Song," "A Forgotten Man's Song About the Winds," "Bird Song," "Delight in Nature," "Moved" and "Delight in Singing" from *Eskimo Poems*, translations copyright © 1973 by Tom Lowenstein. Reprinted by permission of Tom Lowenstein.

"The Hawk Is Hungry" from *The Hawk Is Hungry and Other Stories* by D'Arcy McNickle. Copyright © 1992 Arizona Board of Regents. Reprinted by permission of The Newberry Library.

Acknowledgments

Acknowledgments

Excerpt from *Cheyenne Memories* by John Stands in Timber and Margot Liberty. Copyright © 1967 Yale University. Reprinted by permission of Yale University Press.

Excerpt from *To the American Indian: Reminiscences of a Yurok Woman*, by Lucy Thompson. Copyright © 1991 by Heyday Books. Reprinted by permission of Heyday Books. All rights reserved.

"Windmills & Crazy Papers" from *The Trickster of Liberty* by Gerald Vizenor. Copyright © 1988 by Gerald Vizenor. Reprinted by permission of the University of Minnesota Press.

"The Warriors" from *The Sun Is Not Merciful*, copyright © 1985 by Anna Lee Walters. Reprinted by permission of Firebrand Books, Ithaca, New York.

Photography Acknowledgments

Cover *Double Woman*, 1971. Oscar Howe (1915-1983). Casein on paper, 18 1/2 x 22 3/4 in. Courtesy The Collection of the Oscar Howe Family, Copyright Adelheid Howe 1983.

vi Chris Arend/AlaskaStock Images; **1** Museum of Anthropology, University of British Columbia, Canada/Werner Forman Archive/Art Resource, New York; **2** Jerry Jacka; **6** Ohio Historical Society; **7** (l)Mark Burnett, (r)Ohio Historical Society; **8** David F. Barry/State Historical Society of North Dakota; **17** Lesley Woodfin; **21** Grenville Goodwin/Arizona State Museum/University of Arizona; **26** Shako'wi Cultural Center, Verona, NY/The Oneida Nation/© 2002 Dan Umstead; **30** Jay Ann Cox; **40** Richard & Susan Day/Animals, Animals; **41** (l,c)Icon Images, (r)SuperStock; **42** John Pflug; **50** (l)Scala/Art Resource, New York, (r)Giraudon/Art Resource, New York; **54** La Fonda Indian Shop and Gallery, Santa Fe, NM/Jerry Jacka; **55** Founders Society Purchase with funds from Richard A. Manoohian, New Endowment Fund, Joseph H. Boyer Memorial Fund, and Mr. and Mrs. Walter B. Ford II Fund. 1991.205/The Detroit Institute of the Arts; **56** Library of Congress; **61** Cynthia Farah; **67** Ed McCombs; **80** Courtesy Bently Quast/McClelland & Stewart Inc.; **86** Lawrence Migdale/Stock Boston; **87** (tl)courtesy Gary Auerbach, www.platinumphotographer.com, (tr)Lawrence Migdale/Stock Boston/PictureQuest, (b)Mark Burnett; **88** Paul Rosado; **94** David Muench/Stone; **95** (t)William Johnson/Stock Boston/Picturequest, (b)Wood River Gallery/Picturequest; **96** CORBIS; **103** Courtesy Manny Skolnick; **110** Courtesy Barney Bush; **114** Jerry Jacka; **115** Chuck Place/Stock Boston; **116** Sun Valley Photography; **126** (l)Hulton Getty Picture Collection/Stone, (r)Superstock; **130** Courtesy Larry Littlebird; **135** Gary Isaacs, courtesy of Scribner; **141** Sun Valley Photography; **144** Don Pitcher/Stock Boston; **145** David Brooks/The Stock Market; **146** Christopher Little/Outline Press; **152** Jerry Jacka; **153** (t)The National Anthropological Archives/Smithsonian Institution, (b)Paul Grebliunas/Stone;

154 The Newberry Library; 164 Courtesy Houghton-Mifflin; 170 The Heard Museum, Phoenix, AZ/Jerry Jacka; 171 The Brooklyn Museum of Art; 172 William Ready Division of Archives and Research Collections, McMaster University Library, Hamilton, Ontario, Canada; 176 SuperStock; 177 (t)Icon Images, (c)©TNT/The Everett Collection, (b)©20th Century Fox/The Everett Collection; 178 Archive Photos; 183 National Portrait Gallery, Washington DC/Art Resource, New York; 192 UPI/Bettmann/CORBIS; 199 Cynthia Farah; 205 Courtesy John Stands-in-Timber; 224 Anthony Cassidy/Stone; 225 (t)CORBIS, (b)William Taufic/The Stock Market; 226 courtesy Gerald Vizenor; 234 The Turquoise Tortoise, Sedona, AZ/Jerry Jacka; 235 Jerry Jacka; 236 Marilyn "Angel" Wynn/Sun Valley Photography; 237 (t)Ruth Dixon/Stock Boston, (b)Richard A. Cooke III/Stone; 238 Miriam Berkley; 247 Cynthia Farah; 251 261 Nancy Crampton; 267 Courtesy Duane Big Eagle; 273 Steve Greiner; 278 Coco McCoy/Rainbow/Picturequest; 279 (l)Icon Images, (r)Christie's Images; 280 Nancy Crampton; 284 Hulton Getty Collection/Stone.